# The Glory of Arthur

T0055262

# The Glory of Arthur

*The Legendary King
in Epic Poems of
Layamon, Spenser and Blake*

JEFFREY JOHN DIXON

McFarland & Company, Inc., Publishers
*Jefferson, North Carolina*

LIBRARY OF CONGRESS CATALOGUING-IN-PUBLICATION DATA

Dixon, Jeffrey John.
    The glory of Arthur : the legendary king in epic poems of Layamon,
Spenser and Blake / Jeffrey John Dixon.
        p.      cm.
    Includes bibliographical references and index.

    ISBN 978-0-7864-9456-9 (softcover : acid free paper) ∞
    ISBN 978-1-4766-1609-4 (ebook)

    1. Arthur, King—In literature.    2. Epic poetry, English—History
and criticism.    3. Arthurian romances—History and criticism.
4. Great Britain—In literature.    I. Title.

PR328.D59 2014
820.9'351—dc23                                              2014025186

BRITISH LIBRARY CATALOGUING DATA ARE AVAILABLE

Front cover image: *Dying King Arthur*, 1860, John Mulcaster Carrick (©
2014 PicturesNow)

Printed in the United States of America

*McFarland & Company, Inc., Publishers*
    *Box 611, Jefferson, North Carolina 28640*
        *www.mcfarlandpub.com*

For my mother Louisa,
who always believed I could do it.

For Anthony and Sass Tuffin,
who walked with me those Arthurian streets.

For Stephen Packer and Martin Williams,
my first readers.

And for Steven Harris,
whose friendship sustained me throughout the writing.

# Table of Contents

The British Antiquities are now in the Artist's hands;
all his visionary contemplations,
relating to his own country and its ancient glory,
when it was, as it again shall be,
the source of learning and inspiration.
—William Blake, 1809

# *Preface*

This work, although it stands alone, also represents to some degree a companion piece to my first book, *Gawain and the Grail Quest: Healing the Waste Land in Our Time*, published in 2012. In that work, I tried to show that the Grail legend was the creative response of the poetic imagination to centuries of iconoclasm and religious literalism that had created the modern wasteland. We could only begin to heal the land, I argued, by restoring the imagination to its central position in human consciousness.

In doing so, I was inspired by the work of the English prophet of the imagination, the poet and artist William Blake, whose image of a fallen Albion reflects that of the maimed Grail king. In this new book, I explore some of the ways in which Blake was himself inspired by an earlier poet, Edmund Spenser, to create a fresh reading of those legends of their native island, and mine, which are known collectively as the Matter of Britain. I further show how Blake's and Spenser's use of "fairy" lore places them in an English tradition that can be traced back to the early thirteenth-century poet Layamon, who wrote the first English-language epic of Arthur.

While Blake continues to be well served by Geoffrey Keynes's one-volume edition of the *Complete Writings* (and is widely available both in popular editions and in facsimiles of his *Illuminated Books*), Spenser is less well known to the general public. The publication at the beginning of the twenty-first century of an annotated edition (by A.C. Hamilton) of *The Faerie Queene,* Spenser's Arthurian epic, is therefore most welcome to those who wish to become better acquainted with this sixteenth-century masterpiece.

Even more obscure is my third principal source, Layamon, who wrote in a form of Middle English (that is, intermediate between Anglo-Saxon and modern English) that can now be appreciated only by scholars. In order to represent the salient aspects of his contribution to the narrative of Britain's ancient glory, I have, therefore, made use of two modern translations: that of Rosamund Allen, who renders into English verse the entire *Brut*, and Barron and Weinberg's edition of its "Arthurian section," in which the original text is accompanied by a prose translation on the facing pages. Until such time as a major contemporary poet such as Simon Armitage (who has already provided us with exciting new translations of two other Arthurian alliterative poems) undertakes a new translation, these must suffice.

Original texts with facing-page translations are now also available for the chroniclers on whom Layamon drew: Geoffrey of Monmouth, whose *History of the Kings of Britain* kick-started the Arthurian craze of the twelfth century, and Wace, whose French version of the same legends led to the proliferation of continental romances, with many ingredients of which we are still familiar. The easy availability of accessible editions of Spenser, Layamon, Wace, and Geoffrey of Monmouth means, I hope, that the general readers who may be unfamiliar with them can follow up my researches into this literature with investigations of their own.

What I have *not* done in this book is adduced evidence either for or contra the historical existence of Arthur. Despite the sterling work of independent scholars such as Geoffrey Ashe to establish the Once and Future King in British history—and of scholars such as Thomas Green to establish him in mythology—the jury is still out. I have therefore preferred to avoid the issue (what has been called the "banal dualism" of myth and history) by focusing on what I believe is most important for us about the figure of Arthur: that is, the stories that we tell about him. I prefer to imagine Arthur than to believe in him.

Another line of research that I broached in my earlier book and that I therefore touch upon only briefly in this work is the contested relationship between the Arthurian legends and the ancient heresy of the Gnostics; here I have limited myself to exploring the Gnostic Arthur of Blake's vision. Access by the general reader to an understanding of Gnosticism has been greatly facilitated by the discovery of a cache of parchments in Nag Hammadi in Egypt in 1945, which are now available in English translation under the direction of James Robinson. Those wishing to make up their own minds about the possible influence of such ideas on the development of Arthurian legends and on Blake's reworking of the Matter of Britain would do well to start there.

As with my earlier work, this book speaks to my continuing engagement with the ideas of the French philosopher Henry Corbin, whose rediscovery of the lost world of the imagination acts as a theoretical counterpart to the poetry of Blake. On a more personal level, it also speaks to my continuing engagement with the Arthurian streets of the obscure public-housing estate in South East London where I was brought up. The street where I lived, Pendragon Road, was surrounded by Roundtable Road; around the corner, by the bus stop, was Merlin Gardens. To the effect on the imagination of a young boy of these evocative names, the present work can testify.

# Introduction:
## Imagining Arthur

In February 2012, Britain celebrated the sixtieth anniversary of the accession to the throne of the United Kingdom of Queen Elizabeth II, and in June 2013, we celebrated the sixtieth anniversary of her coronation. The second Elizabethan Age, as it has become known, began almost four hundred years after the first was inaugurated by the accession of Elizabeth Tudor in 1558, and during the last sixty years, Britain has lost the empire which it had built up since the first Elizabethan Age.

It is perhaps too soon to know which writers and creative artists will be remembered by future generations as emblematic of the second Elizabethan Age, although it is doubtful that we will ever have another Shakespeare. It was another poet, however, rather than the Bard of Avon, who most specifically celebrated the glory of the first Elizabeth: Edmund Spenser, who died in 1599, four years before the death of the monarch whom he celebrated as "Gloriana." Spenser's imagination transformed Elizabeth I into a "faerie queen," as the title of his most famous poem indicates, and he also constructed a genealogy that makes Elizabeth Tudor the direct descendant of Igerna, the mother of King Arthur (though not of the legendary king himself, who was believed to have died without surviving issue).

In making his monarch a part of Arthur's family tree, Spenser was identifying Elizabeth I with a glorious past, when Britain ruled most of northwestern Europe and humbled the Roman Empire—a past, unfortunately, that cannot be corroborated by historians. For the problem with King Arthur is that he is everywhere and nowhere.

Today, not just King Arthur but also Merlin the Magician, the Lady of the Lake, Morgan the Fay and various Knights of the Round Table stride

5

through the pages of novels and comic strips, academic studies, translations of medieval texts and narrative retellings, and are impersonated on stage and screen. Symbolic sites such as Camelot, which has never been conclusively found on a map, draw the archaeological researcher and excavator as much as sites such as Tintagel and Glastonbury, which we can visit. Symbolic objects such as Excalibur and the Holy Grail are claimed by pagans and Christians alike and are venerated equally by neo-fascists and by New Age occultists.

But none of this has much to do with the historical Arthur, if in fact he ever existed. So who was—or perhaps we should ask: *where is*—Arthur?

•••

In the early ninth century, a Welsh monk known as Nennius compiled a legendary *History of the Britons* in which Arthur is presented as a post–Roman warlord (*dux bellorum*) who led the resistance to the Anglo-Saxon invasion that would eventually turn the south and east of this island into "England." The eighteenth-century historian Edward Gibbon (much maligned, as we will see, by the prophetic poet William Blake for his advocacy of "reasoning" over "spiritual agency") could still accept Arthur as the triumphant deliverer of twelve victories over the invaders, although he believed that the fantastic stories that accumulated around the king were imported from the Orient by returning crusaders in the twelfth century, when there was a literary explosion of Arthurian romances.

In the intervening centuries, however, the figure of Arthur was at the center of a Welsh literary tradition that combined ancient mythology with historical chronicles in an eschatological hope that the legendary king would, one day, return to liberate his people and restore the hegemony of this island to its native Britons.

In the twelfth century, the Norman and Angevin dynasties were happy to promote stories of the Celtic resistance to the Anglo-Saxons in order to strengthen their own rule over the kingdom of England, and in 1138, during the troubled reign of King Stephen, the Welsh cleric Geoffrey of Monmouth published a *History of the Kings of Britain*, in which the skeleton of Nennius's account was fleshed out with stories and characters drawn from Welsh legend to provide the first full-length narrative of the birth, noble deeds, and passing to Avalon of a king who was now seen, not just as the conqueror of the English, but of the Romans as well!

When Geoffrey's Latin prose chronicle was translated into the courtly language of Norman-French by the Jersey cleric Wace, in 1155, it was dedicated to the Angevin queen Eleanor. But the ruling dynasty may not have been so happy to foster the belief (referred to by Wace, but already the subject of popular speculation) that Arthur would return from Avalon to lead his people to rise up against their conquerors and restore the island to its native inhabitants, the ancient Britons. When the monks of Glastonbury, in 1191, claimed to have found the bones of King Arthur in a tomb in the Abbey grounds, the announcement soon received royal sanction. Avalon *was* Glastonbury, and it would be the reigning monarch who would be the new Arthur, returned *in spirit* to unite all his subject peoples and restore their ancient glory.

After Wace, the Arthurian legend was developed on the continent in the form of verse romances that promoted one or more of the king's knights, rather than the monarch himself, as their hero, while Arthur himself was increasingly presented as a *roi fainéant,* allowing his champions to steal his glory. By the time this process was halted, if not reversed, in the fifteenth century, by Sir Thomas Malory, who contributed "the whole book of King Arthur" to the canon of English literature, there is no doubt that Arthur is a King of England, who, in the words of Malory's editor Caxton, "ought most to be remembered among us Englishmen to fore all other Christian kings." It is this exemplary *English* monarch who is celebrated in the famous poetic cycle of the Victorian Poet Laureate Alfred, Lord Tennyson: the *Idylls of the King.*

By now it is clear the historical Arthur, if he ever *was,* has been buried under the accretions of literary legend, and although scholars still hotly debate the matter of his historicity, it is the *mythical* Arthur, a supernaturally endowed defender of this island against its enemies, both human and monstrous, who has the most vivid presence in medieval Welsh poems and tales, in European verse romance and in post–Victorian English-language prose fiction. The Arthur of myth was and will be again: *rex quondam rexque futurus.* He *is.*

But *where* is he?

•••

From Geoffrey of Monmouth onwards, everyone agrees that Arthur was taken, after the last battle, to Avalon. For some historically minded commentators, as we have seen, Avalon was Glastonbury, the site of the king's burial, but for those in whom the mythic sense is more developed, Avalon cannot be found on any map. It is an elf realm, a region of Faerie, where Arthur, healed of his wounds, awaits the call to return in his country's hour of greatest need.

Sometimes Arthur is presented as the Sleeping Lord, an archetypal image that was also developed by William Blake (1757–1827) in his image of Albion as a fallen Titan seduced into a deathlike sleep, a slumbering giant who must awaken. If Blake's Arthur is only the "spectre" of what Albion once was, it is nevertheless prophesied that, in the Last Judgment, the Eternal Man and his spectre will once more be united: Arthur will return when Albion awakes.

In the meantime, the king and his knights still ride out from Camelot in the service of the queen or their ladies or on a higher, spiritual quest, encountering magicians and fays, dragons and monsters, in an endless stream of stories that continually reimagine Arthur's Kingdom of Logris. This realm bears only a tangential relationship to the post–Roman Celtic Britain in which the historical Arthur would have lived, or to the medieval England and Brittany into which many of the stories were displaced in order to make them contemporary with the *conteurs* who told them. Arthur's Logris is meant to be an earthly kingdom, but it is contiguous with a kingdom of the imagination, for it is bordered by, or encloses, wastelands and paradisiacal islands, valleys of no return, enchanted lakes, magical castles, and perilous forests. Somewhere beyond Logris, in an indeterminate direction, is Corbenic, the Kingdom of the Grail.

If Logris is, in many of its features, recognizably our world, nevertheless it slips imperceptibly into another world; the quester finds himself no longer in the fields we know, but in the Otherworld, the realm of giants, elves, and fays. It is here, then, that we, travelling the path between Camelot and Faerie, must look for Arthur.

•••

But if Arthur's kingdom is a realm of the imagination, it is also a land of promise. The chroniclers reveal Albion to be the land promised *to* the Trojan exile Brutus, the eponym of Britain, *by* the goddess Diana. As the Promised Land of the Goddess, Albion is the inversion of Canaan, the Promised Land of God the Father, in the Christian understanding of the Biblical myth.

It is this understanding that is explored by Blake in his greatest poem, *Jerusalem.* Albion exists in Eternity in harmony with his consort, Britannia. He loves his "emanation" (or feminine aspect) Jerusalem, but he becomes divided against himself and falls into a deathlike sleep. The giant Ancient Man originally encompasses the whole Earth, but in his fall, he shrinks down to the island we now know as Great Britain. Jerusalem becomes divided from Albion as East becomes divided from West, but although Albion and Canaan are now separated geographically, the spirit of Canaan still hovers over the island of Britain, so that Britain is a reflection on Earth of the spiritual Promised Land.

It is, therefore, through the imaginative eye of William Blake that we can read the British legends, not as a collection of tales historical and fantastical about kings and their conquests, but as the story of a fall that holds out the hope of restoration to a lost wholeness. For the island of Albion is the Promised Land both of a pagan goddess and of the Christian God, and although the medieval writers struggled to reconcile these contrary aspects of the mythical tradition they had inherited, Blake saw that the "gods of the heathen" are the poetical "emanations" of the Eternal Prophet, who personifies the imaginative faculty of the Ancient Man. It is only when the imaginative vision is lost that God and the gods become negations; that Man and his Spectre become adversaries; that Arthur is deemed to be dead in a tomb, rather than sleeping in Avalon, as Albion sleeps.

For Blake, Arthur *is* the fallen Albion as Albion *is* the spirit of the island of Britain, sleeping but awaiting the promised call. Thus the myth of Arthur's promised land is the story of the Eternal Man's "fall into division & his resurrection to unity." In what follows, we will journey with Arthur from Albion to Avalon and explore the meaning of the promise of resurrection for the land and its people.

Our principal guides in this exploration will be three English poets whose work, for one reason or another, is not as well known as it arguably should be. The first is a medieval cleric from the Welsh marches called Layamon, who wrote the first epic account in the English language of the birth, noble deeds, and doubtful death of Arthur. The second is Edmund Spenser, who presented Arthur as a young prince in quest of the Faerie Queen in his Elizabethan epic. The third is Blake, a great admirer of Spenser, whose prophetic poem *Jerusalem* should also be ranked as an Arthurian epic, since it tells the story of the giant Albion who, after his fall, *becomes* Arthur.

In the writings of these three great English epic poets, the figure of Arthur is reimagined—the warlord becomes a messianic redeemer; the world conqueror becomes a King of Faerie—and his kingdom becomes "the source of learning and inspiration." For Blake, it is "mental fight," rather than "corporeal" war, which is the true basis for our "ancient glory," and following Blake, perhaps we can imagine that the end of empire can mean the beginning of a new inspiration.

# Prologue:
# The Lost Ancient Britons

On the 20th of April 2009, Tate Britain, the national gallery of British art in London, opened an exhibition of the work of the English artist and prophet of the imagination William Blake. In contrast to its millennial retrospective of his work (held in November 2000), the 2009 exhibition had a much more limited objective: to recreate, as much as it is possible to do now, Blake's one-man show of 1809, on its two-hundredth anniversary.

William Blake was born in London in 1757, the year in which, the visionary Swedenborg (1668–1772) declared, the Last Judgment was realized—not as the dead literally rising up from their tombs, but as the awakening of the spirit in life: resurrection *in,* not *of,* the body. Blake was, in his youth, much influenced by Swedenborg, and although he always maintained a critical independence ("Opposition," he stated, "is true friendship" [*BCW* 157]), he would always acknowledge the older man as his "divine teacher" (Bentley, 413). The Last Judgment was a theme to which he would return over and again in both his art and his poetry.

It is in fact for his poems—and, of them, only a handful of his shorter works—that Blake is best known, though how well the casual reader understands even his short, early poems is doubtful. Of his later, voluminous long poems, usually referred to as his Prophetic Books, the wider public remains ignorant. This is in part because Blake eschewed the lyric form, so popular with his Romantic contemporaries, in favor of sprawling, discontinuous, and highly symbolic epics, but also because he developed his own idiosyncratic mythology, peopling his narratives with eternal beings who love, war, and create both this and all other possible worlds until they can be reunited with the source of their existence. This restoration of, or *awakening to,* wholeness is Blake's Last Judgment.

In 1808, Blake painted an enormous (seven feet by five) work that he entitled "A Vision of the Last Judgment." This painting, according to the artist, depicted "Eternal Creation flowing from The Divine Humanity in Jesus: who opens the Scroll of Judgment upon his knees before the Living & the Dead" (*BCW*, 444). Unfortunately this painting is now lost, but other versions, in different media, have survived. Blake, in fact, continued working on the subject of the Last Judgment until his death.

Blake had intended to exhibit his painting in 1810, and he accordingly wrote a detailed description of the work that was to be printed in a catalogue, but the planned exhibition was cancelled when the one-man show of 1809 proved to be a failure.

## Infernal Illuminations

William Blake was over fifty years old when he arranged with his brother James to put on an exhibition of his work in a room above the hosier's shop that had been their father's and where William had been born.

He was, at this time, working on what is now acknowledged as the greatest of his "Illuminated Books," so called because, like medieval manuscripts, they are lit up by colored illustrations that interact meaningfully with the words. Blake's unique method of "illumination" was an inversion of the usual process of etching. Instead of covering bronze plates with an acid-resistant wax and then etching into it, Blake painted and wrote directly onto the plate. He then covered his designs with an acid-resistant varnish and corroded the background. This caused his words and pictures to stand out; hence the technique is known as "relief-etching." Because it was the opposite of the conventional method and because it compelled him to write backwards, Blake referred to it as his "infernal" method (Viscomi, 41).

The greatest of the works he produced by this method is the long poem called *Jerusalem: The Emanation of the Giant Albion*—an enormous work in four chapters, taking up a hundred relief-etched plates, and one that should not be confused with the famous hymn, the lyrics to which are in fact part of the preface to an earlier epic poem called *Milton*.

Milton, the eighteenth-century poet, author of *Paradise Lost*, is himself the central character in the earlier poem. In *Milton*, which is in two books covering over forty plates, the eponymous hero experiences his own Last Judgment, by reuniting himself with those parts of his whole self from which he has (like all of us) become alienated. The first of these is a shadow-self, which Blake calls a "spectre," and the second of these is the split-off feminine side of his personality, which Blake calls an "emanation."

Both the spectre and the emanation are aspects of the whole being, which nonetheless, due to an internal conflict that Blake characterizes as a "fall," manifest themselves on the outside as if they were separate, distinct beings, whereas their true place is inside, living together in holistic harmony. Blake's longer poems are filled with spectres and emanations, their interactions in love, seduction, and conflict making up the dramatic narratives that spill out from Eternity into the productions of Time. Some of them are identified with Biblical figures, some with pagan deities, and others with legendary or historical people—including some of the main characters from the Arthurian chronicles, whom Blake found in his reading of Spenser, although his use of figures such as Arthur, Merlin, and Guinevere takes little from his sources in constructing his own system, something he claimed he had to do in order not to be a slave to anyone else's.

In constructing his personal mythological system, Blake had no problem including historical characters, sometimes even his contemporaries (who might be patrons or enemies, or sometimes both). Thus in *Milton* the poet is presented as having a six-fold emanation, personified as his three wives and three daughters—biographically accurate, but, more importantly, symbolically resonant, given how often archetypal female figures are grouped in threes or seen as threefold in British legends (beginning, as we will see in the first chapter, with the goddess Diana, who presides over the founding of the British nation). In the course of the poem, Milton's descent into the Deep to redeem his emanation, his overcoming of his spectre, and, at last, his restoration to wholeness, is seen as an image in microcosm of the journey that not just each individual but all of creation must make.

The macrocosmic myth that Blake unveils while recounting Milton's personal journey to regain Paradise is one that he explores in several of his poems, but it finds its fullest and most detailed exposition in *Jerusalem*. In this, his last epic poem, the process of at-one-ment is related to a creation myth of the cosmos and to the prehistory of Britain, as Blake would have known it both from Milton (whose prose work, *The History of Britain, that Part especially now called England, from the first Traditional Beginning* ... was first published in 1670) and from earlier authors.

*Milton* and *Jerusalem,* though published as Illuminated Books, made no money for their author. The enormous poem called *Vala: or, The Four Zoas* (a work-in-progress that he eventually abandoned in favor of *Jerusalem,* in which many of the same themes are explored), was never even published in his lifetime, the first edition appearing at the end of the nineteenth century under the direction of the poet W.B. Yeats, who championed what he saw as Blake's transforming of Christianity into a religion in which the imagination is experienced as a divine manifestation and the forgiveness of sins is awakened by the imaginative arts (Gorski, 22f).

*Vala* makes fascinating, if difficult, reading, but Blake had a living to make. Further, he wanted to make money by the paintings that he considered to be his own, personal productions and not just by commercial engravings or commissions for illustrations. But the art establishment of his day, exemplified by the Royal Academy and the British Institution, considered his most visionary works to be "an unscientific and irregular Eccentricity, a Madman's Scrawls." They were not alone, as Blake would discover. But, initially confident that the public, if allowed to see the works that the official exhibitions rejected, would recognize their "Genius and Inspiration," Blake decided that it was no more than the duty he owed to his country (for "Art is the glory of the Nation") to exhibit his paintings himself (*BCW*, 561).

## Pictures at an Exhibition

It was thus that Blake came, in May 1809, to organize his one-man show at his brother's shop in Broad Street (now Broadwick Street, London W1) in the Parish of St. James, Westminster. Entrance was a shilling, but, for half-a-crown, one could also purchase a copy of the *Descriptive Catalogue* that he produced for the occasion: a powerful work in its own right, in which he makes the most of the opportunity to justify the ways of a divinely inspired artist to his fellow men.

Of the sixteen pictures ("Paintings in Fresco, Poetical and Historical Inventions" [*BCW*, 560]) he assembled for the exhibition, several were on Biblical, some on historical, subjects; some were the depictions of spiritual visions. Although it is the fifth picture in the exhibition that most concerns us, it is worthwhile also discussing the first four pictures, since they present us with themes that dominate much of Blake's work and help us to put into context his approach to British myth and history—and consequently to the Arthurian legends, which partake of both.

The first two pictures Blake describes in the catalogue were, moreover, significant in combining all three of his principal subjects at once, being spiritual visions of historical events seen in a Biblical light. "The Spiritual Form of Nelson guiding Leviathan" and its companion piece, "The Spiritual Form of Pitt guiding Behemoth," are "compositions of a mythological cast" that combine the Biblical monsters of the Deep with political figures (Nelson, the admiral who secured Britain's naval supremacy during the Napoleonic Wars, and Pitt, the prime minister of the day) in a way that would be typical of his later epic poems, in which contemporary politics and even Blake's personal relationships are filtered through the light of Eternity.

Blake claims to have been "taken in vision" to Asia to see the monumental depictions of oriental deities that are known in the Bible as the Cherubim and that are "sculptured and painted on walls of Temples, Towers, Cities, Palaces, and erected in the highly cultivated states ... among the Rivers of Paradise." These "sublime conceptions" are the products of inspiration and imagination, "all containing mythological and recondite meaning, where more is meant than meets the eye." This, of course, is a description of Blake's own paintings, and he writes that, in his "spiritual" portrayal of Nelson and Pitt, he "has endeavoured to emulate the grandeur of those seen in his vision" (*DC*, 45f). To emulate the grandeur of his visions was Blake's artistic credo throughout his life.

The third picture described in the catalogue is, on the surface, taken from a more conventional literary and historical subject: Chaucer's *Canterbury Tales*. However, even here Blake is keen to demonstrate that he is not just depicting a collection of idiosyncratic characters: Chaucer's pilgrims, for Blake, are archetypal beings, "the physiognomies or lineaments of universal human life" (49).

Blake returns to this point later in the catalogue, when he writes that these characters describe "eternal Principles that exist in all ages" (55). Blake believed that the Everlasting Gospel was given to humanity at the dawn of time, but that the Daughters of Memory, who act as Muses to a narrow artistic vision, have preserved it only partially; the fuller vision is vouchsafed only to true poets by the Daughters of Inspiration. Thus it is that poets throughout history have been given visions of these eternal principles, which they then present in their artistic creations as characters bearing the lineaments of universal human life—human but eternal beings which constitute the members of the pagan pantheons against which the Biblical prophets fulminated.

For Blake, then, the gods of Greek mythology were no different to "the ancient Cherubim of Phoenicia"—angelic beings when in service to a higher God, but all too often, throughout history, elevated to become the objects of idolatry. The hubris of these pagan gods must be subdued, but the Greeks failed to do this when their poets saw them in vision. The classical pantheon, which Blake calls "the gods of Priam," was brought to Albion by the Trojan exile Brutus (as we will see in the first chapter), and, although we, "the Moderns," do not worship them under their ancient names, they live on in other guises. We, too, have "neglected to subdue" them.

> These Gods are visions of the eternal attributes, or divine names, which, when erected into gods, become destructive to humanity. They ought to be the servants, and not the masters of man, or of society. They ought to be made to sacrifice to Man, and not man compelled to sacrifice to them; for when separated from man or humanity, who is Jesus the Saviour, the vine of eternity, they are thieves and rebels, they are destroyers [56].

Here we have one of the clearest and most powerful statements Blake ever made about his understanding of the relationship between human beings, the gods who "reside in the human breast" (*BCW*, 153), and the Eternal Man. Blake was an unconventional monotheist whose poetic inspiration obliged him to recognize the intermediary beings whom he saw in his visions.

In this respect, he seems to have agreed with the Kabbalists, whose ideas, like those of the Christian Gnostics, he may have encountered through his reading of the mystical shoemaker Jacob Boehme (1575–1624), whom Blake considered to be divinely inspired (Thompson, 35). Blake is referring to the Kabbalistic figure of Adam Kadmon, the Primordial Man, when, in his address to the Jews at the beginning of the second chapter of *Jerusalem,* he says that they "have a tradition, that Man anciently contain'd in his mighty limbs all things in Heaven & Earth" (*BCW*, 649). "Tradition" is in fact a good translation of the Hebrew word "Kabbalah," which more specifically refers to the secret doctrines of Jewish mysticism (Scholem, 20f), which had a significant influence on western esotericism in the Renaissance period (Faivre, 111–4), and is currently undergoing its own "celebrity renaissance" thanks to its espousal by stars of stage and screen (whose idolatrous worship, it could be argued, we Moderns have also neglected to subdue).

Following the attempt in the Renaissance to equate the pagan Mysteries with those of Judaism, as exemplified by the Kabbalah (Wind, 19f), late eighteenth-century scholars such as the antiquarian Jacob Bryant (1715–1804) argued that the sacred traditions of the "heathens" are derived from the first chapters of Genesis. Blake read Bryant, whose "new system" of mythology was published in 1774, and worked as an apprentice to the engraver of the book. In his Catalogue, Blake claims that Bryant has proved that the antiquities of all nations are "no less sacred" than those of the Jews and are therefore no more worthy of being "neglected and disbelieved." If they are "the same thing" (*DC*, 71), then there is spiritual truth in the ancient myths, as there is in the Bible, and the many gods of the polytheistic pantheons, such as those of the ancient Greeks and Phoenicians, are really personifications of the divine names of the One God rather than demons, as more conventional Christians would have claimed. It is only when these aspects of the godhead become separated from the whole—and claim for themselves supremacy over it—that they become rebels, thieves, and destroyers.

This mystical theology is one that Blake depicted in vivid, narrative form in his later epic poems. Jesus is Divine Humanity as redeemer, but, as the Kabbalists believed, Divine Humanity is also fallen and must be redeemed (Scholem, 279f). Fallen Humanity is called the Eternal or Ancient Man in *The Four Zoas,* where the "zoas" are the "living beings" (from the Greek *zoon,* pl. *zoa*) who, in a time before time, live in harmony within the Man, but who, when he falls, become antagonistic and/or seductive towards each other. There is war in Heaven, and the Divine Names compel humankind to sacrifice to them as gods. Through the intervention of Jesus, the separate, warring "attributes" or Zoas find their way back to wholeness: a cosmic journey, which is explored on many metaphorical levels in the poems and which is the archetypal basis of all pilgrimage.

Blake also makes an interesting analogy between the way Chaucer's archetypal pilgrims are debased in some, more conventional, renditions and the way Shakespeare's witches (from the "Scottish play," *Macbeth*) are similarly degraded on stage. For Blake, the Three Witches are not "wretched old women" but "the Goddesses of Destiny" (*DC*, 53). These goddesses are the Three Fates familiar from Greek and Norse mythology, also known as the Weird Sisters, but what is less well known is that the Latin original of the word "fate" (*fatum*) also gives us the words "fay," "fairy," and Faerie (the land of the fays). Already, by the early nineteenth century, fays or fairies were being seen as the twee, gossamer creatures familiar from children's picture books and moralizing "fairy tales," rather than as the powerful and implacable goddesses of antiquity. Thus, Blake reminds us that Shakespeare's and Chaucer's fairies are "the rulers of the vegetable world" (54), that is to say, the rulers of this mortal realm, mistresses of everything that is born and dies. They are the Ladies of Life and Death. But they also open the door to the Otherworld, which is contiguous to this one, and they and their realm of Faerie will play an important role in the chapters that follow, especially when we come to the life of Arthur, a king blessed by the fays.

Fate, however, is a pagan concept that applies, to Christians such as Blake, only to the Vegetable World and the human psyche. There is also a spiritual world that is the source of Destiny, but is not bound by it. Those humans who are in touch with this higher world are not witches or fays, but prophets, and it is as a prophet that Blake depicts the Welsh bard who is the subject of the fourth picture in his catalogue. The title ("The Bard, from Gray") refers to a poem written in the year of Blake's birth by the eighteenth-century English poet, Thomas Gray, from which Blake quotes.

The poem is set at the time of the invasion of Wales by the English army under Edward I in the late thirteenth century. Edward's advance through a deep valley is halted by the appearance of a bard, atop an inaccessible rock, who denounces the king's murderous assault on his country, prophesies the ruin of the Anglo-Norman monarchy, and divines that the poetic genius will never be extinguished by the cruelty of the powerful. In Blake's painting, Edward and his queen cower before the bard, who, assisted by the spirits of his murdered brethren, is "weaving the deadly woof" (*DC*, 66) which is the fatal destiny of the Norman conquerors.

In Gray's poem, the bard, after delivering his prophecy, hurls himself into the rushing torrent below. This event is not depicted by Blake, but a dying bard does appear in the battle scene that constitutes the fifth painting described in his Catalogue: here the last of the warrior-bards was apparently depicted as falling among the casualties of King Arthur's Last Battle and was shown singing and playing his harp, like a true artist, even at the point of death.

This painting was entitled "The Ancient Britons."

## A Naked Civilization

Visitors to the Tate's bicentenary recreation of Blake's 1809 exhibition will have been confronted with five empty spaces, representing pictures now lost. Of these the biggest ("the Figures full as large as Life") was "The Ancient Britons," which Blake considered to be the most important and which he listed first in his advertisement for the exhibition.

Here, also, he printed the following description in a poem, using the unrhymed septenarian (seven beats to the bar) verse form familiar from his epic Illuminated Books:

> In the last Battle that Arthur fought, the most Beautiful was one
> That return'd, and the most Strong another: with them also return'd
> The most Ugly, and no other beside return'd from the bloody Field.

> The most Beautiful, the Roman Warriors trembled before and worshipped:
> The most Strong, they melted before him and dissolved in his presence:
> The most Ugly they fled with outcries and contortion of their Limbs.

The story on which he based his picture, the largest Blake ever made, he said was "From the Welch Triades" (*BCW*, 560)—the Welsh Triads being a traditional poetic form in which fragments of legendary tales are grouped together in threes, as a mnemonic. The picture had been commissioned by William Owen Pughe, a Welsh scholar of whom Robert Southey, later to become Poet Laureate, said that his memory was a "great storehouse of all Cymric tradition and lore of every kind." Owen Pughe had asked for a painting of the three warriors who, according to Welsh tradition, were the sole survivors of the Battle of Camlan, where the legendary Arthur fell, and he apparently provided for Blake a translation of the Triad, in which the three survivors are referred to (Bentley, 327).

This Triad, numbered Eighty-Three, is found in the Third Series in the

Second Volume of the *Myvyrian Archaiology* (1801), the first attempt to publish the Welsh Triads, but unfortunately, it shows all the signs of having been tampered with by Owen Pughe's fellow editor, Iolo Morganwg (*TYP*, 12), whose infamous forgeries and fabrications misrepresented ancient Welsh literature and religion (Hutton 2003, 6) and set back genuine scholarship for many years to come.

As with all the Welsh Triads, the references are to a body of learned and popular lore, most of which is now lost. Blake therefore had plenty of room to exercise his imagination, although we cannot know how much information on the subject Owen Pughe gave him. For example, in all the surviving versions of the battles of King Arthur which mention his war with Rome, the British King defeats the Romans on the Continent before returning home for the Last Battle. Blake, then, has conflated two episodes in the legendary life of the king to produce a depiction of "Three Ancient Britons overthrowing the Army of armed Romans" (*BCW*, 560), but whether he did this at Owen Pughe's suggestion, or using his own poetic license, we cannot tell.

We also cannot tell what ultimately befell the painting. According to one of Blake's recent biographers:

> "The Ancient Britons" was not quite finished when it was exhibited in 1809, or at any rate Blake was still adding finishing touches to it two years later....
> When the great picture was finally delivered, Owen Pughe presumably took it to his estate at Nantglyn, near Denbigh, Wales, and it has never been recorded since [Bentley, 329].

Consequently, all that we now know of the picture, apart from what Blake himself wrote about it, is what the artist's contemporaries said of it. Of all the pictures at the exhibition, this was the one which attracted most attention from visitors, such as the poet Charles Lamb, while Southey considered it to be "one of his worst pictures,—which is saying much" (Raine, 170). But then, Southey held Blake "for a decided madman" (Speck, 143).

Most of what we know about the painting and its inspiration, however, comes from the artist's own description. "The Ancient Britons" is the subject of the fifth entry in the *Descriptive Catalogue,* in which Blake also takes the opportunity to outline his plans to transform the "British Antiquities" into a "source of learning and inspiration" through his own "visionary contemplations." For what are now in his hands, he tells us, are "all the fables of Arthur and his round table; of the warlike naked Britons; of Merlin; of Arthur's conquest of the whole world; of his death, or sleep, and promise to return again; of the Druid monuments, or temples; ... of the Giants of Ireland and Britain; of the elemental beings called by us by the general name of Fairies" (*DC*,

68f)—all, in other words, that is sometimes referred to as the Matter of Britain; the legendary, alternative history of this island.

The Matter of Britain is a term commonly used to contrast with the Matter of Rome (the classical legends that tell how the fall of the Trojan civilization led to the creation of a new one) and the Matter of France (the legends attached to Charlemagne, who was the next of the great Christian "worthies" to follow on after Arthur). For Blake, this imaginative "matter" is "self-evident action and reality" that cannot be turned, twisted or disarranged by the "artifice" of the "reasoning historian" (71), that is to say, of the apostles of Enlightenment Rationalism, such as the eighteenth-century English historian Edward Gibbon.

But Blake is happy to call on the evidence of conventional historians for his view that the ancient Britons were "naked civilized men" (an oxymoron to the rational mind, but the kind of poetic paradox that Blake delighted in). Our ancestors were "learned, studious, abstruse in thought and contemplation" and, in fact, "wiser" than their descendants, which must include us Moderns, but at the same time they were "naked, simple, plain in their acts and manners" (68)—the epitome of the "noble savage" as philosopher.

"Enlightened" historians such as Gibbon may have concurred with Blake's rosy view of the ancient inhabitants of Britain as the embodiment of a "naked" civilization, but it is unlikely that they would have attributed the Britons' "abstruse" wisdom, as Blake does, to the closeness of the Age of the Druids to the primordial revelation that produced the first, universal religion: "All had originally one language, and one religion, this was the religion of Jesus, the everlasting Gospel" (71).

Blake claims to have in his possession "poems of the highest antiquity," which show that Adam and Noah were Druids—although it is not at all clear at this point whether Blake is referring to ancient Welsh poems (such as those found in the *Book of Taliesin,* in which Biblical characters such as Adam and Noah are mentioned alongside ancient British pagan mythological characters and which Owen Pughe could have translated for him) or to his own poem *Jerusalem,* on which he had begun work in 1804 and which was reported by a journalist in 1820 to be "an ancient, newly discovered, illuminated manuscript" (69&*n*56).

According to Blake's revision of Biblical and British history, the story of Abraham takes place at the end of the Age of the Druids, by which time the "naked civilization" had become corrupted, its "abstruse thinkers" beginning "to turn allegoric and mental signification into corporeal command, whereby human sacrifice would have depopulated the earth."

The first Christianity on earth, therefore, is the primordial religion of the Druids, but it falls prey to the curse of literalism, the letter that kills the spirit. Sacred truths that must be interpreted *metaphorically* are debased and corrupted when understood *literally*. This, at least, is one possible symbolic meaning of one of the most striking passages in the Book of Genesis, when God appears to call upon Abraham to sacrifice his only son; but, at the last moment, commands him to sacrifice a ram instead. Sacrifice to God is a symbolic act: it does not require the murder of human beings. Thus, when the Druids are portrayed, in later ages, as practitioners of human sacrifice, this is not an indication of how "primitive" they are but, on the contrary, of how far they have fallen from their aboriginal state of grace.

It is in the fallen state that the "corporeal" supplants "allegoric and mental signification," the symbolic truth of revelation is supplanted by a literalist misunderstanding, and a new revelation is required so that "the world of vegetation and generation may ... be opened again to Heaven" (69). Thus God condemns human sacrifice on Mount Moriah and restores the spiritual truth of metaphor: the Age of the Druids is succeeded by the Age of Abraham. And so it is that, when Joseph of Arimathea comes to preach Christianity among the rocks of Albion (a popular legend that is the subject of an early engraving by Blake), he is not bringing a new revelation but restoring a primordial truth that has long been lost.

Albion, meaning "the White Island," is a poetical name for the island now called Britain, but how it acquired its new name, the subject of an early poem by Blake, we will explore in the first chapter. According to the legend with which Blake was probably most familiar (through Spenser), this island took its first name from a giant son of Neptune, but to this tradition Blake adds his own original—one might say inspired—interpretation: "The giant Albion," he writes, "was Patriarch of the Atlantic; he is the Atlas of the Greeks, one of those the Greeks call Titans" (70).

The Titans (in Greek mythology the sons and daughters of Heaven and Earth) attempted to defend the rule of Saturn against the usurpation of the Olympian gods. The reign of Saturn on Earth was the Golden Age, and, in his attempt to restore this blissful state, Atlas, the leader of the Titans, can be seen, like Blake himself, as a "conservative revolutionary" (King, 28). Atlas is defeated and, as a punishment, is condemned to carry the weight of the heavens on his shoulders. Both Atlas and Blake can be seen as suffering Titans, carrying on their shoulders the spiritual burden of maintaining the connection between Heaven and Earth in an age when they are separated and hoping to restore that Golden Age, which is Heaven on Earth.

There is a classical myth in which the hero Hercules temporarily takes on Atlas's burden for him, and this is especially interesting as Hercules is often equated with King Arthur. We will revisit the connections between the two heroes later, but what is important for our purposes now is to see that, for Blake, Arthur was also someone who, temporarily, took on the burden of attempting to restore, in his limited time and place, that connection between Heaven and Earth that is the essence of true *religion* (meaning, according to one etymology, that which "binds" us to the sacred [Skeat, 398]).

If Arthur, like Atlas, is condemned to the herculean labor of carrying the weight of the heavens on his shoulders, it is because he is an incarnation of the giant Albion, albeit a mere "spectre" of the fallen Titan: "The stories of Arthur are the acts of Albion, applied to a Prince of the fifth century, who conquered Europe, and held the Empire of the world in the dark age, which the Romans never again recovered" (*DC*, 70).

## A Dark Age Prince

Most English-speaking people nowadays are familiar with the Arthurian stories from the fifteenth-century retelling by Sir Thomas Malory, generally known as *Le Morte Darthur*, and the nineteenth-century poetical version by Alfred, Lord Tennyson: the *Idylls of the King*.

Here we find the familiar Arthurian tropes and characters: Uther Pendragon, Merlin the Magician, the Sword in the Stone, Excalibur, the Lady of the Lake, Morgan the Fay, the Quest of the Holy Grail, the adulterous affair between Arthur's wife Guinevere and his greatest knight Lancelot, and the final battle between Arthur and Modred, after which the wounded Arthur is transported to Morgan's island of Avalon, from which it is believed that he will one day return to save Britain in its hour of greatest need.

Needless to say, none of the above elements has any basis in known history, although it is possible that some of the characters such as Arthur himself, Merlin (under different names) and Medraut (the original Welsh name of Modred) were real people. Other historical characters crop up from time to time, often anachronistically, in the stories, while some famous names such as that of Gawain, Arthur's nephew and champion, have been seen to derive from folklore or mythology.[1] Blake's identification of Arthur with Albion and Atlas, on the other hand, forms part of his own private, poetical mythology; they are symbolic characters in the religious (spiritual and psychological) narratives that constitute his epic poems.

The sources of Blake's own knowledge of the Arthurian legends can only be guessed at; nothing in Blake's art or writing indicates a specific knowledge of Malory's *Morte Darthur*. The direct inspiration for "The Ancient Britons," as we have seen, came from the Cymric scholar Owen Pughe, who may have supplied all of the relevant detail from Welsh-language sources that were not then available in English. It was almost certainly from Owen Pughe (Damon, 29) that Blake derived one of his most astonishing beliefs about the king: that Arthur was a name for Arcturus, the Guardian of the Bear, the principal star in the constellation Boötes, and therefore "the Keeper of the North Pole" (*DC*, 68).

We will return to the polar symbolism of Arthur later. What we do know for certain is that Blake knew Spenser's *The Faerie Queene*. This unfinished work was composed over a period of some fifteen years, between 1579 and 1594, about a hundred years after Malory's prose masterpiece was written, but it appears to owe little to the *Morte Arthur* beyond a few borrowed names.

*The Faerie Queene* purports to tell the hitherto-unknown story of the young Prince Arthur, who, before he became king, had a vision of the beautiful Gloriana, the Queen of Faerie (the land of the fays and elves). He sets off to find her, and the adventures he meets with on the way constitute the narrative of the surviving six (of a proposed twelve) books. All the characters and incidents related are susceptible of a fairly precise and explicit allegorical interpretation, unlike Blake's symbols, which are never fixed and perhaps for that reason appeal more to the modern taste, having something in common with late nineteenth- and early twentieth-century movements in art and poetry such as Symbolism and Surrealism, where meaning can seldom be precisely pinned down.

When Blake says that Arthur is the Spectre of Albion, for example, he is relating one symbolic character to another and weaving strands of thematic thread into ever more complex patterns. When Spenser, on the other hand, says that Prince Arthur personifies the virtue of Magnificence, then his pursuit of a queen whose name suggests that she personifies Glory is fairly easy to interpret.

As well as abstract virtues, Spenser's heroes and heroines signify political figures of the day: Gloriana is, of course, the first Elizabeth, and Prince Arthur may, at least in part, be meant to signify Robert Dudley, the Earl of Leicester. By contrast, Blake's symbolic figures include not just famous Biblical, mythological and historical characters, but also personal friends and enemies, all of which makes the process of exegesis partly dependent on knowledge of Blake's biography. The poet William Hayley, Blake's friend and patron who himself features as a character in one of the Prophetic Books, commissioned Blake to produce portraits of literary figures, including Spenser, and he did a watercolor of "The Characters of Spenser's *Faerie Queene*," the sale of which, after the artist's death, helped to secure Blake's widow's financial future (Bentley, 443).

The most important influence of Spenser on Blake's use of the Matter of Britain comes from one of the least poetical sections of the *Faerie Queene*. In Book Two, Canto X, Spenser provides us with what is primarily a versification of Geoffrey of Monmouth's *History of the Kings of Britain* from the reign of the eponymous Brutus to the accession of Uther Pendragon, Arthur's father.

The Welsh traditions about Arthur had been developing for hundreds of years after the Anglo-Saxon conquest of what was to become England, traditions that were primarily transmitted orally, but that also included written chronicles and poems. It was not until the early ninth century, however, that the first complete "history" of the island, from its settlement by Trojan refugees in the twelfth century before the Christian era to the Anglo-Saxon conquest, was attempted, and this sketchy narrative, which included an account of Arthur's military triumphs, was considerably augmented after the Norman Conquest, when Geoffrey wrote his *De Gestis Britonum* ("Concerning the Deeds of the Britons," better known as the *Historia Regum Britanniae*) in 1136–8. His history of the Kings of Britain was ostensibly the translation into Latin of an ancient book written in the indigenous British language, and clearly based on native traditions, myths, and legends, along with a certain amount of literary embellishment to flesh out the scanty historical facts that hold the patchwork together.

Geoffrey's "history" begins with the settlement of the island of Albion by the descendants of refugees from the Siege of Troy, led by Brutus, the great-grandson of Aeneas, who had fled the burning city and settled in Italy. The Latin descendants of Aeneas had founded Rome, while his British descendants founded a kingdom that was twice able to humble the mighty Roman Empire—or such, at least, was the claim of Geoffrey's *Historia*.

Thus when Spenser's Knight of Temperance, Sir Guyon, accompanied by Prince Arthur, chances upon an ancient book, entitled *Briton Moniments,* which contains a chronicle of British kings from Brutus to Uther, it may be intended to be the very book on which Geoffrey based his history.

It was around the year 1138 that Geoffrey's work was first published, and it quickly became a best-seller. It was translated from prose into verse and from Latin into Norman-French, the courtly language of the ruling classes in Britain, by 1155 (when its translator, the Jersey-man Wace, dedicated it to the queen, Eleanor of Aquitaine), and within three decades, some of the greatest poems of the Middle Ages had been written, inspired by stories that were circulating about the heroes of Arthur's court: sometimes, in origin, contemporary knights thinly disguised as mythical warriors. The Fellowship of the Round Table had been born.

By the end of the decade, however, the stories had taken on a whole new complexion with the introduction, in an unfinished poem by Chrétien de Troyes, of a mysterious vessel, a *graal,* which soon, in the hands of Chrétien's continuators, became "the Holy Grail." Now, Arthur's humbling of the Roman Empire, as described by Geoffrey and Wace, took second place to a spiritual quest that could only be achieved by the most perfect of his knights, leaving the royal court a shadow of its former self, unable to recapture its past glories and soon to fall prey to fratricidal fury.

In the first decades of the thirteenth century, verse adventures gave way to increasingly vast prose compilations, in which the heroic adventures of the Knights of the Round Table were assimilated into the story of the Grail. As they did so—and as the mysterious and mythical elements in the stories were subordinated to Christian dogma—the battles and loves of the knights were increasingly viewed as diversions from the true path; *eros* was devalued in favor of *agape,* earthly in favor of spiritual chivalry. By the middle of the century, the astonishing creative outflow that Geoffrey and Wace had undammed had all but dried up.

The beginning of the thirteenth century also saw the beginning of an alternative tradition of Arthurian verse, however, one that used not the clerical language (Latin) nor the courtly language (French), but rather the vernacular language of the English people. This tradition begins with a reworking of the Anglo-Norman chronicle of Wace into Middle English, that is, the intermediate form of the language that straddles the centuries between the disappearance of Anglo-Saxon (or "Old English") with the Norman Conquest and the emergence of modern English in the fifteenth century. The English poet who reworked Wace appears in the surviving manuscripts as Laȝamon, usually transliterated as Layamon, and it is by this name that I will refer to him, even though it might be more accurate to call him (as his translator Rosamund Allen does) "Lawman," which is what his name means.

What little we know of Layamon is that he was a Worcestershire clergyman, brought up on the banks of the Severn, as he himself tells us in the prologue to his poem. Layamon's *Brut* is almost double the length of his main source, Wace's *Roman de Brut* ("Romance of Brutus"), and among the additions that he brings to his version are elements derived from Welsh oral traditions about the bard Taliesin and what is sometimes called "fairy lore"—a set of beliefs about a nonhuman race with magical powers who exist side-by-side with mortals and share the land with us.

Unfortunately, as I have said, despite its origin in the Latin word for the Goddess of Fate, the word "fairy" has whimsical connotations, evoking images of winged sprites in Victorian illustrations (not to mention photographic forgeries!), and so, when J.R.R. Tolkien tried to revive the power and the glory of this tradition in his fiction, he used the alternative word "elves," which derives from Germanic mythology, and this is in fact the term that Layamon uses. Spenser refers to a male "Elf" and a female "Fay" as the ancestors of the fairies and to their realm as the land of Faerie. Their mutual interest in fairy lore is one of the principal links between Layamon and Spenser, and it is also found in Blake.

All three poets also develop the mythology of the giants, another non-human race who share the island with mortals as well as with the Little People, as the elves are sometimes known. Layamon, following Wace, shows the giants inhabiting Albion before the arrival of Brutus the Trojan; Spenser presents them as monstrous enemies of humans and elves alike, but Blake reveals that this enmity is precisely due to their separation from the human. For Blake, giants are an image of a primordial (antediluvian) energy that has been suppressed, with destructive consequences. Albion himself is a sleeping giant who will become whole, fully and eternally human, only when he awakes.

Thus we can see that Layamon is the originator, not just of the Arthurian epic in English, but also of its mythology of giants and elves. As such, he deserves to be much better known than he is, but unfortunately the Middle English in which he wrote is inaccessible except to scholars. Another obstacle in the way of a fuller appreciation of Layamon is his use of an outmoded style of versification. Like the Anglo-Saxon poets before him, most famously the author of *Beowulf*, Layamon writes in a form of verse called "alliteration," meaning that words "rhyme," not because their endings sound the same, but because they begin with, or put the stress on, the same consonants. Thus each of Layamon's lines includes several words beginning with the same consonant, rather than having two lines which both end with the same sound, which is what we usually think of as rhyming poetry. Alliteration is nowadays only used for tongue-twisters, and its unfamiliarity as a vehicle for serious poetry means it can put off modern readers. Allen, in her translation, has powerfully reproduced Layamon's alliterative style, and it deserves to be explored, benefitting (as does the original) from being read aloud.

Layamon's alliterative verse style was archaic even in the early thirteenth century, but it was not a dead end. About a hundred and fifty years later, there was an Arthurian revival in the north of England, producing such alliterative masterpieces as a *Morte Arthure* and the more famous *Sir Gawain and the Green Knight* by the end of the fourteenth century. Both of these works have been recently translated by the northern English poet Simon Armitage, but whether this will spark a new alliterative renaissance, only time will tell!

After 1400, however, English literary investment in the Arthurian legends was sporadic. When Malory produced the *Morte Darthur* in the fifteenth century, he mainly relied on the French prose compilations, although even a cursory reading of his Book Five, dealing with the war with Rome, reveals that he is paraphrasing an alliterative poem. In fact, he has reworked a section of the alliterative *Morte Arthure* while barely attempting to conceal his source, so that it reads very differently to the rest of his "whole book." Malory did, however, produce a very English masterpiece by toning down the magical and mystical elements in his French sources in favor of the personal, human tragedy of the king, his wife, and her lover; his *Morte* became an epic account of the death of chivalry, in which earthly glory passes, like the king himself, to another, more doubtful state.

Spenser, in the sixteenth century, took up the characters of Arthur and Merlin, but it was only to place them within an allegorical setting in which the battles of heroic champions defending gentle ladies threatened by sorcery and monstrosity become exemplars of human virtue.

As a young man, John Milton, the greatest English poet of the seventeenth century, had contemplated writing a national epic based on the legends of King Arthur; he abandoned this idea in favor of a work based on the Book of Genesis (*Paradise Lost*), but the research he had done in the ancient chronicles found its way into his *History of Britain,* where he declares himself unconvinced of the historicity of Arthur. Edward Gibbon, writing a hundred years later, was, by contrast, inclined to accept a historical Arthur, but only as a battle-leader, not as the fabulous figure of the romances.

William Blake, however, eschewed the merely historical, preferring to give "the historical fact in its poetical vigour" (*DC*, 71) so that Merlin becomes an embodiment of the imagination (see Chapter Four) and King Arthur the historical incarnation of the giant Albion.

Blake's Albion is a cosmic being who is the British counterpart of the Anthropos, or "Divine Humanity." The myth of the Anthropos is found in many cultures, in polytheistic religions (the Vedic Purusha and the Norse Ymir, for example, are both primordial giants who are dismembered in order to create the world) as well as on the margins of the monotheistic Abrahamic faiths, where he is described as the "original" or "spiritual" Man, the Adam of Light— the Adam Kadmon of the Kabbalists. Where the Adam of Genesis "falls" through sin and is expelled from Paradise, the "cosmic" Adam falls into division and self-limitation, becoming the earthly reflection of his own, higher self. In the Gnostic version of this myth, the shattered parts of the whole Man survive as sparks of light trapped in the darkness of a world that is created by his falling, but the sparks are in each of us created beings so that, in a sense, we *are* the fallen Man who has forgotten his spiritual origin until he awakes in us.

Thus Blake's Albion falls, as the primordial human being always does, because in doing so he creates the fallen world we know. At first, the fallen Albion stretches across the whole world, but as the Fall continues, the giant is contracted to the size of the island that bears his name. In the fifth century of the Christian era, his Spectre appears in human guise as the greatest king of the native Britons.

Warfare and sexual strife are the enduring characteristics of fallen Humanity, according to Blake (who predates Freud by almost a century in seeing war as the result of repressed sexuality), and they are the leitmotifs that span the life of Arthur, the fallen Albion. It is fitting, therefore, that Blake's first portrait of the Arthurian Age should be the depiction of a battle—of his Last Battle, in fact, although, by incorporating his victory over the Romans, Blake is perhaps suggesting that corporeal must give way to mental fight. By making the scene of Arthur's greatest earthly victory the scene of his departure from this Earth, Blake is showing us that the incarnation of his Spectre in the Dark Age is only a temporary, "herculean" interlude in the transformations of the giant Albion. Arthur's fabled return can only be Albion's Last Judgment.

This also, perhaps, explains why in Blake's painting Arthur himself is not portrayed: he has already passed on, changed his life. What interests Blake in "The Ancient Britons" is what survives on Earth of the spirit of Albion, and this he shows us in the three figures who survive the warfare. The Beautiful Man represents feeling ("the human pathetic"); the Strong Man, sublimity; and the Ugly Man, human reason (*DC*, 70).

It may surprise the reader, therefore, to learn that Blake portrayed the Ugly Man as a bestial creature who loves carnage and delights in "the savage barbarities of war" (74). But, for Blake, Reason must always be part of a balanced whole, or it turns ugly. Here, Reason is separated from Feeling and Sublimity and runs amok.

None of the three can function properly—be fully human—without the others.

> They were originally one man, who was fourfold; he was self-divided, and his real humanity slain on the stems of generation, and the form of the fourth was like the Son of God [70].

The original fourfold Man is the giant Albion, and his hidden, godlike "fourth" aspect is Arthur, who, in the Matter of Britain, becomes a Messiah, as we will see in Chapter Eight.

The story of how the Eternal Man became divided was the subject of *The Four Zoas,* a poem that Blake had abandoned by the time he held his exhibition. But its theme and even some of the earlier poem's verses were incorporated into *Jerusalem,* and it is to this "voluminous" work that Blake refers when he says that he has "written it under inspiration," an inspiration that enabled him to combine his two great influences—sacred history (the Biblical and Miltonic world of Satan and Adam) and legendary matter (which he saw as "the ancient history of Britain")—into one seamless whole.

Blake announces his intention to publish *Jerusalem,* but states that meanwhile he has painted a picture of "those naked Heroes" who have survived in the Welsh mountains from the fifth century to the present day: "they are there now ... there they dwell in naked simplicity; happy is he who can see and converse with them above the shadows of generation and death" (70). One such happy poet is Gray, whose vision of the heroic bard on Snowdon was the subject of the fourth picture in the exhibition; another, of course, is Blake himself, for the subject of his fifth painting is something he himself had seen in his visions.

So "The Ancient Britons" can be seen as an announcement, or a statement of intent, heralding the appearance of the Illuminated Book that would be the summation of his life's work. But although, unlike with *The Four Zoas,* he would produce the plates, fully colored, in his trademark "infernal" relief-etching, few people would ever see *Jerusalem* in his lifetime.

One of the few who did, Robert Southey, considered it a "perfectly mad poem" (Raine, 156), and we can assume that he would not have been alone in his opinion. It was, after all, not dissimilar to the reaction Blake got to the paintings he exhibited in 1809. The only published critical review was that which appeared in the progressive periodical *The Examiner,* whose art critic talked of Blake's "wretched pictures, some of which are unintelligible allegory," while the Catalogue itself was dismissed as "a farrago of nonsense, unintelligibleness, and egregious vanity, the wild effusions of a distempered brain" (*DC,* 32).

The Catalogue does at least give us a description, albeit "effusive," of the picture that no one has seen for about two hundred years. The three survivors (the Most Strong, the Most Beautiful and the Most Ugly of the naked heroes) march through the field of the Last Battle *unsubdued, as Gods* (68), while the defeated Roman soldiers are rolled together as if by a whirlwind and left in an "affrighted" heap before them, each of them showing one of many different expressions—not just fear or horror, but also "amazement, or devout wonder and unresisting awe." Naked Britons and armed Romans strew the field, where also sings the dying warrior-bard, the ancestor of Gray's. In the distance, among the mountains, Druid temples have been erected, which are similar to Stonehenge. "The Sun sets behind the mountains, bloody with the day of battle" (74). But the sun of Britain *shall arise again with tenfold splendor when Arthur shall awake from sleep, and resume his dominion over earth and ocean* (68).

In the chapters that follow, we will explore the story of the lost ancient Britons which constitutes the Matter of Britain, and I will focus above all on those poets who have allowed us to imagine the "ancient glory" that was Britain's and to believe in the promise of renewal, which is the awakening of the Sleeping Lord. In doing so, I will highlight the work of those three English poets—Layamon, Spenser, and Blake—whom I have selected, not only because their versions of the legends are relatively unfamiliar to the modern reader, but also because between them they present us with an archetypal transformation of the figure of Arthur through literary history.

Working in the early thirteenth century, Layamon rewrote the stories he found in the Norman French "romance" of Wace to produce the first account in the English language of the birth, life, and death of King Arthur. It remains an open question as to whether or not Spenser was familiar with Layamon,[2] but we do know that they both stressed the importance of the world of Faerie to the early development of a king who would return to that world on his passing. If both Layamon and Spenser told of a world of Faerie just beyond the fields we know, Blake showed us visions of a reality that transforms those fields, the spiritual realm of Albion that is both here and now and in Eternity.

Layamon's image of Arthur is that of one of what Blake would call the "kings in wrath," but the medieval poet also portrayed the king as one blest by Faerie. In doing so, he opens the door to the Elizabethan poet Spenser's Faerie mythology, and Spenser's portrayal of Arthur's encounter with Faerie opens the door to Blake's portrayal of Arthur as the fallen Albion who shall arise again with tenfold splendor. For if Layamon's wrathful king shows Albion at the depth of his descent into time, Spenser's prince enchanted by the Faerie Queen shows Albion awaking to his true nature and destiny, that of a king in two worlds: the everyday world and the Otherworld.

That Otherworld has its roots not in medieval or Renaissance Christianity, but in an older, indigenous British paganism that left its mark on early Celtic Christianity in this island and whose traces survive in the Welsh literature of the Middle Ages, where the figure of Arthur is first transformed from a warlord to a mythical hero: a guardian of the island against both human and supernatural threats. In exploring the ways in which Layamon, Spenser and Blake present the Matter of Britain, I will, therefore, also explore some of the Welsh traditions on which all three, directly or indirectly, drew.

If the early Welsh poets mythologized Arthur, and Layamon and the other chroniclers historicized him, Spenser took Arthur into the elven Otherworld, while Blake restored the Once and Future King to the archetypal reality from which he had fallen: to his true identity as the Ancient or Eternal Man who awakes upon the rocks of Albion.

# One

# *The Founding of Britain*

"Britain was active and awake and alive long before Caesar saw it. Nor was it a country of blue-painted savages in bear-skins. It had an old culture of its own, older than the little hill of Romulus."[1]
—D.H. Lawrence, 1932

The Matter of Britain preoccupied William Blake from an early age. As a teenager, working as an apprentice engraver, he produced a copy of a figure in a painting by Michelangelo, "The Martyrdom of St Peter." The figure was originally a centurion, looking away from the crucifixion scene, whom some have seen as a self-portrait of the artist, but Blake has transformed him to look like one of the Druids whom antiquarians were "rediscovering" at this time. The title he gave the picture, when he re-engraved it at about the time he held his exhibition, was "Joseph of Arimathea among the Rocks of Albion."

Joseph was believed to have come to Britain (as indeed was St. Peter himself) and to have founded the first Christian church here: "This is One of the Gothic Artists who Built the Cathedrals in what we call the Dark Ages" (*BCW*, 604). One of Blake's biographers has suggested that, while it would be "too easy" to see Joseph, like his centurion model, as a self-portrait of the artist, nevertheless "Joseph of Arimathea was, in many respects, Blake's true ancestor" (Ackroyd, 49). If Blake always acknowledged Michelangelo as *il miglior fabbro,* he could also see Joseph as the "better craftsman," building a church and establishing the religion of Jesus in rocky Albion. Blake, who sought to renew that religion in an Age of Enlightenment, was Joseph's heir as Gothic artist—those artists who sought to delineate Eternity in the now, whether through painting or building.

About twenty years after he did his youthful engraving of Joseph, Blake, by now a published poet but concerned that his art was not receiving the recognition it deserved ("The Labours of the Artist, the Poet, the Musician, have been proverbially attended by poverty and obscurity" [*BCW*, 207]), issued a "Public Prospectus," in which he extolled the virtues of his method of relief-etching and announced that he had for sale works on Biblical and historical subjects, along with his own prophecies and illuminated books. Among the historical works was an engraving depicting Edward I and Queen Eleanor, the monarchs who were challenged by Gray's Bard—a descendant, Blake suggested, of those naked heroes in the Welsh mountains who survived the Last Battle of King Arthur.

He also produced, in 1793, a small book of engravings for children, entitled "The History of England." The work has not survived, but we do have a handwritten list of the subjects he depicted. Of these, the first eight do not refer to "English" history at all, in the sense that they are all set before the Anglo-Saxon settlement, but Blake, like Layamon before him, saw a direct line of continuity from modern England back to the ancient Britons.

In the first eight subjects we can also see that, for Blake, there was no valid distinction between history and legend (counter-history), any more than there was between body and soul:

1. Giants ancient inhabitants of England.
2. The Landing of Brutus.
3. Corineus throws Gogmagog the Giant into the Sea.
4. King Lear.
5. The Ancient Britons according to Caesar.
6. The Druids.
7. The Landing of Julius Caesar.
8. Boadicea inspiring the Britons against the Romans [208].

The first four subjects, of course, have no basis in known history, but they had been dealt with in prose by Milton and in poetry by Spenser; they are foundational stories of the Matter of Britain. The story of King Lear, reprised from Geoffrey of Monmouth by Spenser, is more famously the subject of a tragic play by Shakespeare, but the landing of Brutus is also the subject of a minstrel's song in Blake's early, unfinished dramatic poem "King Edward the Third" (1783). It is with this story, the story of the genesis of the British nation, that we will begin our exploration of this island and discover how, by English poets from Layamon to Blake, it has been seen as a Promised Land.

## An Unpeopled Savage Wilderness

As in the Biblical story of the Promised Land, the aboriginal inhabitants have to be depicted as unworthy of their territory, in order to justify the divine choosing of another race to settle there. In Book II, Canto X of *The Faerie Queene,* Spenser sets the scene:

> The land, which warlike Britons now possesse,
> And therein haue their mighty empire raysd,
> In antique times was saluage wildernesse,
> Vnpeopled, vnmannurd, vnproud, unpraysd,

a desolate region, not yet an island, still attached to the European continent ("the *Celticke* mayn-land" [*FQ,* II.x.5]). This is the land of Albion, so named by mariners because of the white rocks on its southern sea coast that have saved many a ship from wreck. There is a reason, however, why even the most adventurous could not further invade the territory

> But far in land a saluage nation dwelt,
> Of hideous Giaunts, and halfe beastly men,
> That neuer tasted grace, nor goodnes felt,

and who live like wild beasts in shameless nakedness, hunting their prey with the swiftness of deer, despite being

> Of stature huge, and eke of corage bold,
> That sonnes of men amazd their sternesse to behold [7].

Spenser declares himself unable to affirm "whence they sprong, or how they were begott" (8) and, indeed, neither Geoffrey of Monmouth nor his translators tells us the story of their origin. Wace, in his *Roman de Brut* (l.1063), laconically announces that there were giants in the island, in a perhaps conscious echo of Genesis VI: 4: "There were giants in the earth ..."

It is also from this chapter of Genesis, where we are told that the Sons of God consorted with the daughters of men, producing the mighty men of old, that is likely to have been derived the legend Spenser refers to, without committing himself to its veracity, of the birth of the giants from the fifty daughters of Dioclesian, who had been driven into this land by chance:

> Where companing with feends and filthy Sprights
> Through vaine illusion of their lust vnclene,
> They brought forth Geaunts and such dreadful wights,
> As far exceeded men in their immeasurd mights [*FQ,* II.x.8].

Thus the giants, the offspring of mortal women and demonic beings, are the first inhabitants of this island, and it is they who build Tintagel, the "fairy castle" where Arthur will be conceived (Walter, 64).

One of these giants, Spenser tells us, is himself called Albion, but his father is neither a fiend nor a filthy sprite, but the sea god Neptune. One of the brothers of Albion named by Spenser is Pelasgus, who gave his name to the Pelasgians, the mythical pre–Hellenic peoples of Greece, as Brutus will give his name to the Britons. Spenser thus contrives a far more exalted lineage for "mightie *Albion*" than is accorded to the other aboriginal giants, and he alone among them can be considered to be "father of the bold/And warlike people, which the *Britaine* Islands hold" (IV.xi.15).

Albion, however, does not live to meet the hero who will replace him as the island's eponym. The giant son of Neptune,

> for the proofe of his great puissance,
> Out of his *Albion* did on dry-foot pas
> Into old *Gall* ...
> To fight with *Hercules,* that did aduance
> To vanquish all the world with matchlesse might,
> And there his mortall part by great mischance
> Was slaine: but that which is th'immortall spright
> Liues still ... [16].

This will have occurred at some time when the island was still attached to "the Celtic mainland," since Albion can pass across to Gaul with dry feet: translating these events into known history, we would therefore date the cataclysmic event of the death of our first ancestor to at least eight thousand years ago, during the Mesolithic period, when the island was finally separated from the mainland by the rising sea levels that marked the ending of the last Ice Age.

Death at the hands of world-vanquishing semi-divine heroes apart, the giants were clearly a long-lived race, since Godmer, the son of Albion, is still alive when Brutus and "the remnant of Troy" arrive. The Trojan War is traditionally dated to the late twelfth century before the Christian era, by which time the "mortal part" of Hercules is also slain and his spirit has joined the Olympians, although his sword remains on earth to be claimed by Arthur, according to the French prose romances (*LG* 1, 293f).

Spenser describes Brutus as being "anciently deriu'd/ From roiall stocke of old *Assaracs* line" (II.x.9), Assaracus being a son of Tros (who gave his name to Troy) and the great-grandfather of Aeneas (who is in turn the great-grandfather of Brutus). Aeneas, the semi-divine son of the goddess Venus, famously flees the burning city and, after many adventures, is guided by his mother to Italy, the land that his descendants are destined to rule. The progeny of Aeneas will, in the nationalist myth developed by the Augustan poet Virgil, be the founders of Rome; and it is in imitation of, and in some respects opposition to, this foundational myth that the chroniclers of the Matter of Britain developed an alternative one, in which the island that Rome was to come to dominate for hundreds of years has a similar, but much older history.

Aeneas in Italy is united with Lavinia, the Princess of Latium, and their descendants rule the country until Romulus, the last of the line, founds Rome. The royal line of Britain, meanwhile, begins with Silvius, the grandson of Aeneas, who learns from a prophecy that his wife will give birth to a boy who will cause the death of both his parents, but that after a period in exile, he will gain the highest honor.

All comes to pass as predicted: the wife of Silvius dies giving birth to a son, who is named Brutus, and so it is that Brutus and his progeny can be seen as "anciently derived" from the same royal stock as the ancestors of Romulus. When he is fifteen years of age (the age at which Arthur will become King of Britain), Brutus accidentally kills his father in a hunting accident. As a result, he is sent into exile.

Brutus makes his way to Greece, where he finds thousands of Trojan men, the descendants of those taken as prisoners of war, living as slaves with their women and children. Brutus soon establishes himself as their leader, through his wisdom and valor, and promises to win them their freedom. This he accomplishes through a combination of bravery and cunning: he defeats the Greek army and takes their king captive, demanding the hand of the king's daughter in marriage. The King of Greece takes some comfort from the fact that his daughter will marry a man of such prowess, one who has shown himself to be a true heir of Troy, and the princess Ignoge, whom Blake will count among the twelve Daughters of Albion, is duly wed to Brutus.

Like Moses, Brutus has freed his people from slavery; he must now lead them to the Promised Land.

## The Dream Vision of Diana

On their way to their unknown destination, the Trojans arrive first at an uninhabited island where, in a deserted city, they find a Temple of Diana, whom Layamon describes as "queen of all the wood groves" (*LB*, 15). Brutus, accompanied by a priest and twelve wizards, enters the temple and stands before an oracular statue of Diana, which used to answer the questions of the previous inhabitants of the island. Brutus holds up a vessel filled with wine mixed with the milk of a white hind—an animal sacred to Diana and one that will figure frequently in the Arthurian romances as the precursor to otherworldly adventures. He then repeats nine times the following invocation, as rendered by John Milton in the First Book of his *History of Britain:*

> Goddess of shades, and huntress, who at will
> Walk'st on the rolling sphere, and through the deep

> On thy third reign the earth look now, and tell
> What land, what seat of rest thou bid'st me seek,
> What certain seat, where I may worship thee
> For aye, with temples vow'd, and virgin choirs.[2]

Brutus now lies down upon the skin of the sacrificed hind and falls asleep. In a dream the goddess appears to him, saying that he must seek an island in the far west where he can build a New Troy: "there shalt thou find a lasting seat," she tells him,

> And kings be born of thee, whose dreaded might
> Shall awe the world, and conquer nations bold.

In Layamon's version, the "Lady Diana, beloved Diana, lofty Diana" names the island "Albion" and evokes its pre-human beauty where humans will be blest: it is full of birds, fish and animals to hunt, woodland and wilderness to explore: "The land is very welcoming," the goddess tells him, "with wells of sweet water" (*LB*, 16f).

Here we have a picture of Albion as the Promised Land—but, as the Israelites discovered in Canaan, the land of milk and honey, there are giants living there, and Brutus will be obliged to deprive them of what Spenser calls their "vniust possession"—unjust, because they "with their filthinesse/Polluted this same gentle soyle long time" (*FQ*, II.x.9).

This island has been chosen for Brutus and his Trojans as Canaan was chosen for Moses and his Hebrews by the God of the Old Testament. But the divinity who has chosen Albion for Brutus is a goddess, Diana, as it is the goddess Venus who chooses Italy for Aeneas. This may be a literary embellishment of the chroniclers, inspired by Virgil's *Aeneid,* but it will become an important factor in the later development of the Arthurian romances, in which the presence of Diana, the huntress of the woods, stands behind the figure of the Lady of the Lake (*LG* 1, 281).

The Christian chroniclers could not place as positive a slant on the role of a heathen goddess (whose powers, according to Layamon, come from the Devil) in the founding of Britain as the pagan Virgil did in his account of the founding of Rome, but the implication is that Britain is the Promised Land of the Goddess and that she will preside over its destiny in the Arthurian mythos in many different guises. Spenser describes Brutus's arrival here as being "Driuen by fatall error" (*FQ*, II.x.9) and this wandering, guided by Fate, sets the scene for the role of the fays in Arthur's life, from Layamon's Argante to Spenser's Faerie Queen. But for Blake, all such pagan goddess figures must give way, ultimately, to the spiritual emanation Jerusalem.

## Upon the Rocks of Albion

> ... a British record ...
> ... revealed
> The marvellous current of forgotten things;
> How Brutus came, by oracles impelled,
> And Albion's giants quelled,
> A brood whom no civility could melt ...[3]
> —Wm. Wordsworth, "Artegal and Elidure" (1815)

Traveling on, Brutus discovers another colony of Trojan exiles living on the Iberian coast. Their leader is a certain Corineus, strong as any giant, whose help becomes indispensible to Brutus when he decides to join up with him. Together they take on the twelve kings of Gaul (foreshadowing Arthur's own later conquest of the country) but, anxious to avoid losing any more of his men in battle, Brutus decides it is time to find the island of the divine prophecy. So, taking advantage of favorable winds and smooth seas, he sets sail for the promised island and comes ashore at what is now Totnes.

This event was commemorated by William Blake in several ways, both in words and pictures. In his first published book of poetry, the *Poetical Sketches* of 1783, Blake included a fragment of a dramatic poem entitled "King Edward the Third," in which a minstrel sings to the assembled British troops before the Battle of Crécy in 1346, reminding them of their ancient glory.

Invoking the troops as "Sons of Trojan Brutus," the king's minstrel reminds them that their ancestors came from "the fires of Troy" to land "in firm array upon the rocks/Of Albion" which will be from thenceforth their mother, nurse, and grave: "The sepulchre of ancient Troy, from whence/Shall rise cities, and thrones, and arms, and awful pow'rs."

The wild, naked giants ("enormous sons/Of Ocean") emerge roaring like "savage monsters" from the hills, rocks and caves. They are struck down like trees felled by lightning, and as our fore-fathers view the blood streaming from the "mighty dead" upon "the melancholy shore," Brutus speaks with prophetic inspiration:

> The flowing waves
> Of time come rolling o'er my breast ...
> And my heart labours with futurity:
> Our sons shall rule the empire of the sea.

Brutus has a vision of the sons of the Trojans spreading their wings across the globe like giant birds of prey; the gleaming of their swords will block out the dawn. Even Liberty has eagle's wings that cover Albion, while her spear stretches over distant lands (*BCW*, 31–3).

There is little here either of Blake's poetic genius or of the "prophet against empire" of the later illuminated books, but we must bear in mind that Brutus's prophecy has been filtered through the song of a royal minstrel, steeling the troops to battle by invoking the triumphs of their ancestors. Earlier on in the same dramatic poem, we hear that "death is terrible, tho' borne on angels' wings!" (30). Even, Blake seems to be saying, when the wings are borne by the Angel of Liberty.

Blake returned to the subject of the landing of Brutus, as we have seen, in one of the engravings he did in 1793 for his (now lost) children's history book. But what has survived is a much earlier watercolor, dating from 1779, on which the later engraving was probably based. It is entitled "The Landing of Brutus in England," for Blake consistently and anachronistically gave the modern name "England" to the land south of Scotland and east of Wales and Cornwall, a land that the Arthurian legends usually refer to as Loegria or Logris.

The chroniclers will tell us how Logris and the other parts of the island get their names, but first, they describe the settling and naming of Britain itself. Diana had extolled the virtues of the land she was giving to them, and the Trojans are not disappointed. Having driven off the giants in the coastal areas, they start to feel the island is theirs; they build houses and till the soil.

With the land cultivated and fruitful, the people grow prosperous and multiply. Brutus is the master of all he surveys, and he rejoices in his domain:

> He beheld the mountains, beautiful and mighty,
> He beheld the meadows which were most magnificent,
> He beheld the waters and the wild creatures,
> He beheld the fishes and all the birds and fowl,
> He beheld the grasslands and the lovely groves,
> He beheld the woodland flowering and beheld the cornfields growing;
> All this he saw in the country and his heart was light and happy ... [*LB*, 27].

Brutus decides to name the land he loves and rules after himself: Albion becomes Britain. Corineus, likewise, gives his name to Cornwall, the part of the island that is allotted to him. It is, however, an area where many of the surviving giants have congregated, and Corineus, to establish his sovereignty, must engage in hand-to-hand combat with their leader, Gogmagog.

## God's Own Adversary

The name Gogmagog is derived from Biblical prophecy, where Gog and Magog are nations who will fight against God at the end of time; hence Layamon describes Gogmagog as "God's own adversary, but the Evil One did love him" (24). But the Gogmagog of the legendary chronicles is not just a harbinger of the Last Judgment; he also has a cosmogonic role. Like the giants in Greek mythology, Gogmagog and his horde must be destroyed so that a new order may come into being. Chaos must give way to cosmos; the wasteland of the giants of Albion must become the settled order of the men of Britain.

The point is made most clearly by Wace (*RB*, ll.1169–74): it is only when the giant race is "cleansed" (*neïee*) from the land that the Britons feel secure enough to build cities and plant seeds. The cleansing is not total, however; there are still giants, even in Arthur's day. They lurk on the edge of civilization, threatening to reduce all to chaos once more.

Layamon tells us how the bold giant-hunter Corineus wrestles with Gogmagog on a cliff-top and hurls him out to sea. The giant is dashed into a thousand pieces on the rocks below, and his monstrous soul is dispatched to Hell; to this day, the place where he fell is called "Gogmagog's Leap." The site was identified in the sixteenth century with Plymouth Hoe; hence Spenser can write of the giant's death:

> That well can witnes yet vnto this day
> The westerne Hogh, besprincled with the gore
> Of mighty Goëmot ... [*FQ*, II.x.10].

Now, the creation of the world through the dismemberment of a primordial giant is also found in Hindu and Scandinavian mythology; seen from this traditional perspective, creation is always conceived of as a "fall" from one state into another. Thus, the "leap" of Gogmagog is structurally equivalent to the Fall of Albion in Blake's mythology.

The primordial giant falls from spiritual harmony into a fractured material existence. At first he straddles the whole world, but as his (and our) vision shrinks, he becomes a mere island in the sea, a son of Neptune. Nevertheless, from this nadir (the sleep of Albion) comes "the great leap forward" that is the foundation of British civilization. Thus it is that, in the chronicles, the death of Gogmagog is followed by the founding of New Troy, now London, where Brutus will be buried and which will become the capital of Britain.

For Blake, however, the spirit of Gogmagog lives on in the oppressive institutions that develop in the capital's "chartered streets" in opposition to the true spirit of Albion, when the mercantile and industrial Britain of the poet's own day was denounced by him as carrying war abroad while inflicting poverty on its own citizens. Although Gogmagog's material body was destroyed by the Trojans, his destructive spirit is kept alive by the literalist misunderstanding of religious revelation, a misunderstanding that arises when "the eternal principles or characters of human life" are no longer recognized as divine names but "erected into gods," that is to say, worshipped as idols.

The "gods of Priam" that the Trojans brought with them to Britain, although in essence no different from the Biblical Cherubim, are no longer understood to dwell in the human breast. They have become objectified, idolized, and therefore "destructive of humanity." They are no longer visions of the eternal, but allegories of "moral virtue," which has always been used to deny the gratification of desire in order to channel its energy into corporeal war.

Thus in *Milton,* as the eponymous poet prepares to go down into the Deep in order to annihilate his limited "selfhood," which prevents him from becoming whole, he declares:

> I go to Eternal Death! The Nations still
> Follow after the detestable Gods of Priam, in pomp
> Of warlike selfhood contradicting and blaspheming.
> When will the Resurrection come to deliver the sleeping body
> From corruptibility? O when, Lord Jesus, wilt thou come?

The second coming of Jesus alone can rescue us from Eternal Death, bringing about the Resurrection that, for each of us, if we have annihilated our selfhood, follows the Last Judgment. For Blake, this must happen while we are still alive, or else, as is the case with Milton, the soul must make the journey into the Deep after the death of the body to seek spiritual rebirth:

> I will go down to self annihilation & eternal death,
> Lest the Last Judgment come & find me unannihilate
> And I be siez'd & giv'n into the hands of my own Selfhood [*BCW*, 495].

But the Last Judgment comes whenever we awake to the knowledge of who we really are: children of eternity who have fallen in love with the productions of time and been seduced into believing that *they* are all there is.

The Second Coming is always here, has already happened in the visionary imagination—which, as we will see in Chapter Four, is very different to being merely an *imaginary* experience. In Blake's imagining of the coming of Jesus, at the very end of *Jerusalem,* the detestable gods are dissolved into One Man through "the wonders Divine/Of Human Imagination" and the cry is heard from the Living Creatures of all the earth:

> Where is the Covenant of Priam, the Moral Virtues of the Heathen?
> Where is the Tree of Good & Evil that rooted beneath the cruel heel
> Of Albion's Spectre, the Patriarch Druid? Where are all his Human Sacrifices
> For Sin in War & in the Druid Temples of the Accuser of Sin, beneath
> The Oak Groves of Albion that cover'd the whole Earth beneath his Spectre?

Where are the Kingdoms of the World & all their glory that grew on Desolation,
The Fruit of Albion's Poverty Tree, when the Triple Headed Gog-Magog Giant
Of Albion Taxed the Nations into Desolation & then gave the Spectrous Oath?
[746].

Here the giant Gogmagog is triple-headed, as if he is a monstrous parody of the Trinity: for Blake, as we are told in "A Vision of the Last Judgment," beings with three heads represent Vegetative Existence, as opposed to Eternity, which is embraced by those "who are blessed with Imaginative Vision" (609). In the same passage, we find that the Great Red Dragon (of Revelation, not of Wales!), who carries Satan's Book of Accusations, has been bound in chains by the demonic Gog and Magog, "who have been compell'd to subdue their Master."

It would seem, then, that at the Last Judgment, even Gogmagog can be redeemed, or at least made an agent of "the Saviour, the True Vine of Eternity, the Human Imagination" (606). For insofar as he symbolizes both the founding of Britain and the restoration of its ancient glory at the Last Judgment, he can be seen as the shadow of Albion, in whom all things begin and end, and we can imagine that, at the end of time, Gogmagog and Albion will become as one. But as long as we are still rooted in the dualism of Moral Virtue, Gogmagog manifests as the spirit of unimaginative materialism, demanding the "spectrous" oath of loyalty from the rulers of the nations, who tax their subjects into the desolation of poverty in order to pay for their "pomp of warlike selfhood."

Both poverty and warfare are forms of human sacrifice, as though the leap of Gogmagog becomes a hideous distortion of the self-sacrificial fall of Albion, inaugurating the false Covenant of Priam, whereby divine names and attributes degenerate into detestable gods who are worshipped in oak groves and Druid temples as the idols of a literalist religion—in which the gospel of Jesus, the forgiveness of sins, is forgotten and replaced by the moral virtues of the Accuser of Sin.

For we must remember that, for Blake, the gospel of Jesus was the original, primordial revelation, not something that was announced for the first time in the Roman province of Judaea. We will see in the next chapter how news of the birth of Jesus was first brought to these shores; in the meantime, we must return to the story of those Trojan exiles who were the first to bring the gods of Priam here.

## Brutus's Sacred Progeny

Brutus has now established his sovereignty over the whole island: His empire reaches to "the vtmost shore" (*FQ*, II.x.10) of what was Albion but is now Britain.

Twenty-three years after his landing at Totnes, Brutus dies, leaving three sons to inherit the kingdom he has founded: Locrinus, Camber, and Albanactus.

Locrinus, the eldest son, is made sovereign over the other two (14), but Camber is given the land west of the river that is now called the Severn, a country that is henceforth called Cambria. Layamon adds: "And this is that wild land which the Welsh people love" [*LB*, 28]). Meanwhile, the youngest son, Albanactus, rules the land north of the River Tweed, and this is henceforth known as the Kingdom of Albany. The land south of Albany and east of Cambria and Cornwall is ruled directly by the High King Locrinus and is henceforth called Loegria after its founder. *Lloegr,* it is worth noting, is still the Welsh word for "England."

The first challenge to the peace of the realm comes from the Huns, who have been conquering and pillaging the western world and who at last come to Albany. They kill King Albanactus and then march south to meet the combined forces of Locrinus and Camber. This time it is the King of the Huns who is killed, drowning in the river that is named the Humber after him, and for the first time, the Britons are taught the lesson that Arthur above all will learn: A nation united cannot be defeated.

The victory has its price, however. One of the spoils of war is a German princess, Astrild, who had been captured by the Huns and who, in turn, captures the heart (or, at least, the loins) of Locrinus. The High King is prepared to marry her, if that is the only way he can bed her; but his courtship offends Corineus, to whose daughter, Gwendolen, Locrinus is engaged to be married. Locrinus is not prepared to defy the giant-killer, so he duly marries Gwendolen, but comes up with an ingenious method of satisfying his lust for Astrild: He has an earth-house built in one of the many caves beneath New Troy, and there he hides the Princess Astrild, who is kept locked up for seven years! Whenever Locrinus finds an excuse to visit his capital city, he tells his wife that he must spend seven days in seclusion, performing secret rites to his underworld god, but all the time he is enjoying the Lady Astrild's body. It is while she is still in prison that the princess bears him a daughter, whom she names Sabrina (or Habren).

It is only when Corineus dies that Locrinus feels able to dispense with secrecy and take Astrild as his queen. The deserted Gwendolen, however, has something of her father's temperament and raises a Cornish army against the man who abandoned her and her young son, Madan, who is the legitimate heir to the throne. Locrinus, who had fallen "to vaine voluptuous disease," in Spenser's evocative phrase, is struck by an arrow, and the first High King of Britain dies on the field of battle. His German wife ("Whose wanton pleasures him too much did please" [*FQ,* II.x.17]) and "sad virgin innocent" daughter are soon captured and, on Gwendolen's orders, drowned in the river that to this day bears Sabrina's name, the River Severn (or Afon Hafren in Welsh). "Such was the end, that to disloyall loue did fall" (19).

Gwendolen rules the country on behalf of her son for fifteen years, during which time she displays throughout the realm a power which reveals "the glory of her sex." As the queen who "first taught men a woman to obay" (20), she is the archetype of later female monarchs, in Spenser's time as in our own.

Eventually she retires to Cornwall, leaving her son to rule, but, according to Spenser, he was "vnworthie of his race:/For with all shame that sacred throne he fild" (21). Unfortunately we do not learn how he defiled the throne, but we have more specific information about the sins of his two sons, Mempricius and Malin, whom their father intended should share the throne, but whose rivalry turns murderous.

Having killed his brother and seized sole power, Mempricius rules tyrannically, destroying all those who stand in his way. What is worse, having fathered a son, a fine young man called Ebraucus, Mempricius grows tired of his wife and gives himself up to unnatural vice—the same vice, the chroniclers assure us, that led to the destruction of Sodom. Layamon adds the salacious detail that he took his serving-men to bed (*Brut* l.1290). But if Mempricius's reign has the effect of tearing the country apart, it ends with *him* being torn apart—by wolves, in a hunting trip that goes horribly wrong.

Mempricius is succeeded by his admirable son Ebraucus, who does a lot to restore British confidence, most notably by what will become a time-honored tradition of attacking the Europeans. At the same time as King David is writing the Psalms, Ebraucus is establishing his reputation as the first British king to go abroad on raiding expeditions. But just as David is founding Bethlehem (*RB*, l.1513), the High King of Britain is using his plundered wealth to build cities that will last to the present day—notably Caer Ebrauc, which the Romans knew as Eburacum and which we call York, and Alclud, modern Dumbarton, in Strathclyde.

Ebraucus, perhaps determined to avoid any suspicion that he has inherited his father's unnatural proclivities, fathers fifty children by twenty different wives: twenty sons and thirty daughters, of whom the most beautiful is Galoes, who gives her name to Wales (*Brut*, l. 1357). All thirty are sent by their father to Italy, to his kinsman Silvius Alba, who finds husbands for them among the nobility of Trojan descent. Their brothers (with the exception of Brutus Greenshield, the heir to the throne) travel with them and, with the aid of the King of Italy, conquer Germany.

Meanwhile Brutus Greenshield succeeds his father Ebraucus as High King of Britain and is in turn succeeded by his son Leil, who founds the city that bears his name (Caer Leil, modern Carlisle) at about the same time that King Solomon is building the first Temple of the Lord in Jerusalem.

Leil is succeeded by his son Hudibras, the founder of the cities of Canterbury and Winchester. He also builds Shaftesbury Castle on the Walton Downs. As the walls are being built, an eagle lands on them and speaks, prophesying the king's death. To the distress of Hudibras's people, the eagle's prophecy is fulfilled (ll.1411–6), and Bladud the Necromancer succeeds his father to the throne.

## Terrible Family Feuds

Sadly, the seven hundred years of British counter-history that follow the landing of Brutus are characterized as much by internal dissension as by glorious deeds. Of the list of legendary kings who succeed Brutus, Blake names only two before Arthur—Bladud and Belin—and these he characterizes as "satanic" rather than heroic, for they are "Kings in wrath" whose deeds make of Albion a "Fourfold Desart," that is, a place where the four Zoas no longer live in harmony.

Against them, in Blake's mythology, stands Los, the Eternal Prophet, who demolishes their false beliefs as the Hebrew prophets denounced the kings of the Israelites when they abandoned God. Los personifies the principle of imaginative creativity who tries to preserve the sense of Eternity in Albion. Hence he is described as "Permanently Creating," but part of his creativity is the destruction of the productions of time, such as "all the Kings & Nobles of the Earth & all their Glories" who are "to be in Time Reveal'd & Demolish'd." For Los, destruction is a creative act, so he is holding true to the creative potential of Albion when he "with his mighty Hammer demolishes time on time/In miracles & wonders" the wrathful kings and their pagan religion (*BCW*, 713).

The first of the British kings whom Blake identifies to be "revealed and demolished" is Bladud the Necromancer, the ninth High King of Britain. Spenser tells us that he learned his magical arts in Athens,

> From whence he brought them to these saluage parts
> And with sweet science mollifide their stubborne harts [*FQ*, II.x.25].

Athens is the city of Athena, whom the Romans called Minerva, the goddess of wisdom, and it is this goddess whom Bladud reveres above all others. Consequently, when he builds the City of the Healing Baths (Caer Badon, modern Bath), it is Minerva that he chooses as its tutelary deity, building a temple to her in which the fires are never allowed to go out. But his skill leads to hubris:

> Yet he at last contending to excell
> The reach of men, through flight into fond mischief fell [26].

Using the knowledge he has gained from the Devil (*Brut*, ll.1419–20), Bladud builds for himself a pair of wings, boasting that he can fly, but he comes crashing down onto the roof of the Temple of Apollo in New Troy and is dashed to pieces.

The fall of Bladud appears to prefigure that of Simon Magus, who appears in the Acts of the Apostles as well as in the Christian apocrypha. Bladud, according to Geoffrey of Monmouth, lived at the time of the Prophet Elijah; while Simon Magus was baptized by John the Baptist (who was himself believed to be a manifestation of the Prophet Elijah). Simon Magus, in apocryphal tales, tries to fly to demonstrate his superiority to Simon Peter, but, like Bladud, he comes crashing down and ends up denounced as the godfather of Gnostic heresy. Thus it is that for Bladud, as for Simon Magus, luciferian pride comes before a fall.

The son of Bladud is perhaps the most famous of all the kings of the House of Brutus, and it is not surprising therefore that he was the fourth in the list of subjects that Blake had intended to make engravings of, to illustrate his "History of England." We know him best as Shakespeare's King Lear, but he may originally have been a British sea god, Llŷr (*TYP*, 419), whose daughter Creiddylad (Cordelia) is loved by Gwyn, the King of Faerie.

Gwyn has a rival for her affections, however, and we must assume that their rivalry has an archetypal and timeless character, for, hundreds of years later, King Arthur is obliged to intervene to end their dispute. He decrees that the two rivals must fight each other every year on May Day, and whoever is the victor on Doomsday will win her love for all eternity (*MMWT*, 151).

Nothing of this mythological coloring, it should be said, survives in the traditional tale that Shakespeare dramatized, but Cordelia resurfaces as a mythological figure in Blake's *Jerusalem,* where she—along with Brutus's wife Ignoge and Arthur's wife Guinevere[4]—is described as one of the twelve Daughters of Albion.

The chroniclers tell us that King Lear, the founder of Leicester (Caer Llŷr) on the River Soar, has three daughters, among whom he intends to divide his realm: To determine which of them should have the lion's share, he invites them to outdo each other in telling him how much they love him. The two eldest play the game and are rewarded with marriage to the Dukes of Albany and Cornwall respectively. Cordelia, the youngest, replies simply and honestly and is punished, for refusing to flatter the old man's vanity, by being disinherited. Fortunately she finds a loving husband in the person of one of the kings of Gaul, and it is they who, when Lear's two ungrateful daughters cast him out ("The wretched man gan then auise to late,/That loue is not, where most it is profest" [*FQ*, II.x.31]), raise an army to restore him to his throne. They are successful and, unlike in Shakespeare's tragedy, Cordelia lives to bury her father, curiously, in an underground chamber that she orders to be dug beneath the River Soar and which she dedicates to the god who looks both forwards and backwards, Janus. But Cordelia's story still has a tragic ending: Her nephews, the sons of her elder sisters, rise up against her and overthrow her; she hangs herself in prison.

After the death of Cordelia, two grandsons of King Lear divide the island between them, until what is only one among many interfamilial conflicts leaves one of the cousins, Cunedagius, undisputed ruler of Britain. It is during this period that the twins Romulus and Remus found Rome, the city that will develop into Britain's greatest adversary. The traditional date for the founding of Rome is April 21, 753 BCE. Meanwhile, in the Holy Land, Isaiah is prophesying the birth of Emmanuel (*RB*, ll.2111–20), whose incarnation will transform both empires.

But while the city of Rome is on the rise, Britain appears to be in decline. Fratricide (Romulus's killing of Remus) is part of the founding myth of Rome, but in British mythology it inevitably leads to the weakening of the nation and contributes to its conquest by Rome. To Blake, this family feuding is consuming the fallen body of Albion.

> The Spectres of the Dead howl round the porches of Los
> In the terrible Family feuds of Albion's cities & villages,
> To devour the Body of Albion, hung'ring & thirsting & rav'ning [*BCW*, 714].

It would be tedious to list all the undistinguished kings who succeed Cunedagius; suffice it to say that Gorboduc, the sixteenth High King of Britain, has two sons who, having thrown their senile father into prison, turn on each other. "Stout Ferrex" is killed by "stern Porrex," thanks to "the greedy thirst of royal crown,/That knows no kindred, nor regards no right"; and in revenge, Porrex is killed by his own mother (*FQ*, II.x.34f ).

With the death of Porrex, the eighteenth High King of Britain, the first royal dynasty comes to an end.

> Here ended *Brutus* sacred progeny,
> Which had seuen hundred yeares this scepter borne,
> With high renowme and great felicity;
> The noble braunch from th'antique stocke was torne
> Through discord, and the roiall throne forlorne:
> Thenceforth this Realme was into factions rent,
> Whilest each of *Brutus* boasted to be borne,
> That in the end was left no moniment
> Of *Brutus,* nor of Britons glorie auncient [36].

However, Brutus's Promised Land, at its nadir, would show, not for the last time, its ability to renew itself.

# Two

# *The Conversion of Britain*

Where be the temples which in Britain's Isle,
For his paternal Gods, the Trojan raised?
Gone like a morning dream, or like a pile
Of clouds that in cerulean ether blazed!
Ere Julius landed on her white-cliffed shore,
They sank, delivered o'er
To fatal dissolution; and, I ween,
No vestige then was left that such had ever been.[1]
    —William Wordsworth, "Artegal and Elidure" (1815)

The unity of the realm established by Brutus has been shattered by the fratricidal hatred of Ferrex and Porrex, but it is re-established by Dunwallo, the King of Cornwall, who is elected High King of Britain by "the Princes of the people" and brings the whole country to "ciuile gouernaunce." It is he who restores Britain's "quiet state" through "sacred lawes, which some men say/Were vnto him reueald in vision" (*FQ*, II.x.37–9), and it is his immediate descendants who extend our ancient glory abroad through foreign conquest. I refer to this as the Molmutine dynasty, after Dunwallo's surname (*Moelmud* in Welsh, latinized by Geoffrey of Monmouth as "Molmutius"), which also gives us the name by which his sacred law-code is thenceforth known.

Dunwallo has two sons who, despite their prowess, are sadly possessed of the same spirit of rivalry that characterizes so many of the mythical kings of Britain. On the death of their father, Belin and his younger brother Brennus fight for the kingship, eventually agreeing to divide the kingdom between them. Belin, however, as the eldest, holds Cambria, Cornwall and Loegria and is overlord to Brennus, who rules Northumbria.

When Brennus rebels against his brother's authority, Belin seizes the whole island, defeats Brennus in battle, and drives him into exile. Belin, who is the second of the British "kings in wrath" whom Blake names as preceding Arthur, is nevertheless also a peacemaker: He establishes the Molmutine Laws over the whole island and, travelling over all of it, beholds its beauty (*Brut*, ll.2402–6) as Brutus did before him, suggesting that Belin is the true heir of the founder.

To improve the realm he has inherited, Belin builds great highways that crisscross the island from north to south, east to west, and diagonally and takes personal responsibility for the safety of travellers on these new roads, the King's Highways.

The peace and security of Belin's rule does not last long, however, for Brennus invades Britain with a continental army. This time their mother makes peace between the brothers.

## Subject to Britain

Once they have stopped fighting each other, the brothers decide to displace their aggression abroad and, in what is becoming a familiar pattern, attack their neighbors across the Channel. What follows is an elaboration of a historical event—the capture of Rome by Celtic (but not, as far as we know, British!) tribes early in the fourth century BCE, one of the few dates that enable the legendary events to be firmly situated in the historical record.

First of all, the brothers conquer Gaul, and then they turn their attentions to Rome, intending to avenge the death of Remus at the hands of Romulus (ll.2612–5). Even though this would have happened hundreds of years earlier, the sibling rivalry of Belin and Brennus must have made them overly sensitive to the subject. The Roman consuls, hearing that the brothers have crossed the St. Bernard Pass, determine to save their possessions by trickery—they offer them gold, silver and hostages in the form of the children of their nobility, but this is just a delaying tactic since, they claim, if Tervagant wills it, they will destroy them before they can return home (ll.2670–2).

Had the Romans realized that the Kingdom of Brutus is specially favored by Tervagant, they might have reconsidered their treachery—for, as the philologist Skeat originally observed, the medieval Tervagant is *Trivagarans*, the "thrice wandering" moon: that is, Diana in her three aspects of ruler of sky, earth, and underworld.[2] This Triple Goddess is not just she who reveals the Promised Land to Brutus in a vision—taking many different forms, she will guide its destiny until she receives its greatest king, Arthur, into her sacred island of Avalon, to await his second coming. The Romans will soon discover that she does *not* will the destruction of her chosen people.

It is Layamon who, of all the chroniclers, revels in the extent to which the Romans are prepared to abase themselves in their treacherous servility. Carrying in their hands golden goblets, the nobles ride to where the brothers are encamped and fall to their knees before Belin, exclaiming that they will give up all their territory and treasures. This they swear in the name of their god Dagon, "who is mighty in his fame" (*LB*, 70).

The naming of the Semitic deity Dagon as one of the gods of Rome as far back as the fourth century BCE, long before the fashionable syncretism of the imperial period, is especially surprising when we consider that Dagon (whom Milton calls "Sea Monster, upward man/And downward fish" [*PL*, Book I, ll.462f]) was one of the Baalim, the principal gods of the Phoenicians and Canaanites, who were also "worship'd o'er the sea" in the Phoenician colony of Carthage—Blake names Dagon and Baal as two of the twelve monstrous gods of Asia who oppose the divine vision preserved by Los (*BCW*, 528).

The legend was familiar from Virgil. Ever since their Queen Dido was spurned by Aeneas, the Carthaginians had resented the Romans as upstarts in their Mediterranean hegemony, and the rivalry between the two powers would eventually lead to three wars and, ultimately, the *deleting* of Carthage from the map. *Carthago delenda est!* was the clarion call in the Roman republic, but, not content with sowing salt on their fields (or so the story goes), the Romans rubbed salt into the Carthaginians' wounds by accusing them of child sacrifice—and it may be this dubious accusation (typical of those used by conquering powers to demonize the enemy, but still hotly contested to this day) that inspired one of the least edifying episodes in the career of Belin.

The Romans agree to be vassals of Belin, giving him in token of good faith twenty-four noble children to be held as hostages. The brothers now march on Germany, but as soon as they do so, the treacherous Romans send an army against them, so the brothers turn back to besiege Rome itself. Having found it impossible to undermine Roman resistance by other methods, the brothers finally resort to erecting gibbets and hanging twenty-three of the children in front of their parents.

Like most war crimes, however, this atrocity does not have the desired effect; if anything, the determination of the Romans is strengthened. But to no avail: the walls of Rome are broken, its defenders struck down, and its treasure looted.

The brothers now rebuild the walls of Rome and restore its ancient laws. Before returning to Britain, the High King Belin appoints his brother to be his regent in Italy. Brennus rules Rome until his death, fifteen years later—when, presumably, the Republic is restored. The Romans, of course, will have their revenge, but King Arthur will later quote the sack of Rome by Brennus and Belin as justification for his own resistance to imperial domination.

The role of Brennus in our chronicles appears to have been inspired by that of the Gallic chieftain Brennus, who sacked Rome in 390 BCE, and who should not be confused with another Brennus who led the Celtic tribes that, a hundred years later, founded the realm of Galatia in Asia Minor. Both heroes may, however, have been named after their god-king Brân the Blessed, an important figure in Welsh mythology, who, scholars have argued, was "a divine figure, probably originally the pagan Brittonic god of death" (Green, 58), and this constitutes one of several connections between Arthur and Brân that make the one the true successor, if not the incarnation, of the other.

As for Belin, he returns to Britain to preside over a period of peace and plenty, unexcelled before or since. In Wales he founds on the river Usk a city, the capital of Demetia, which after the Roman conquest will be known as Caerleon, the "City of Legions." He also causes a gate and tower to be constructed in New Troy, which is known to this day as the Gate of Belin (Billingsgate). When he dies, Belin is cremated and his ashes placed in a golden barrel, which is in turn set atop his tower.

The son of Belin is Gurgunt. When he hears that the King of Denmark, who paid tribute to his father, claims to owe the son no allegiance, Gurgunt sails to Denmark, kills the king, and reestablishes British sovereignty. It is while he is returning home from this expedition that he encounters a group of exiles from Iberia, who have been looking for a land where they could settle. Gurgunt sends them to the island to the west of Britain, which we now call Ireland but which, at that time, is completely uninhabited, and which, as Spenser puts it, "they should hold of him, as subiect to *Britayne*" (*FQ*, II.x.41).

The subjection of Gaul and Germany by the brothers Brennus and Belin, as well as their defeat of the Romans—along with the winning of Denmark and the subjection of Ireland to British rule, achieved by Gurgunt—are all feats that will be reprised by Arthur, who combines in a single lifetime all the greatest exploits of his predecessors. In him is personified Britain's ancient glory.

## A Human Awful Wonder

The Molmutine Dynasty continues to rule Britain until the coming of the Romans. Notable among its sons are Morindus, whose main claim to fame is that he is swallowed by a sea monster; Artegal and Elidure, another pair of warring brothers, who were the subjects of a narrative poem by the middle-aged Wordsworth; and "Heli," whose name is a corruption of Beli.

We are now firmly in the realm of Welsh mythology, for Beli the Great (*Beli Mawr*) is an ancestral deity who may be identical to the Gaulish god

Belenos (*TYP*, 288); he fathers a daughter, Aranrot, on the Welsh mother goddess (284). Beli also has sons, the eldest of whom, Lud (Lludd or Nudd in Welsh), is in origin the Romano-British deity Nodons, the remains of whose temple on the banks of the Severn survive to this day at Lydney in Gloucestershire (419), while the youngest, Caswallon or Cassibellaunus, is the only one who can be firmly established as a historical character.

It is Beli's eldest son who succeeds him as High King of Britain. Lud refurbishes the walls of New Troy, surmounting them with countless towers in imitation of the Tower of Belin, and, to match Billingsgate, he creates Ludgate. But Lud must face three great challenges, or plagues, that afflict his reign. First, the realm has been invaded by the Coraniaid, a race possessed of magical knowledge. Second, every May Eve, a cry resounds through the lands that strips people of their strength and the land of its fertility. Third, provisions gathered for the king's table disappear mysteriously after the first night.

Lud overcomes these threats with the aid of his younger brother, Lleuelys, King of Gaul, who tells him, firstly, how to defeat the Coraniaid, by using vermin homeopathically diluted in water; the Coraniaid themselves are a plague of vermin, and in order to rid the land of this pestilence, *similia similibus curentur.*

Secondly, Lleuelys explains that the cry is caused by the sacred dragon of Britain, which is being attacked by a foreign one. Lud, following his brother's advice, finds the dragons in the exact center of the island, intoxicates them with mead, and then shuts them up in a stone chest, which he buries in Snowdonia. "As long as they remain in that secure place," explains Lleuelys, "no oppression shall visit the isle of Britain from another place" (*MMWT*, 115). Sadly, King Vortigern will later uncover them, an act which will constitute one of the Three Unfortunate Disclosures of the Island of Britain (*TYP*, 94f).

Thirdly, Lleuelys reveals that a powerful magician is stealing Lud's food and drink, after putting his guards to sleep. Once more following his brother's advice, Lud himself keeps watch after organizing a feast. In the early hours of the morning, beautiful music starts to lull him to sleep, but he immerses himself in cold water and is still awake when the magician enters the hall and starts filling up his basket. Lud confronts him, fights him, and defeats him; he spares his life on condition that the magician owes him allegiance.

After overcoming these supernatural threats to his realm, King Lud rules the land in peace and prosperity. When he dies, he is buried at Ludgate, and the city of New Troy, which he made the most splendid in the kingdom, is renamed Caer Lludd, "Ludscastle." The Romans called it Londinium, and we know it as London.

Blake will later walk London's chartered streets, lamenting that it has become a new Babylon. But just as Jerusalem must be built anew in England, so "the spiritual Four-fold London" (*BCW*, 485) will be restored when Albion wakes up to his eternal nature. Hence Blake hears London, "a Human awful wonder of God" crying:

> Return, Albion, return, I give myself for thee.
> My streets are my Ideas of Imagination.
> Awake, Albion, awake! and let us awake up together [665].

## The Island at the World's End

Lud's sons, according to the chroniclers, are too young to rule the land when their father dies, so Lud's brother Cassibellaunus is chosen by the nobles to be High King. It is during his reign that Julius Caesar first has designs upon this island.

Standing on the coast of Flanders, Caesar looks across the sea and, the weather being fine, discerns an attractive-looking island. When he is told that it is the land conquered by Brutus, Caesar recalls what he knows of the history of the Britons: "We all come from one common tribe," he exclaims and, remembering the shame inflicted on Rome by Brennus and Belin, vows to spare the Britons the pains of war if they will bow to him and pay him tribute (*LB*, 94f). For Spenser, Caesar envied "the Britons blazed fame" and was possessed by "hideous hunger of dominion" (*FQ*, II.x.47).

But Caesar has not reckoned with the pride of the British. Cassibellaunus is only too well aware that the Romans and the Britons are descended from one race, and so, to the man who wishes to make himself overlord of all the Earth, the High King proclaims:

> We are on an island, and at the world's end it stands,
> Which Brutus acquired and on which we reside,
> And freely we hold it against all kings of the world [*LB*, 95].

They will never send Rome tribute; on the contrary, Cassibellaunus foreshadows Arthur's defiance of Rome by claiming that the conquest of that city by the Molmutine brothers gives him the right to demand tribute from Caesar: "So you must bow to me!" (96).

Caesar, not surprisingly, is enraged and launches an invasion, but his army is met by the united forces of the British and is repulsed. Caesar himself loses his sword to Nennius, the High King's younger brother, who is nevertheless fatally wounded. Caesar flees Britain, and Nennius is buried at the north gate of Ludscastle with the sword of Caesar beside him.

## Mysterious Doctrines

Two years later, Caesar tries again. He is again repulsed, but the Britons, in the midst of their celebrations, start to fall out. Caesar, having learnt that the Britons, united, can never be defeated, is only too happy to take advantage of another "terrible family feud." Cassibellaunus is forced to make terms with the Romans, finally agreeing to pay the tribute Caesar demanded in order for the island to be left in peace. Despite the hostile resentment of successive British kings, this arrangement will continue "Till *Arthur* all that reckoning defrayd" (*FQ*, II.x.49).

Lud's son Tenantius succeeds his uncle Cassibellaunus as High King when the latter dies, seven years later, and Tenantius is in turn succeeded by his son Cymbeline (familiar from Shakespeare's play, but better known to historians as Cunobelinus), who, having been brought up in the household of Augustus Caesar, maintains good relations with the Romans throughout his life.

It is during the reign of Cymbeline that Jesus is born in the town of Bethlehem. The High King hears "mysterious doctrines" concerning the events in Judaea and summons the wizard Taliesin, who has witnessed at first hand the birth of the Divine Child ("And I was with my lord in the manger of oxen and asses") and will witness his death ("I was atop the cross of the merciful son of God" [*MMWT*, 172f]).

Taliesin was a historical character, a sixth-century poet who worked as court bard for the kings of Powys and Rheged, but later poems that have been credited to him (but which more likely date from about the ninth century onwards) present him as a poet-seer or a shamanic figure like Orpheus, who descends into the Underworld to enchant its denizens. In the case of Taliesin, he is believed to have undertaken a journey to Caer Sidi, a castle in the Otherworld whose name—"the Fortress of the Sídh" or "the Fairy Castle"—identifies it as a dwelling of the elven folk who were once pagan gods. It is there, beside unearthly waters, that Taliesin gains his poetic chair, and it is perhaps in his position as Underworld initiate that Taliesin is enrolled for expeditions to the Otherworld led by Brân and Arthur, as Orpheus was enrolled by Jason to guide the Argonauts to the Land of the Golden Fleece.

In one story, Taliesin as a boy is swallowed by the witch Ceridwen and, after spending nine months in her womb, reborn as a poet and seer who can remember countless incarnations at different periods of history and in different locales, both mythical and geographical. He is imbued with the wisdom of the ages, and it is this secret knowledge, some believe, that is encoded in the cryptic poems attributed to him that have survived to the present.

One of Taliesin's incarnations involves a journey to Judaea, where he witnesses the birth of Jesus, after which he appears in the court of the King of Britain. Cymbeline says to the bard that there are terrifying signs and tokens in the heavens of the birth of a great and powerful child, provoking "awe among the race of men" (*LB*, 118). Asked by the king to explain what these portents mean, Taliesin replies that they indicate the coming to earth of the Savior, who will release the patriarchs from Hell. The Britons never forget these words.

After a long reign, Cymbeline resigns the throne to his eldest son, Guiderius, who refuses any longer to pay the tribute to Rome negotiated by Julius Caesar; as a consequence, the Emperor Claudius launches an invasion. Guiderius is killed by treachery, but his brother Arviragus leads such a strong resistance in his place that Claudius is forced to negotiate: he will give Arviragus the hand of his daughter Genvissa if, in return, Arviragus will accept Roman suzerainty. This is agreed, and Arviragus and Claudius then join forces to subdue the thirty-two islands of Orkney.

Shortly thereafter, Arviragus and Genvissa are married, thus uniting the royal families of Britain and Rome. The emperor, meanwhile, fathers a son on a native British woman, a wise virgin whom his soldiers have captured (*Brut*, ll.4786–8). This son, Gloius or Gualun, will later be made duke of the city which was founded on the eastern banks of the Severn and which will be named after Claudius's bastard child: Caer Gloyw, or Gloucester. But Claudius does not live to see the ducal instatement of his only son. Having subdued Britain and brought it within the Empire, Claudius returns to Rome, where he dies ten years later, to the great sorrow of the British royal family and the nobles of the island he conquered.

For nearly four hundred years thereafter, the south of the island will be the Roman province of Britannia, and its kings will rule in more or less willing deference to a greater power. But a higher power is also about to make its presence felt in Britain: the power of the Christ, who demands that people do not only render unto Caesar what is Caesar's, but also unto God what is God's.

## Christian Conjectures

The origins of Christianity in Britain are shrouded in the mists of legend. Scholars have struggled to separate myth from history, as theologians have struggled to define the relation between the human and divine aspects of the Savior. The faithful willingly suspend their disbelief and accept that Christ is both God *and* man, or that legend is both myth *and* history. Poets delight in the paradox.

William Wordsworth—in a series of *Ecclesiastical Sonnets,* which he wrote in 1821—traces the progress of the Christian faith in this island. The second sonnet, "Conjectures," as its name suggests, refers to two little-known legends (as well as a much more famous one) concerning the source of the holy river of British Christianity. The sonnet begins with Wordsworth asking whether there are prophets who can reveal the past as well as the future. If so, they might be able to tell us when "this savage island" was first blest with waters from "the sacred well/Of Christian faith"; whether, for example,

> Wandering through the west,
> Did holy Paul a while in Britain dwell,
> And call the Fountain forth by miracle,
> And with dread signs the nascent Stream invest? [*WPW*, 329].

In answer to his own question, Wordsworth appended a note to this poem in which he professed himself unconvinced by the arguments (put forward by Edward Stillingfleet, author of *Origines Britannicae; or, Antiquities of the British Church,* in the late seventeenth century) that the apostle Paul ever came to Britain (721). But he then refers to the possibility of an evangelical mission led by "He, whose bonds dropped off, whose prison doors/Flew open, by an Angel's voice unbarr'd" (329).

The idea that Jesus's disciple Peter (who in Acts XII: 7–11 is delivered from prison by an angel) might have come to Britain was a popular belief in the Middle Ages, and it is interesting to speculate whether or not this belief influenced, or was influenced by, the story of another Peter (*Petrus*)—a disciple of his cousin Joseph of Arimathea, rather than of Jesus—coming to Britain as a Christian missionary.

The story is first told by the Burgundian knight Robert de Boron, in a late twelfth-century poem (later reworked into prose) called *Joseph of Arimathea,* in which Joseph sends Peter to the Isle of Avalon with a letter from Christ about the Holy Grail. We do not know, any more than Peter does, what the letter contains, but he is supposed to wait in Avalon until the Grail Hero arrives (*MG*, 41). The unfinished story of Peter is picked up in a huge prose compilation called, because of its popularity, the Vulgate Cycle. Here we learn that, on the way to Avalon, Peter is shipwrecked on the Orkney Isles, converts their pagan king to Christianity, marries the Orcadian princess, and founds the Christian dynasty that will eventually produce the Arthurian princes Gawain and Modred (*LG* 1, 149–55).

It is not clear that Peter ever reaches Avalon, which by the late twelfth century was identified with Glastonbury, but he is instrumental in converting to the Christian Faith Lucius, the High King of Britain (154). Spenser is also familiar with the legend of the good king who first received the "sacred pledge of Christes Euangely" and with the story that it was Joseph of Arimathea who brought the Holy Grail to these shores, where he "preacht the truth; but since it greatly did decay" (*FQ*, II.x.53).

Joseph of Arimathea appears in the New Testament as a Christian disciple who gains permission from the Roman governor Pilate to bury Jesus after his crucifixion, but abundant apocryphal stories soon grew up to flesh out his story. He becomes, for example, the uncle of the Virgin Mary and therefore the great-uncle of Jesus himself. Joseph is purported to be a tin trader, and it is in this capacity that he is supposed to have first visited Britain, then famous for its tin mines, bringing with him the young Jesus.

This, of course, is the ostensible subject of the well-known lines in the poem by Blake from the Preface to *Milton,* better known as the words to the hymn "Jerusalem":

> And did those feet in ancient time
> Walk upon England's mountains green?
>
> And was the holy Lamb of God
> On England's pleasant pastures seen?
>
> And did the Countenance Divine
> Shine forth upon our clouded hills? [*BCW*, 481].

It is not safe to assume, as many do, that Blake believed the legend to be literally true. For Blake, holy lambs can always be seen in England's pastures, and the divine countenance is always shining forth, for those who have eyes to see. He might well have agreed with Wordsworth, who, in a poem celebrating the momentary renewal of the "visionary splendour" of his youth, declares: "An intermingling of Heaven's pomp is spread/ On ground which British shepherds tread!" The poem, "Composed upon an Evening of Extraordinary Splendour and Beauty," dates from 1818, some fourteen years after Blake wrote *Milton.* In it, Wordsworth expresses his gratitude at having been allowed, one last time, a "glimpse of glory" won from "worlds not quickened by the sun" (*WPW*, 359f).

For Blake, the miracle of the Incarnation was not about an event that happened once only, in Judaea, and the miracle of the Divine Presence is not about an event that may or may not have happened in the youth of Jesus, but about one that is happening eternally in the Divine Imagination. For the man of vision, as Wordsworth was in his youth—and as Blake was until he died—the Kingdom of Heaven is always about us.

## The Precious Current

The latter half of Wordsworth's second Ecclesiastical Sonnet is concerned with a second supposed visit of Joseph to Britain—carrying this time, not the child Jesus, but His blood (the Sangreal). Were some, he asks, "of humbler name" than Peter and Paul, driven by storms to these shores? Some "who, having seen the cup of woe/Pass from their master, sojourned here to guard/The precious current they had taught to flow?" (329).

After the death of Jesus, Joseph is believed to have gone to Gaul with the Apostle Philip and Mary Magdalene and thence to have been sent to preach the Gospel in Britain, where he founded the earliest Christian oratory at Glastonbury.

The story is summarized in Tennyson's nineteenth-century poem, "The Holy Grail," part of the sequence known as the *Idylls of the King,* when a monk tells Percivale (one of the three knights who achieve the Grail quest) that Arviragus, a "heathen Prince," gave Joseph "an isle of marsh whereon to build;/And there he built with wattles from the marsh/A little lonely church in days of yore" (*PT,* 1663). This legend was also the subject, as we have seen, of the first engraving Blake ever made, when he was a mere fifteen years of age, showing Joseph of Arimathea walking alone among the Rocks of Albion. Some ten years later he did an etching of "Joseph of Arimathea Preaching to the Inhabitants of Britain," and Blake's biographer Peter Ackroyd considers that Blake would have felt himself to be the heir of Joseph, walking alone his solitary path, wandering, unable to rest from his great task:

> To open the Eternal worlds, to open the immortal Eyes
> Of Man inwards into the Worlds of Thought, into Eternity
> Ever expanding in the Bosom of God, the Human Imagination [*BCW,* 623].

As Blake imagines him, Joseph was not bringing a new revelation, but reminding humanity of what it had forgotten. For Britain was the "Primitive Seat" of the "One Religion" in which all the inhabitants of the earth find their unity: "The Religion of Jesus, the most Ancient, the Eternal & the Everlasting Gospel" (649).

This was the primordial, antediluvian religion of the Druids, who were the sons of Albion when he and his emanation Jerusalem lived together in harmony. After the Flood, Albion and Jerusalem became separated, but the Biblical patriarchs such as Noah, his son Shem (eponymous ancestor of the Semitic peoples) and Heber (the great-grandson of Shem and eponymous ancestor of the Hebrews) were Druids, as was Abraham.

It is in the story of Abraham that Blake finds a key to the degeneration of the patriarchal religion: when God commanded Abraham to sacrifice his son, this was not meant literally (corporeally) but allegorically (mentally), which became apparent when God substituted the ram for the child. Here Blake sees Biblical justification for his dislike of the kind of religious fundamentalism, only too prevalent today, which sees nothing but literal truth in sacred scriptures.

Unfortunately, with the separation of Albion and Jerusalem, the Druids fall prey to precisely this dangerous literalism, leading to the danger that the practice of human sacrifice will depopulate the earth! As a result, Abraham is called to succeed the Age of the Druids and restore the Everlasting Gospel.

But the Jews, no less than the Britons, have forgotten the original unity of Albion and Jerusalem, so, in his address "To the Jews," which prefaces the second chapter of *Jerusalem,* Blake points out that Albion is none other than the Anthropos, Divine Humanity, the figure that the Kabbalists call Adam Kadmon:

> You have a tradition, that Man anciently contain'd in his mighty limbs all things in Heaven & Earth: this you reciev'd from the Druids.
> "But now the Starry Heavens are fled from the mighty limbs of Albion."

> Albion was the Parent of the Druids; & in his Chaotic State of Sleep, Satan & Adam & the whole World was Created by the Elohim [*BCW*, 649].

For Blake, the material creation is not wholly good; it is an act of divine mercy. To prevent Albion from falling into non-existence, the world is created to be a couch on which he sleeps, and while he does so, there are dire consequences, which are elaborated in the poem that follows.

Where London now stands, there once stood the pillars of Jerusalem, who then walked side by side with the Lamb of God amongst our green meadows, so that every English child can be seen as a child of Jesus and his bride, Jerusalem. But Satan wins his "first victory," and as a result, the Druids start offering up human life as "sacrifice for sin." Albion groans, the Mountains of Atlantis shake, and Satan stretches his Druid pillars across those of Jerusalem. But even though the Human Form is withered up into "a Mortal worm," it is still "translucent all within," revealing its true parentage.

> The Divine Vision still was seen,
> Still was the Human Form Divine,
>     Weeping in weak & mortal clay,
> O Jesus, still the Form was thine.

> And thine the Human Face, & thine
> The Human Hands & Feet & Breath,
>     Entering thro' the Gates of Birth
> And passing thro' the Gates of Death [650f].

When the Jews also take up "compulsory cruel Sacrifices," the Age of Abraham has also passed and needs to be succeeded by a new Divine Vision.

For this purpose Jesus becomes "apparent on Earth" as the prophets have foretold (652): through him, the Human Form Divine is restored to its primordial glory.

But when Blake asks, "Art thou return'd to Albion's land?/And is Jerusalem thy Bride?" (651), we must not assume that he is giving literal credence to the legend of the young Jesus visiting Britain with Joseph. Jesus and his bride Jerusalem were here before the fall of Albion and will be together again when Albion awakes at the Last Judgment.

Nor would Blake have been attracted to the cult of the Holy Blood, the Sangreal, for he rejected the idea that Jesus was incarnate in order to shed his blood for our sins. He calls this the doctrine of the False Tongue, with "its sacrifices and/Its offerings," and bemoans the distortion of the Eternal Gospel, in which

> Jesus, the image of the Invisible God,
> Became its prey, a curse, an offering and an atonement
> For Death Eternal in the heavens of Albion & before the Gates
> Of Jerusalem, his Emanation ... [481].

This may be the reason why, despite his knowledge of Spenser, Blake never mentions the Holy Grail.

By the time of Tennyson, whose poem presents us with the modern form of the Glastonbury Grail legend, the nature of this mysterious, protean vessel has become fixed. It is, according to Tennyson's Percivale, the cup from which Our Lord drank at the Last Supper and which Joseph of Arimathea "journeying brought/To Glastonbury, where the winter thorn/Blossoms at Christmas, mindful of our Lord./And there awhile it bode," until evil grew so powerful throughout the land that this miraculous vessel, which could instantly heal anyone who saw or touched it of all that ailed them, was taken up to Heaven and seen no more on Earth (*PT*, 1663).

But if the Grail is, for Tennyson, the most Christian of vessels, others have traced its origins in pagan antiquity, classing it among the wonder-working vessels of Celtic mythology, or seen it as an exemplar of Gnostic heresy.[3]

Just as there are many different versions of the Grail, so there is no agreement as to when Christianity first came to these islands. If, indeed, Paul or Peter came here as missionaries—and if Arviragus gave Glastonbury to the Christians—nevertheless the faith remained a minority one, as elsewhere in the Roman Empire.

According to the chroniclers, Arviragus and his successors Marius (during whose reign the Picts, a people of Scythian origin, first settle in Albany) and Coilus remain steadfastly pagan. But ever since the days of Cymbeline, when the bard Taliesin prophesied the birth of the Savior, the good news has been spreading.

The first British king to be converted is the son of Coilus, good King Lucius, during whose reign paganism is eradicated almost throughout the entire island. Those of his retinue who refuse baptism are executed, and the pagan temples are cleansed of their heathen attributes. Interestingly, their statues, Layamon tells us (*Brut*, l.5079), are called "Mahun" (i.e., "Mohammeds"): an instance, not uncommon in Christian medieval literature, of an inability to differentiate paganism from Islam: (The French prose romances of the Vulgate Cycle even claim that there were mosques in the cities, the tallest being at Camelot, at this time [*LG* 1, 136].) Either way, the buildings are re-sanctified in the name of the Savior.

Lucius has no son to succeed him. When, after a reign of forty-two years, he dies in Gloucester (Layamon dates the event one hundred and sixty years after the birth of Our Lord), the Molmutine dynasty founded by Dunwallo about six hundred years earlier comes to an end, and there follows a period of confusion, both in the country and in our sources. The chronicles simply jump straight ahead to the year 208, when the Emperor Septimius Severus came to Britain, and the Matter of Britain once more intersects, however obliquely, with the known historical record.

# Three

# *Dreaming of Sovereignty*

Tell me the Acts, O historian, and leave me to reason upon them as
I please; away with your reasoning and your rubbish.[1]
—William Blake, 1809

At those points in our narrative where the imaginative counter-history
that is the Matter of Britain intersects with the known historical record, it
will be useful to call upon the services of a "reasoning historian," one of those
such as Edward Gibbon whom Blake dismissed as a "turner and twister of
causes and consequences" who disbelieve what they think "improbable or
impossible."

Blake, in his angry response to Enlightenment Rationalism, may have
agreed with the assertion of the Church Father Tertullian: that the Resurrec-
tion is certain, *because* it is impossible. Historians, writes Blake, "cannot see
either miracle or prodigy" because they are "weakly organized," that is to say,
because their reasoning faculty is not in harmony with the inspired imagina-
tion, a harmony which is the natural organization of the Eternal Man. They
do not see "spiritual agency," as a result, "all is to them a dull round of proba-
bilities and possibilities; but the history of all times and places, is nothing else
but improbabilities and impossibilities."

Blake is happy for the historian to give him "the Acts" (we would say, the
*facts*), but claims that he can find out "the Why, and the How" for himself.
Thus, in his now lost painting of "The Ancient Britons," Blake "has done, as
all the ancients did"; he has "given the historical fact in its poetical vigour"
(*DC*, 71f). In the remaining chapters of this book, we will endeavor to give
the historical facts, as much as they are known, and try to distinguish the
"probabilities and possibilities" from the vigor of the poets. For history and

**61**

counter-history are not mutually exclusive opposites, but rather "contraries," without which, as Blake himself argued, there is no progression.

We can do no better than to allow Edward Gibbon to be our guide to the "acts," for his *History of the Decline and Fall of the Roman Empire,* completed towards the end of the eighteenth century, remains, though some of its interpretations may have been called into question by subsequent scholarship, one of the greatest works of historical literature in the English language. His elegant, "reasoning" prose will, I hope, balance out the "poetical vigour" of Blake and the chroniclers of the Matter of Britain, without adding too much rubbish to the landfill of history.

## The Empire in the West

We saw, in the last chapter, that Britain first becomes a Christian country in the reign of good King Lucius, who dies (according to Layamon) in 160 CE. It may seem surprising that the opinion of our imperial Roman overlords about this conversion passes unremarked, but we must remember that, in our counter-history, the Kings of Britain are largely left to their own devices as long as they keep paying the tribute imposed by Julius Caesar.

Layamon does not resume his narrative until the arrival of the Emperor Septimius Severus in the early third century, and this means that he misses out an important stage in the fluctuating relations between Britain and the empire. For, although it is never mentioned by the chroniclers, we learn from the historical record that the arrival of Severus was preceded by the first of several usurpations of the Empire of the West by military commanders who, if not actually British natives, were nevertheless stationed in Britain and had the support of the legions there.

The most famous of these historical figures is Constantine the Great; his most famous legendary successor is Arthur. The first to gain the title of Caesar and claim the imperial purple, however, was the little-known Clodius Albinus.

Born in North Africa, Albinus won fame as a commander in his battles against the "barbarians," i.e., any cultures that had not yet received the benefits of Roman civilization. By the year 192, he had become governor of Britannia and had the task of defending the province against the barbarian Caledonians, who frequently attempted to encroach south of the Antonine Wall, which was then the northernmost limit of Roman power. In 193 the new emperor, Septimius Severus (who, like Clodius Albinus, was a native of Africa), promoted Albinus to the rank of Caesar, making him his regent and, effectively, his heir. Within two years, however, an (alleged) attempt by Severus to assassinate his regent led Albinus to declare himself emperor, cross over to the continent, and make a futile bid for supreme power. Albinus was decisively defeated at the Battle of Lyons (197 CE) and, in true Roman fashion, committed suicide.

It is a shame that the Emperor Albinus, whose uncanonical reign from 193 to 197 constitutes the first attempt of a ruler of Britain to lay claim to the throne of the world, was never counted among Geoffrey's Kings of Britain. His name alone seems to imply that he could be seen as the embodiment of the spirit of Albion, despite his North African origin.

Be that as it may, with the defeat of Albinus, the Emperor Severus set about the restoration of Hadrian's Wall, which had fallen into disuse, but on hearing of an invasion of the Roman province by the Caledonians in 208, he set off in person for Britannia, accompanied by his whole court and his two sons, Bassianus and Geta. After (temporarily) subduing the north of the island, the Emperor Severus died at York in 211, and his sons, declared joint emperors, returned to Rome, where, within a year, Bassianus (whom the chroniclers consider to be born of a British mother) had murdered his brother.

Sixty years after Bassianus, later known as the Emperor Caracalla, was murdered in fulfillment of a prophecy, Britain declared its independence from Rome. In 287 CE, Carausius, the commander of the Channel fleet, rebelled against the authority of the Emperor Maximian and usurped the throne of Britain. The chroniclers would have it that Carausius was British, and the eighteenth-century antiquarian William Stukeley, who wrote an unreliable *History of Carausius,* considered him to be "native of St. David's, and a prince of the blood royal of Britain" (*DF* 1, 364*n*25). But according to Gibbon, he was of Belgian origin; it was only when he was accused of fraud by Maximian that he fled to Britain and declared himself its emperor.

During the seven years of Carausius's reign, Gibbon tells us, the island prospered both artistically and monetarily. Not only did the British Emperor drive back the Caledonians, but it was at this time that Britain first began to rule the waves:

> His fleets rode triumphant in the channel, commanded the mouths of the Seine and of the Rhine, ravaged the coasts of the ocean, and diffused beyond the columns of Hercules the terror of his name. Under his command, Britain, destined in a future age to obtain the empire of the sea, already assumed its natural and respectable station of a maritime power (366).

In 294, however, Carausius was murdered by his first minister Allectus, who declared himself Emperor of Britain.

Meanwhile, Maximian had adopted a Dardanian nobleman, Constantius, as "Caesar" (Regent) of the West and entrusted him with the task of restoring

Britain to Roman sovereignty. It took Constantius three years to prepare a fleet adequate to the task. In 296 he sent his principal squadron, under the command of his prefect Asclepiodatus, to launch the invasion; the usurper Allectus was slain, and Britain, after ten years of independence, was reabsorbed into the main body of the empire.

In 305, Constantius succeeded Maximian as Emperor of the West and returned to Britain to suppress a Pictish rebellion. His eldest son Constantine, who was already a successful warrior, joined him there, and when, like the Emperor Severus nearly a century before him, Constantius died in the Imperial Palace at York, his son was immediately proclaimed emperor by his legions. The date was 25th July, 306.

In 307, Constantine married the daughter of Maximian and for six years ruled in Gaul, Spain and Britain, while his brother-in-law, the tyrannical Maxentius, ruled Italy and Africa. In 312, war broke out between the two emperors for supremacy in the west, a war which Constantine won.

Legend has it that Constantine became converted to Christianity on the eve of his decisive battle against Maxentius at the Milvian Bridge.

> In one of the marches of Constantine, he is reported to have seen with his own eyes the luminous trophy of the cross, placed above the meridional sun, and inscribed with the following words: BY THIS, CONQUER.

The skeptical Gibbon tells us that the emperor, who had not yet converted to the new faith, was as astonished as his army by this "amazing object in the sky"; but when, the following night, he has a vision of Christ "displaying the same celestial sign of the cross," he makes it the standard under which he will march to victory against Maxentius (741). By this sign, he will go on to conquer all his enemies.

This miracle notwithstanding, it was not until twelve years later that he began actively to promote, rather than simply to protect, Christianity, after his victory over the Eastern Emperor Licinius united the empire under his sole rule. "The foundation of Constantinople," Gibbon writes, "and the establishment of the Christian religion, were the immediate and memorable consequences of this revolution" (445). It was also at this time that Constantine's mother, whom he honored by the title of "Augusta" (Empress), undertook a pilgrimage to Palestine, during which she is believed to have discovered the True Cross of Jesus.

The historical acts that are so elegantly outlined by Gibbon become hopelessly confused by the chroniclers, but their alternative account reconnects us with the mythological underpinnings of British history.

According to our counter-historians, after the death of Allectus, Asclepiodatus rules Britain on behalf of the Empire and imposes Roman justice, which means that, during his reign, the persecution of the Christians is enforced. On the command of the Emperor Diocletian, churches are torn down, sacred scriptures burned, priests and their congregations martyred; the faith that has been sustained since the days of good King Lucius is almost wholly wiped out in these islands.

But divine providence intervenes at last and, after ten years of tyranny, Asclepiodatus is overthrown by the Christian Coel, the Earl of Gloucester, whom Layamon describes as "the highest born man who was living here in Britain" (*LB*, 140), for he is a descendant of the Emperor Claudius himself. Coel, who may be the "old King Cole" of the English nursery rhyme, is, according to Spenser, the first native-born High King of Britain since King Lucius. It is he who builds the city that bears his name, Colchester, and it is from this time forth that this realm began to "renew her passed prime" (*FQ*, II.x.58). Coel is eager to make a rapprochement with Rome, so he offers to Constantius, in the person of his daughter, the Sovereignty of Britain.

## The Most Holy Queen

The legendary events by which the sovereignty of this island was taken away from Rome—and restored to it, not in the form of conquest, but as a mythical act of union—figure largely in the British imagination from Geoffrey of Monmouth to Edmund Spenser. As a result of this union, between a noble Roman and a Christian British princess, there will emerge a hero who is born in Britain and elevated to the purple there and who will use it as a springboard from which to conquer, by the Sign of the Cross, his pagan adversaries and unite the empire under Christ.

Spenser neatly summarizes the legend, telling us that Coel gave to Constantius his "bright" daughter:

Fayre *Helena,* the fairest liuing wight;                          [= being
Who in all godly thewes and goodly praise      [godly thews = spiritual qualities
Did far excell, but was most famous hight                      [= named
For skil in Musicke of all in her daies,
Aswell in curious instruments as cunning laies [*FQ*, II.x.59].

Helena is the only child of Coel, and he has brought her up to rule the land after his death, as Layamon puts it, "the whole of his kingdom he placed in that young girl's hand" (*LB*, 141). Thus, when Constantius marries her, he is uniting himself with the Sovereignty of Britain. The child of this union is marked from birth as "divinely chosen" (143); his parents call him Constantine, but history will call him "the Great." He will grow up to become the most powerful man in the world and its greatest Christian monarch until Arthur.

Layamon tells us that the child flourishes, being "with God's favour cherished," respected by the British and well-advised by his Roman relatives, but war with Rome comes about because noblemen disinherited by Maxentius ("the Devil's favourite" [143]) flee to seek protection from Constantine. They tell him that the King of Britain is the only man powerful enough to take on the empire and beg him to march on Rome, overthrow the tyrant, and restore to them their rightful possessions. This he does and subsequently makes himself sole ruler of the known world.

Unfortunately, nothing in the story of old King Cole and "Helena of Britain" can be verified by the historical record, and the legend was effectively discredited by Gibbon, who argued that it had been "invented in the darkness of monasteries" (*DF* 1, 403n8). Helena is unlikely to ever have set foot in Britain; she was probably born in Asia Minor, where Constantine named a city in her honor (Helenopolis) after her death (*n*10). Gibbon argues that, far from being a British princess, she was the daughter of an innkeeper, although he defends the legality of her marriage against those who argue that she was merely the concubine of Constantius. Nevertheless, her lowborn status may have been a factor in Constantius's decision to put her aside in order to benefit from "the splendour of an Imperial alliance." In a move that can only have benefited his career, he married the daughter of the Emperor Maximian. By then Constantine, who had actually been born in Naissus in what is now Serbia, was in his late teens. Having been reduced by the divorcing of his mother to "a state of disgrace and humiliation," he allowed his mind to become "engrossed by ambition," and he joined his father in the expedition to reclaim Britain for the empire (403–5).

The historical record, unfortunately, can confirm very few details about the life of a woman who would become a "thrice-blessed" saint, finding herself compared to Mary as the "God-beloved" mother of Christ (Harbus, 19). It is the very paucity of accurate biographical material that has allowed so many legends to accumulate around her, including such "outlandish manifestations" as that she was a pagan Welsh goddess of the dawn (1) or a Jew who tried to convert her "God-beloved" son to Judaism before a miracle turned both of them into Christians (25).

In fact, Constantine himself was only baptized on his deathbed. Apart from the brief interregnum of Julian II, known as "the Apostate," all the emperors were henceforth Christian, but paganism was tolerated until the reign of Theodosius. As for Helena, it is impossible to ascertain whether she was brought up as a pagan, Jew, or Christian, but it does seem probable that her journey to the Holy Land was undertaken, at least in part, as an act of Christian pilgrimage (22). If her trip to Jerusalem was the zealous act of a recent convert, it was believed to have dramatic consequences. For, while there, she was alleged to have found the very cross on which Christ was crucified, a miracle which had the effect of transforming her son's vision of the Sign of Conquest into a material reality.

The event known as the *Inventio Crucis* has occasioned an amusing anecdote recounted by Evelyn Waugh, a British Catholic convert who devoted a novel to the saint whom he presents as both a British princess and the authentic discoverer of the sacred relic. In the Preface, however, he reports that a woman hostile to the Church had been on a visit to Palestine, where, she claimed, even the priests admitted that the chapel that Helena had founded in Jerusalem was the place of the "Invention of the Cross," leading her to get "the real low-down," which was that the whole story "was made up by a British woman called Ellen" (Waugh, 9).

By the time Waugh wrote his novel, in 1950, the legend of Helena's discovery or "invention" had been circulating in Britain for at least twelve hundred years, although it is impossible to find a beginning to what was probably originally an oral legend (Harbus, 28). It might seem curious that Geoffrey of Monmouth, whose "history" relies so much on myth and legend, does not mention what was by the twelfth century a well known story, but he was writing a "patriotic romance" concerned with establishing Arthur's Roman pedigree as the heir to a British Constantine and not "a Christian history" (79). The discovery by Constantine's mother of the True Cross also warrants only four verses from Wace (*RB*, ll.5720–4), but these are expanded by Layamon, who gives us "the earliest existing vernacular account of the British Helena legend" (Harbus, 83).

Layamon tells us that "the most holy queen" Helena goes to Jerusalem, where she meets with the elders of the Jew, promising them much in the way of gifts if they can show her the site where she can find "the Cross/Upon which Christ our Lord from sin released all this world." The Jews, who may have hidden the Cross for religious reasons, hand it over for purely mercenary motives, and Helena not only lives in Jerusalem with the Cross by her side for many years (*LB*, 144), but later becomes Queen of Jerusalem, to general rejoicing (141).

The historical Helena, as she is presented by the chroniclers, is taking on a mythical quality that makes of her a legendary figure. For we now see her as the ruler of three realms: Princess of Britain, Empress of Rome, and Queen of Jerusalem. Insofar as her sovereignty is threefold, is it possible to see behind the legendary figure of Helena of Colchester that ancient threefold goddess of the moon, who also rules three realms—earth, underworld and sky—and who, by conferring Britain on the hero of her choice, establishes herself as the archetypal Lady Sovereignty figure for this island?

One of the names for the moon is Athena (Kerényi 1951, 128), better known as the Greek goddess of wisdom who corresponds to the Roman Minerva, whose cult we saw established by Bladud at Bath. It is, therefore, at the least suggestive that, in British mythology, the Princess Helena is descended from a wise virgin that the Emperor Claudius loved (*Brut*, 1.4787), and she herself is, as Layamon puts it, "the wisest woman who was ever living in Britain" (*LB*, 143). Thus the "British Helen" can be seen as not just a native princess who becomes a Most Holy Queen, but as a symbolic figure who embodies wisdom.

But insofar as the historical Helena has taken on a mythic resonance, it may be because there is also another "British Helen" who is even more clearly mythic and who is sometimes confused with Helena of Colchester,[2] since her story complements and to some extent mirrors that of old King Cole's daughter: she is another British princess whom the Welsh call Elen and who marries Helena's cousin, Maxen the Ruler (*Wledig*).[3] History knows Maxen Wledig as the Emperor Magnus Maximus, but we will now examine his effect on British counter-history, which leads to him being seen as paving the way for the coming of Arthur.

The legendary chronicles continue, after the departure of Constantine for Rome, with a confused account of the reign of a certain "Maximien," one of Helena's cousins, who supports his onetime rival for the throne of Britain, Conan Meriadoc, in crossing the Channel and settling Armorica with Britons. This is the land that will henceforth be known as "Little Britain," or Brittany.

Maximien goes on to conquer Gaul and Germany, then takes Rome itself. It is for this reason that Arthur is later able to claim that his own right to rule in Rome derives from the conquest of the eternal city by his forebears, the family of Helena: her son Constantine and her cousin Maximien.

This "Maximien" was, in fact, the lowborn soldier Magnus Maximus, who served with the Roman army in Britain and had risen to the position of field general when, like Carausius before him, he led a revolt. But unlike Carausius, he did not wait for the island he now ruled to be invaded. Instead, he led a British army across the Channel and was pragmatically accepted as the Emperor of Spain, Gaul, and Britain by the Eastern Roman Emperor Theodosius.

According to the legendary chronicles, however, Helena's cousin Maximien becomes ruler of Britain through his marriage to the daughter of King Octavius (Eudaf in Welsh), who has usurped the throne from one of Helena's uncles. Layamon names Octavius's daughter Orien, but she appears in Welsh tradition as Elen of the Hosts.

According to the Tale of the Dream of the Ruler Maxen, the Emperor of

Rome (Maxen = Maximien = Magnus Maximus) sees Elen in a dream, enthroned and garbed in the red-gold of sovereignty, and knows that he must win her. Following the details of his dream, Maxen finds her in the fortress of Segontium on the North Wales coast, and she gives herself to him on condition that he allows her father to remain King of Britain and that Maxen builds for her three fortresses. She then has highways built to link these fortresses so that the warriors of Britain can assemble for her when she summons them.

This summons comes seven years later, when Maxen's position in Rome is usurped. The hosts of Britain are called to assemble for Elen, and she leads them to Rome to restore her husband's throne. Not for the first time, nor for the last, the walls of Rome fall before a British army in our counter-history.

## Our Lady of the Hosts

It is implicit in this story that Elen is a "sovereignty" figure who confers, on whomsoever she chooses, the power to rule both in Britain and in Rome.

It is instructive in this regard to compare Elen and her father Eudaf with Helena and her father Coel. The two Helens are, as we have seen, cousins by marriage. Their stories, in effect, mirror each other: Helena confers the sovereignty of Britain on her husband, Constantius, and her son, Constantine, goes on to conquer Rome; Elen confers the sovereignty of Britain on her father, Eudaf, and the sovereignty of Rome on her husband, Maxen.

Helena, of course, is a historical character, although her British provenance is contested by historians. Elen, on the other hand, has been seen as a purely fictional character whose name may simply have been borrowed from that of her husband's cousin.[4] The name Helen, however, has mythical qualities that make it a suitable name for the Sovereignty of Britain, despite its Greek origin; as "Elaine," the name is given to many of the female characters in the Arthurian legends.

"Helen" may originally have been one of the many names of the Indo-European moon-goddess, and scholars have certainly seen a commanding divinity behind the seductive figure of Helen of Troy.[5] It is that Helen, we must remember, whose face launched the ships which destroyed Troy, and the fall of Troy is as much a foundational event in the mythology of the rise of the British Empire as it is of the Roman.

The story of Helen of Troy is one of many myths that were reworked in modern times by the Irish poet W. B. Yeats (1865–1939), who also has the distinction of being Blake's first editor, helping to rescue the earlier poet from obscurity at the end of the nineteenth century. But Yeats went much further than mere admiration of Blake: He was one of the first to attempt to locate his idiosyncratic writings within the tradition of western esoteric symbolism, an attempt that would be followed up more systematically by the poet and scholar Kathleen Raine. For Yeats as for Blake (and, for that matter, Raine), myths are symbolic stories that reveal spiritual truths.

In a poem about the divine conception of the Trojan Helen ("Leda and the Swan," 1923), Yeats suggests that the event inaugurates a cycle of destruction that can end a civilization:

> A shudder in the loins engenders there
> The broken wall, the burning roof and tower [*YCP*, 241].

It is the descendants of refugees from broken and burning Troy, as we have seen, who are considered to be the founders of Britain. Whether we call her Helena or Elen, the "British Helen" is the Sovereignty of Albion, who has been fought over ever since refugees from the violence engendered by the Trojan Helen's conception first arrived here.

For it is important to remember here that, no matter how much the claim to sovereignty is a pragmatic issue of power politics, it is also rooted in those myths that underlie our history, that in fact provide historical events with an emotional charge that cannot be wholly accounted for by the "acts" themselves. Myth connects temporal history with the eternal: for Eternity, as Blake has shown us, is always in love with the productions of time.

The Romans, after their conquest of the south of the island of Britain, symbolized their province with the figure of Britannia, an image that borrowed much from that of Minerva, the lunar goddess of wisdom whose cult at Bath was attributed to the legendary Bladud. In creating this figure, the Romans were connecting their earthly rule with that mythic substrate that alone can sustain empires over hundreds of years—the ruled must *believe* in their rulers. The empire created a syncretistic image of the goddess of the land, the Lady of the Sovereignty of Britain, but, in doing so, it was connecting its rule with that of a far more ancient ruler: that Celtic goddess whose antiquity is suggested by her presence in the mythology of Ireland, which was never conquered by the Romans.

For example, in the Irish tale "The Phantom's Frenzy," the hero Conn of the Hundred Battles (who was believed to have lived in the second century after Christ) reaches a house in a mist where he encounters Lugh, the god of light, seated on a throne, beside a beautiful girl on a crystal chair. She has a silver vessel filled with red ale, attached to a golden cup and bowl, with which she serves Conn, while Lugh recites the names of Conn's descendants who will be kings of Ireland. The master of the house tells Conn that the girl represents the eternal Sovereignty of Ireland (Loomis 1956, 27).

This "goddess who rules," like the land itself, can be both fruitful and barren: She can be the mother of her people or, like Minerva, a wise virgin. It was this latter aspect of Britannia that characterized the first Elizabethan Age: As long as Elizabeth Tudor remained a virgin queen, she could maintain her symbolic role as the bride of her people, whom no mortal suitor could replace in her affections.

The earthly representative of Sovereignty can be a monarch in her own right, like the first Elizabeth, or she can choose to bestow her power on the man who wins her love, after he has proved his worthiness. She confers on him, through a sacred marriage, the right to rule; he becomes her champion, the guardian of the land and its treasures or sacred emblems. Among these sacred emblems, for much of our prehistory, may have figured very largely (as indeed they do in the landscape!) the stones of the mythical Giants' Dance, which we now know as Stonehenge, and which William Wordsworth, in an early poem concerning "Incidents Upon Salisbury Plain," invoked as a "fabric of mysterious form":

> Pile of Stone-henge! so proud to hint yet keep
> Thy secrets, thou that lov'st to stand and hear
> The Plain resounding to the whirlwind's sweep,
> Inmate of lonesome Nature's endless year ... [*WPW*, 20f].

Sovereignty has many symbols, but in Celtic mythology especially, we find that a sacred stone establishes the right to rule.

In Irish literature we read of the Stone of Falias, one of the four treasures that the *Túatha DéDanand* (the People of the Goddess Danu) brought with them from their mythical northern homeland to Ireland, which they settled before the arrival of the Celtic Sons of Mil. After the Milesian conquest, the Danaans became the People of the Sídh, the hills of Faerie, dwelling in the ancient pre–Celtic burial mounds and interacting—and sometimes marrying—with mortals. As in Wales, the Irish Otherworld exists side by side and simultaneously with the physical world.

With the Celtic conquest, the Stone of Destiny, as it became known (because it was believed to shriek whenever the true king sat upon it) became the Stone of Sovereignty of the High Kings of Ireland. It was later believed to have been transported to Scotland, where it remained in the Abbey of Scone until 1296, when the English King, Edward I, carried it off to Westminster Abbey, thus symbolically claiming the sovereignty of Scotland (Hutton 1991, 173). More recently, the Stone of Scone has been returned to Scotland, a symbolic act heralding the limited restoration of sovereignty occasioned by the reestablishment of the Scottish Parliament.

A similar symbolic importance attaching to Welsh stones may explain the extraordinary feat, accomplished in prehistoric times, of the transportation of the famous "bluestones" from the Preseli Hills, in modern Pembrokeshire, to Salisbury Plain, where they were used to establish the solstitial alignments of the stone temple. If the Preseli bluestones were "stones of destiny," sacred to the goddess of the land, it seems likely that their removal to the east was symbolic of a major cultural transformation. In political terms, this may have been characterized by the rise to supremacy of the Wessex culture; in religious terms, by the transference of the seat of the Goddess of Sovereignty from southwest Wales to Wiltshire (Darrah, 134f).

This shift in the political and religious center of gravity in Britain may also have corresponded to the transition from a Stone Age to a Bronze Age culture, in which the earlier Neolithic peoples gradually became identified in story as the People of the Otherworld. This would certainly explain how, in later accounts of the erection of the Giants' Dance, the stones were believed to have been brought from Ireland, which in British mythology is frequently seen as a localization of the Otherworld. In this story (which we will return to in the next chapter), the Stones of Destiny are brought by Uther Pendragon to Britain; and it may be that this feat proves his worthiness to win the love of the Goddess of Sovereignty, for it is followed by his marriage to Igerna, who will bear him the son who will become our greatest king.

In the Grail literature, the Stone of Destiny would become transformed into the Siege Perilous, a symbol of spiritual rather than worldly kingship, and it may be this dethroning of Lady Sovereignty by the male God of Christianity and her reduction to a Goddess of Fate who can never be more than an agent of divine providence (along with the reduction of her "giant" people to the "fairy folk," the fays and elves) that leads her to show her angry face, as the Hideous Maiden or Loathly Lady of Arthurian romance.

## A Digression into Some Speculative Tenets

The historical Magnus Maximus was a fanatical Christian who persecuted heretics: "the first," Gibbon informs us, "among the Christian princes, who shed the blood of his Christian subjects, on account of their religious opinions" (*DF* 2, 38). His principal victim was a Spanish bishop called Priscillian, whose heresy, according to Gibbon, consisted not of "the various abominations of magic, of impiety, and of lewdness" with which they were falsely accused, but of an extreme asceticism, coupled with an heretical Christology: "The speculative tenets of the sect, concerning the person of Christ, and the nature of the human soul, were derived from the Gnostic and Manichæan system; and this vain philosophy, which had been transported from Egypt to Spain, was ill adapted to the grosser spirits of the West" (*DF* 2, 38f).

Leaving aside the issue of whether their philosophy was any more "vain" than that of Enlightenment Rationalists, it might be useful at this stage to define what is meant by "the Gnostic and Manichæan system," since these heresies resonate with the work of Blake at several points, although he did not use the terms himself; like most supposed heretics, he saw himself only as a good Christian. It was in fact Blake's friend, the journalist and diarist Crabb Robinson, who claimed after one meeting that what the artist had expounded with great consistency was the Gnostic doctrine of a flawed creation: The creator of this world, the Biblical Elohim, is "a very Cruel Being" who judges his creation; he is not the Father with whom Jesus is one; rather, Jesus is the human face of the God of Mercy, and he comes to heal the suffering creation (*BCW*, 617).

The social historian E.P. Thompson (34f) has suggested that the Gnostic inspiration in Blake's thought might have come from his reading of the German mystic Jacob Boehme or Behmen, who Blake claimed appeared to him and who he considered to be "divinely inspired" (Bentley, 414), but he would also have come across outlines of Gnostic doctrines in the historical writings of his contemporary Joseph Priestley and, of course, in Gibbon. "Gnosticism" as a scholarly term was in fact coined in the Enlightenment, although it is derived from what early heresy hunters denounced as a false "gnosis" being promulgated by people who claimed to possess a salvific "knowledge" that was denied those of simple faith.

At the risk of over-simplification, gnostics are people who seek direct experience of, or intimate acquaintance (*gnosis*) with, the divine. Like mystics, who seek to *merge* with the divine, gnostics are found within all religious practices: There is a pagan gnosis, associated with the Mysteries, which influenced early Christianity (Rahner, 362–7); Jewish gnosis is usually associated with Kabbalism (Scholem, 13); Islamic gnosis with certain tendencies within Sufism and esoteric Shi'ism (which are the particular fields of study of the French philosopher Henry Corbin, whose ideas on prophecy and the imagination I will return to in the next chapter). But the search for the personal encounter with God is not confined to the Abrahamic religions, so it is not surprising to find Corbin describing gnosis as a "world religion" in its own right.[6]

By contrast, the term Gnosticism was coined by scholars in Gibbon's time to refer more narrowly to early Christians who set themselves apart from the merely faithful. They were understood to share the belief that the True God was ineffable; that He was not the same as the Creator of the Cosmos, who was at best ignorant, at worst evil (*DF* 1, 457*n*29); that the creation itself was flawed because it was the result of the fall of a spiritual being from the eternal realms ("aeons"); and that Christ, who was an emanation or emissary of the True God, did not have a material body and therefore did not suffer *physically* on the cross.

Gibbon is at pains to point out that their doctrines derived, at least in part, from their rejection of the divine origin of the Books of Moses, which the Gnostics treated "with profane derision," while the Judaic God of the Law was "impiously represented" as a cruel tyrant. Christ, they argued, appeared on Earth "to reveal a *new* system of truth and perfection" (456f). These ideas we find partly reflected in Blake: it would be "altogether Abominable & Blasphemous," he claims, to defend "the Wickedness of the Israelites in murdering so many thousands under pretence of a command from God," and Christ, having come "to abolish the Jewish Imposture," was murdered because his teaching "that God loved all Man" was "in opposition to the Jewish Scriptures" (*BCW*, 387).

But if the belief that the Jews killed Jesus has been the justification for two millennia of judaeophobia, culminating in the complicity of many Christians with the Holocaust, then the Gnostic rejection of the God of Israel as a Cruel Being has been seen as providing an ideological basis for the extermination of the Jews, who are maligned as the agents of a tyrannical Cosmocrator, or Demiurge. Such beliefs lay behind the "racial gnosis" that developed in the nineteenth century, among groups who taught that it was the Aryans, not the Jews, who were the Chosen People of the Most High God; and for whom Hitler was the Aryan Christ, the "ultimate avatar" who was incarnated in order to reveal the new, anti–Semitic truth: that the Jewish conspiracy is as much cosmological as it is political, economic, and cultural. Such ideas provided a "spiritual wing" for the nascent Nazi Party (Godwin, 585f), and we know what crimes that wing sheltered in the first half of the twentieth century.

But it would be wrong to dismiss Gnosticism because of its misuse by fanatics, just as it would be wrong to dismiss the profound insights of Christianity and Islam (as the proponents of militant atheism are currently doing) because of the fundamentalists who distort their traditions. The sad truth is that the dark side of every culture is reflected, if not magnified, in its counter-culture.

The "reasoning historian" Gibbon, who, in Blake's phrase, "does not see spiritual agency" (and therefore, according to the poet, "is not worth any man's reading" [*DC*, 72]) is skeptical about the value of esoteric exegesis and unorthodox metaphysical speculation, which delivers one to "the guidance of a disordered imagination" (*DF* 1, 458). However, it is important to note that with the finding of many original early Christian texts in 1945, our understanding of the gnosis of antiquity has broadened. As a result, scholars are no longer so quick to dismiss the early Christian Gnostics, as their opponents within the Church did, as elitist, world-denying dualists. Although many of their texts can be read in this way, especially if they are taken literally, it may be more instructive to read them as mythopoeic imaginings, in which characters familiar from Genesis and the New Testament reappear in unfamiliar, dreamlike guises. The texts can then be read as metaphorical, rather than theological, the products of an imagination that, though to an Enlightenment rationalist such as Gibbon it seemed "disordered," is to others the key to understanding the human soul.[7]

Thus, gnostic writers from Blake to the Swiss analytical psychologist Carl Jung have read the biblical Demiurge as the personification of a narrow ego-consciousness; the "I" (Blake's "Selfhood") that sets itself up as the supreme moral authority and condemns all that is "other" (Stein, 47f). The creation of the Demiurge, then, is not the natural world, but a system of consciousness: a rigid materialism that denies the spirit in man and exiles the soul to the wasteland.

In their desire to liberate themselves from the System of the Cosmocrator (Blake's "mind-forged manacles") through spiritual transcendence, the early Gnostic sects are believed to have practiced both extremes of licentiousness ("The soul of sweet delight can never be defil'd") and asceticism ("Enough! or Too much" [*BCW*, 152]). Furthermore, they expressed their ideas in complicated mythological fantasies of which the Prophetic and Illuminated Books of William Blake can be seen as the latest and most idiosyncratic flowering. While he did not share all the beliefs of the early Gnostics, Blake can be seen to have adapted, for "the grosser spirits of the West," some of their most striking ideas into poetic images whose power is not dependent on "vain" philosophical speculation.

The Dutch Jungian scholar Jos van Meurs (275) has seen a gnostic psychology at the heart of Blake's vision: his insistence that "knowledge of reality is based on the personal, inner experience of man ... and not on sense perception or imposed dogma." He has further explored some of the ways in which Blake's cosmology resonates with that of the early Gnostics, in particular his perception that the separation of the spiritual Anthropos (Blake's Albion, the Ancient or Eternal Man) into male Zoas and female Emanations brings about the Fall, and that the Fall precedes and includes the creation, which is the act of a lower demiurge (277).

It is intriguing that some of the most striking correspondences between the Gnostic scriptures and Blake's myth of Albion come from a text that was not discovered until 1945, when the largest ever cache of early Gnostic writings was found by chance in sealed jars buried in the Egyptian desert, and which was therefore unknown to Gibbon, Priestley, or any other of Blake's sources. One of these texts is an untitled work known to scholars as the *Tripartite Tractate* because it is divided by scribal decoration into three sections, which can be seen as the three acts of the cosmic drama: the fall of the primordial being; the creation of the human race; and the salvation of the spiritually enlightened through reintegration into the godhead (*NHL*, 58f). These correspond to the three phases of the drama of Albion announced at the beginning of Blake's *Jerusalem:*

> Of the Sleep of Ulro! and of the passage through
> Eternal Death! and of the awaking to Eternal Life [*BCW*, 622].

Ulro is Blake's name for the region of shadow and emptiness, which the Gnostics call the *Kenoma,* the chaos that exists outside of the *Pleroma,* or divine "fullness." It is into this lightless realm that Albion falls:

> There is a Void outside of Existence, which if enter'd into
> Englobes itself & becomes a Womb; such was Albion's Couch,
> A pleasant Shadow of Repose call'd Albion's lovely Land [620].

Thus the island of Britain itself, or rather its spiritual archetype, is seen as a womb in which the sleeping Albion is protected from the existential void and where he can await rebirth.

In other Gnostic scriptures, it is the female Aeon of Wisdom who experiences a cosmogonic fall. It is a unique characteristic of the *Tripartite Tractate* that this role, as in Blake's mythology, is taken by a masculine being, the Aeon of the Word, or Logos. This is the Word of God, who is equated with Jesus in the Gospel of John, but who here appears as a masculine counterpart of Sophia, being "among those to whom was given wisdom":

> It came to one of the aeons that he should attempt to grasp the incomprehensibility and give glory to it and especially to the ineffability of the Father.

This is the Logos whose error, like that of Sophia in other texts, is to over-reach himself: Acting without restraint, he tries "to bring forth one who is perfect," but this is impossible because he does not have the agreement of the ineffable Father (or Parent) of the Entirety. The Logos is acting "magnanimously, from an abundant love," when he sets out toward "the perfect glory" of the Father (*NHL*, 72); while, towards the end of Blake's *Vala,* it is the Zoa named Luvah (who, as his name suggests, is the personification of Love) who says: "Attempting to be more than Man We become less" (*BCW*, 376), and this seems to suggest that the fall of Albion from a state of spiritual harmony is caused by *hubris.* Albion is Divine Humanity. To seek to become more than human, Blake appears to be suggesting, can in fact make us lose touch with what in us is divine and thus lessen our humanity.

In the Tractate, the Parent withdraws from the Logos and he finds himself beyond the Limit of the Pleroma. He cannot bear to look at the Light, but when he looks into the Abyss, he is filled with self-doubt and falls into "division, forgetfulness and ignorance" (*NHL*, 73). What he brings forth from his confusion is far from perfect: There emerge *hylic* forces (the basis of the material world) that are mere shadows of the spiritual archetypes in the Pleroma. Shocked at what he has produced, the Logos remembers where he has come from, and from his repentance are produced psychic forces (the World Soul). He turns back to the Pleroma, and the brotherly love between him and the spiritual aeons produces the Savior.

In doing so, however, he separates himself from his defective, feminine nature, which is left outside the Pleroma. In Blake's myth, also, the fall of Albion is inextricably bound up with his separation from his female Emanation (Jerusalem) and the alienation of his Zoas from their female selves. Jerusalem is sent into exile, and her place is usurped by Vala who, as her name suggests, symbolizes the Veil of Illusion that separates humankind from Eternity.

Meanwhile the four Zoas fight among themselves and with their Emanations for supremacy. Here again, their actions are paralleled by those of the supernatural beings created by the Logos in the Tractate:

> They thought of themselves that they are beings existing by themselves and are without a source, since they do not see anything else existing before them.

Disobedient and rebellious demiurges who will have no other gods before them, they try to dominate each other, and, as a result, they give birth to fighting, warlike, power-crazed offspring (74).

This War in Heaven, the archetype of the power struggle that is human history, constitutes the bulk of the narrative of Blake's later illuminated books. It is the demiurgic Urizen who, above all others, is the Zoa who typifies the arrogance of those who deny their spiritual origin. After building the Mundane Shell, in an echo both of the Biblical creator and his Gnostic parody, Urizen boasts of his uniqueness:

> "Am I not God?" said Urizen, "Who is Equal to me?"
> "Do I not stretch the heavens abroad, or fold them up like a garment?"
> [*BCW*, 294].

By contrast Los, the Eternal Prophet, tries to preserve the sense of Eternity through the subsequent darkening of the divine vision. In Chapter One of *Jerusalem* Los declares:

... the time will arrive
When all Albion's injuries shall cease, and when we shall
Embrace him, tenfold bright, rising from his tomb in immortality [626].

In the meantime, however: "Albion is dead! his Emanation is divided from him!" (631).

When the female is separated from the whole being, the split-off masculine aspect becomes what Blake calls the Spectre. Thus in Chapter Three we are told, "Man divided from his Emanation is a dark Spectre" (776). With division comes the Fall:

But Albion fell down, a Rocky fragment from Eternity hurl'd
By his own Spectre, who is the Reasoning Power in every Man,
Into his own Chaos,

while his Spectre rises over him, declaring, "I am God, O Sons of Men! I am your Rational Power!"

So spoke the hard cold constrictive Spectre: he is named Arthur,
Constricting into Druid Rocks round Canaan ...
Then Albion drew England into his bosom in groans & tears,
But she stretch'd out her starry Night in Spaces against him like
A long Serpent in the Abyss of the Spectre, which augmented
The Night with Dragon wings cover'd with stars ... [685].

England, an aspect of Albion's wife Britannia and the archetype of the nation that is yet to be formed in the island of Britain, resists Albion's embrace, and her resistance takes shape as a long serpent in the starry night, presumably the constellation of Draco, which once, thousands of years ago, contained the Pole Star.

This passage is complex but also fascinating, for, as we will see in Chapter Six, the polar symbolism of Draco is related to Merlin's vision of the creation of the Pendragon dynasty and the coming of Arthur, who would resist the inroads of the Anglo-Saxons until they amalgamated with the native Romano-Britons and the later Norman conquerors to form the one English nation, "taking refuge/In the Loins of Albion" (739).

The savage warlord Arthur is, for Blake, the embodiment of the spectral Reasoning Power, and it is precisely the predominance of this power over the whole that causes Albion to fall from Eternity into Chaos. The Ancient Man becomes a fallen man, who forgets his divine origin in the chaotic void that is the Sleep of Ulro. The spectral Arthur is himself both the agent of Albion's constriction (the narrowing of vision that is the loss of Eternity) and the embodiment of the process of constriction. He *is* the fallen Albion, constricted "into Druid rocks," that is to say, he becomes the rocky island of the Druids that is also called Albion. The land and the king are one, and Arthur will return (in tenfold splendor) when Albion arises immortal from his tomb (in tenfold brightness).

So we can see that it is, above all, in his image of the fallen Albion that Blake brings a Gnostic perspective to bear upon the figure of Arthur, but Gnosticism has also been identified as a factor in the development of the Grail legends. This was argued most famously by Jessie L. Weston in *From Ritual to Romance,* a book published in 1920 but still in print, which influenced T.S. Eliot's modernist poem *The Waste Land.* However, in the Thirties, the German scholar Otto Rahn pursued the idea that the German Grail legends presented in allegorical form the key figures from the medieval Cathar heresy and that the Cathars had preserved, in their citadel of Montségur, the Grail itself, which Rahn identified as "a precious stone symbolising a dualist tradition which long predated Christianity" (Barber, 208–10).

Rahn's work on the Cathars attracted the interest of Heinrich Himmler and led to his being awarded a commission in the Ancestral Heritage Division of the SS, whereas the interest in such matters of his older contemporary, Déodat Roché, led to the Frenchman's demotion from his position as a magistrate in the Vichy régime. Nevertheless, after the war, Roché continued his researches, which are largely responsible for the modern, popular interest in the Cathars and the belief that Catharism was "the heir of Manichaeism" (203f), an earlier heresy that Gibbon had identified as another source for the "speculative tenets" of the Priscillianist sect.

The Manichaeans were the disciples of the third-century Prophet Mani, whose syncretic system attempted to fuse Gnostic Christianity with Mahayana Buddhism and the Zoroastrian religion of his native Persia. Gibbon (*DF* 3, 424–35) had attempted to show the historical thread that linked the early Gnostics and their Manichaean heirs with the Cathar heresy that developed in northern Italy and southwest France in the twelfth and thirteenth centuries, and more recently the challenge has been taken up by historians such as Yuri Stoyanov. It is true that Catharism has certain points in common with the Manichaean system (notably the belief in two opposing but equal principles of Light and Darkness, of which our world is a mixture), but the once-popular notion that the Cathars were "medieval Manichees" is now contested (Barber, 10–12).

In his conversations with Blake, Crabb Robinson declared that "when a child" he had been convinced of the rationality of the Manichaean doctrine of "two principles"; and Blake had "assented to this." In fact, Blake sounds like a Cathar when he declares that the natural world is "the empire of nothing" (Bentley, 416), for, to the dualists, John 1:3 means that a world of nothingness was created without the involvement of the True God and that this "nothing" was "the transitory world which contrasted with the true reality which was the creation of God" (Barber, 90).

That the Cathar religion developed concurrently with the Grail legends has led perhaps inevitably to twentieth-century authors from Rahn onwards claiming that the stories were intended to express, in a fictional form, heterodox ideas whose open expression would invite persecution. There has even been speculation that the Cathars were Grail Keepers in the sense of guardians of a secret about the bloodline of Jesus (the Sangreal), but it is more likely that the story of the Grail was gradually Christianized as it developed from its obscure beginnings in order to reflect the dogma of transubstantiation, which had been asserted as "a direct answer to the anti-eucharistic views of the Cathars" (111n14). The Grail Quest of Galahad was able to express in more orthodox form the mystical, world-renouncing Christianity that formed such a strong part of the Cathar appeal.

Despite his interest in the figure of Joseph of Arimathea, Blake never refers directly to the Grail legend. But at the heart of the medieval stories is the image of the Maimed King, whose kingdom suffers in sympathy with his wound. And what is this figure of a wounded king at one with his land but Blake's Albion, groaning on his couch of deathlike sleep, whose awakening will also be that of the island that bears his name? The awakening of Albion, one might say, is precisely the Holy Grail of Blake's artistic and spiritual quest.

## The Restoration of Sovereignty

Our excursion into the speculative tenets of Gnosticism began with—and must now return to—the fanatical orthodoxy of Magnus Maximus, the first persecutor of heresy. There may even be a curious reference to his intolerance of the faith of others in the Welsh Tale of Maxen, where we are told that, before he could win the hand of Elen, the emperor had to drive Beli and his sons into the sea. Beli, as we saw in the last chapter, is an ancestral deity who was equated with a legendary king from before the Roman conquest, so we are clearly not dealing here with a historical battle. Rather, the Beli that Maxen drives into the sea can be seen as a symbolic figure representing the vestiges of an ancient paganism that the fanatical emperor would have been as keen on eradicating as he was the Gnostic heresy of Priscillian.

Despite his unimpeachably orthodox credentials, Maximus becomes a figure who can be transformed in story into the chosen one of Sovereignty, and this may indicate the ease with which formerly pagan Britons in the Roman Empire accepted the good news of Christ: prepared as they have been, the legends say, by the prophecies of Taliesin in the court of Cymbeline and by Joseph of Arimathea preaching Christ's "evangely." Thus it is that Lady Sovereignty, in the form of Elen of the Hosts, is willing to transfer her blessing from the pagan Beli to the Christian Maxen, as long as he will serve her, and this is indeed how their relationship is presented in the Welsh tale.

Just as the goddess Diana appeared to Brutus in a dream and conferred on him the Sovereignty of Albion, so Elen appears to Maxen in a dream and makes him love her above all things, so that he has neither "life or being or existence" without her; he wishes only to sleep, so that he can dream of her again (*TM*, 121). The dream is in reality a summons, for its details give Maxen all the information he needs to find Elen; his messengers need only follow the dream itinerary exactly in order to find the princess at Segontium. But when they tell Elen about the emperor's dream and give her the choice of going to Rome or making Maxen come to her, she replies with true regal *hauteur*: "I do not doubt what you say, but I do not believe it overmuch either. If it is I whom the emperor loves, let him come for me" (123).

When Maxen arrives in Britain, he first proves his worthiness by overcoming Beli, the representative of the old pre–Christian dispensation, and then proves his willingness to submit to Lady Sovereignty by granting Elen her every wish. In return, she restores to him the Empire of the West, which he was in danger of losing to a rival due to his extended, seven-year sojourn in the island of his lady-love.

In Welsh mythology Maxen sees only the benign, smiling face of Sovereignty, who gives him Rome, but, for the historical Emperor Maximus, his dream of sovereignty became a nightmare: He over-reached himself, and his hubris led to defeat and execution in 388 CE at the hands of the eastern emperor, Theodosius.

Lady Sovereignty can be loving or angry, helpful or dangerous: a beautiful bride or a monstrous seducer and betrayer. As Fate, she can be fickle. The fate of Maximus prefigures that of Arthur in its broad outlines, as we will see in Chapter Seven. Arthur will quote Maximus's rulership of the Empire of the West in defense of his own claim, but he will also meet his nemesis when the Lady of Sovereignty turns the Wheel of Fortune, after his victory over the Romans.

With his overthrow of Magnus Maximus, Theodosius became sole ruler of the Roman Empire, but on his death in 395, it was divided between his two sons and would never be reunited. The younger son, Honorius, became Emperor of the West, and it was during his reign that Britain was finally separated from the empire.

The chroniclers blame the power-obsessed Maximus for taking away all the able-bodied young men of the island to die abroad in the usurper's ill-fated continental adventures; the Welsh Triads see Elen as responsible for one of the Three Levies that Departed, never to return (*TYP*, 81). Those who remain after the levy are unable to resist the ever-bolder incursions of pagan barbarian tribes, principally the Huns and Picts. "The weary *Britons*," writes Spenser:

> With wretched miseryes, and woefull ruth,
> Were to those Pagans made an open pray,
> And daily spectacle of sad decay:
> Whom *Romane* warres, which now fowr hundred yeares,
> And more had wasted, could no whit dismay;
> Till by consent of Commons and of Peares,
> They crownd the second *Constantine* with ioyous teares [*FQ*, II.x.62].

This Constantine (407–11) was in fact the third of a series of emperors that the British army installed when they revolted against the authority of Honorius, prompted by the latter's inability to defend the province against its traditional enemies, and hoping, Gibbon suggests (*DF* 1, 152), that he would live up to the memory of the great Constantine. Under his command the Roman legions in Britain crossed the Channel into Gaul, never to return; both he and his son Constans, who had been forced to abandon a monastic life, were soon dead at the hands of Honorius.

The death of the usurper Constantine marks the beginning of what is often thought of as "the Dark Ages" of British history,[8] but which, with the final deliverance of the island from the barbarians, ushers in a Golden Age of legend, culminating in the restoration of Britain's ancient glory by Arthur.

Gibbon elegantly summarizes that period about which "reasoning historians" can tell us so little. Abandoned by the legions and exposed to the attacks of Irish and Caledonian "savages" as well as Saxon pirates, the Britons learned to defend themselves, no longer relying "on the tardy and doubtful aid of a declining monarchy. They assembled in arms, repelled the invaders, and rejoiced in the important discovery of their own strength" (*DF* 2, 231). As a result "Britain was irrecoverably lost" to the Roman Empire (232), although, as we will see, the Romans will, in our legendary counter-history, make a last-ditch attempt to regain the island.

Gibbon himself contributes to the legends when he embraces an image that is familiar from the Arthurian story: that of the Pendragon, or "Dragon Head." Gibbon describes Britain after the Roman departure as run by Episcopal synods in which princes, magistrates and bishops regulated affairs of state, "and there is reason to believe," he adds, "that in moments of extreme danger, a *Pendragon*, or Dictator, was elected by the general consent of the Britons" (234).

It is to the legend of the Pendragons—and their relationship with the Prophet Merlin—that we will turn in the next chapter. For in our counter-history, the "second Constantine" arrives, precisely at a moment of extreme danger, when foreign invaders have reduced the Britons to living in pits in the wilderness, to be elected king by universal acclaim of the people.

# Four

# *Immortal Imagination*

The founder of the dynasty that will be immortalized with the surname Pendragon is that "second Constantine" whom history remembers as a short-lived usurper on the imperial throne of the West but who, in the legendary chronicles, is mysteriously transformed into a Breton prince (the great-grandson of King Octavius), who leaves Lesser for Greater Britain at the hour of his ancestral homeland's greatest need.

Following an embassy from the Archbishop of London, Constantine crosses the Channel with a Breton army, landing at Totnes, where Brutus and his Trojans had first disembarked. The beleaguered Britons flock to his side: even the women arm themselves like men, and the foreign invaders (Picts and Huns, Scots and Scythians, Norwegians and Danes) are defeated. Constantine is crowned at Silchester and marries a British noblewoman. She bears him three sons: Constans, Aurelius Ambrosius, and Uther.

Constans is dedicated to the monastic life (this much at least is historical fact, as we know from Gibbon [*DF* 2, 219]), but is tempted to exchange the monk's habit for royal garments when his father is treacherously stabbed to death by a Pict. The man who raises him to the throne is Vortigern of Gwent; it is Vortigern who rules in fact, while Constans merely wields the sceptre, and it is Vortigern who secretly encourages the Picts to murder the king.

In order to exculpate himself, Vortigern has the assassins executed, thus winning the enmity of the Picts, and places himself on the throne when he discovers that those entrusted with the care of Constans's young brothers have smuggled them to Brittany for safekeeping. "For dread of whom," as Spenser puts it, "and for those Picts annoyes,/He sent to *Germany,* straunge aid to reare" ... (*FQ,* II.x.64).

## Strange Aid

Vortigern soon discovers that uneasy lies the head that steals the crown. Aurelius and Uther, the younger brothers of the assassinated Constans, who have taken shelter in Brittany, have come to man's estate and are apparently planning to invade the island that, by rights, is theirs. At the same time the Picts, on whom Vortigern put the blame for the murder of Constans, are plotting revenge. In this atmosphere, the arrival on the coast of Kent of three longships, filled with armed men of enormous stature, could be yet another disaster, but the wily Vortigern decides to turn it to his advantage.

The king receives the leaders of the warriors in his court at Canterbury. They are, he discovers, Saxons, and their leaders are two brothers, Hengest and Horsa. They have been brought to these shores by Woden, their chief god, whom the pagan Romans worshipped as Mercury. The Christian Vortigern is shocked to hear the name of a pagan deity, who has not been openly worshipped in Britain for decades, but curious enough to enquire about their other gods.

The Saxons, it appears, have a pantheon of seven gods, each of whom rules one of the days of the week and who correspond to the seven heavenly bodies (the Sun, Moon and five visible planets) of traditional cosmology. The seven gods, as given in a slightly confused form by Layamon, are: Phoebus Apollo for Sunday; Tervagant (=Diana) for Monday; Tidea (=Tiw, corresponding to the Roman Mars) for Tuesday; Woden for Wednesday; the Thunder (=Thor, corresponding to the Roman Jupiter) for Thursday; Frea (corresponding to the Roman Venus) for Friday; and Saturn (for whom there is no Germanic equivalent) for Saturday (*Brut*, ll.6935–55).

The gods of the fourth and seventh days are invoked together by Hengest when King Vortigern offers him land and wealth if he will lead his men against the Picts: It will all happen as the king desires if it is the will of Saturn and Woden. Vortigern makes it clear that the gods they believe in are, to him, devils (ll.6958–69), but that does not prevent him, after the Saxons have driven off his enemies, from marrying Rowena, the daughter of Hengest, with heathen rather than Christian rites. Here again, history enables us to date the legend, for the marriage of Vortigern and Rowena is said to take place at about the time that St. Germanus, Bishop of Auxerre, along with Lupus, Bishop of Troyes, came to Britain to combat the Pelagian heresy: that is, around 429 CE.

Unfortunately, Vortigern becomes so enmeshed with the pagans that the Christian Britons depose him and install his son (from a previous marriage) Vortimer in his place, but, after signal victories against the encroaching Saxons, Vortimer is poisoned by his stepmother Rowena, and his father is reinstated.

After his son is buried at Billingsgate, Vortigern tries to make peace between Saxons and Britons and calls for the leaders of the two peoples to assemble on May Day in a meadow near Amesbury on the edge of Salisbury Plain. The peace conference turns into a massacre, however, when Hengest calls out *nimeð eowre seax* ("take up your saxes," the "sax" being the short sword or long knife from which the Saxons may have derived their name), and the treacherous Saxons attack their hosts with concealed weapons.

The king's life is only spared on condition that he hands over his cities and fortresses to the enemy. Having agreed to an offer he couldn't refuse, Vortigern flees to Wales, where, on the advice of his astrologers, he starts to build an immensely strong tower on what Layamon calls the Mount of Reir, a last resort should all else fail.

This mountain takes its name from Eryri, the Welsh name for the area of highlands the English call Snowdonia. The Mount of Reir is, therefore, Mount Snowdon, above which, according to Blake, the Council of God meets (*BCW*, 277) and where Arthur will slay the King of the Giants. On such a sacred site we might expect a treacherous monarch to encounter difficulties, and, indeed, whenever the stonemasons try to lay the foundations, they find that whatever they build one day is swallowed up by the earth the next. Vortigern again consults his magicians.

They go to places of enchantment such as crossroads and woodlands to practice divination, casting lots and chanting magical spells over three consecutive nights, but only one of them, a magus called Joram, comes up with a solution: Unlikely as it sounds, if the blood of a fatherless boy is mixed with lime to lay the walls, the tower will stand for all time (*Brut*, ll.7739–51).

Messengers are immediately dispatched to find this miraculous child. Arriving in the town that is now called Carmarthen, they overhear two boys quarrelling: One accuses the other of never having had a father, and the messengers believe they have found the person they are looking for. When they question passers-by about the "fatherless" boy, they are told that his mother is the daughter of Conan, the King of Demetia (now Dyfed), and that she is now a nun, but that no one knows who fathered her son, Merlin.

## A Fatherless Child

Readers who are familiar with the figure of Merlin from Malory will know of his managerial role in the conception of Arthur, but nothing of the origins of the magician himself. This is not the place to explore the development of the character from his putative Druidic or shamanic origins to his later literary career. Suffice it to say that Geoffrey of Monmouth derived his name from a loose translation into Latin of the Welsh Myrddin, a more exact

transliteration would have given him *Merdinus,* roughly meaning "little shit"—
a name that some of the Pendragons' enemies may well have wished to apply
to the chief royal counselor, but which Geoffrey presumably felt lacked the
sense of awe and mystery with which he wished to imbue the character.

Myrddin appears in several medieval Welsh poems unconnected with
Arthur, poems in which he plays a role similar to—and probably borrowed
from—the Scottish prophet Lailoken, the Wild Man of the Woods, who fore-
told that he would die in three different ways at once (Jarman, 121–4). This
theme of the Threefold Death does not appear in the *History of the Kings of
Britain* but is taken up by Geoffrey in his later *Life of Merlin* and in the French
romances.

Myrddin may originally have been a local legendary figure in southwest
Wales, the eponymous founder of the ancient British town of Moridunum
("sea fort"), which later became Carmarthen. It is unlikely, as Geoffrey of
Monmouth implies (by calling it Kaermerdin), that the town of Carmarthen
(Caerfyrrdin in Welsh) is named after the discovery there of the boy Merlin.
It is more likely that the name is formed from the addition of the Welsh *caer*
("castle") to the old Romano-British name for the town. It is easy to see how
Caer Moridun becomes Kaermerdin (137f).

●●●

It is impossible now to estimate how much of Myrddin's ancient lore may
have been preserved in the "British book" that Geoffrey of Monmouth claimed
as his chief source, but the legendary chronicles are now our chief source for
what has survived of the story of Myrddin.

According to these chronicles, the boy and his mother are sent to Vor-
tigern's court, where the truth about Merlin's birth is revealed. At the age of
fifteen, the Demetian princess explains, she was made pregnant by a handsome
young man, who could make himself invisible and who would visit her in her
novitiate's apartment, clothed in gold; he talked like a man, but she did not
know, as Layamon puts it, if he was "a monster, or on God's behalf appointed."

King Vortigern, somewhat dubious about this story, sends for the learned
scholar Magan, who is skilled at incantation and astrology ("the art which
rules in the heavens" [*LB,* 203]). Magan attempts to put the events into con-
text, explaining that fatherless children are not as uncommon as one might
think. There are many beings in the heavens, he says, who will dwell there till
Doomsday; some are good, some evil. Among these are large demonic beings
called *incubi* who play tricks on people: They harass men in their dreams
(Layamon is here referring to the female demons, or *succubi,* who are respon-
sible for nocturnal emissions) and have sex with women (as suggested in an

infamous painting by Blake's friend Fuseli—"The Nightmare" of 1781). This, it would appear, is how Merlin was conceived.

Face to face with Vortigern, the bold child questions why he has been brought there and challenges the magicians to say what lies beneath the foundations of the tower. When they are unable to do so, Merlin reveals that beneath the tower is a pool, which was making the tower unsteady. He further reveals that beneath the pool two dragons lie sleeping; these, of course, are the very dragons that King Lud had buried, and what follows is, according to the Welsh Triads, unfortunate.

The king has the pool drained and discovers that Merlin is correct. The two dragons, one white, one red, emerge from the depths and begin fighting. ("There flew from their mouths fiery flames" [LB, 206]). The White Dragon initially gets the upper hand, but then is beaten back by its opponent. Seeing that the fatherless boy has spoken nothing but the truth, Vortigern has Joram and the other incompetent magicians executed.

Merlin now begins to prophesy, explaining (before his prophecies start to resist easy explanation) that the White Dragon represents the Saxon invaders and the Red Dragon the native Britons who resist them (HKB, 144). He then tells Vortigern to flee, for the brothers of the king he deposed are coming to wreak vengeance on him; they will rule the land in turn, but the youngest brother, Uther, will die at the hands of Vortigern's descendants.

Uther, Merlin continues, will have only one son, who will emerge out of Cornwall like "a wild boar bearing bristles of steel"; he will demolish the towns where the traitors hide in terror and destroy all the kinsfolk of Vortigern. The Boar of Cornwall, he prophesies, "shall be a very valiant man and of noble virtue./From here as far as Rome this same man will rule./He shall fell to the ground all of his foes" (LB, 208).

In these first prophecies concerning the reign of Arthur, we already see the ambiguity in his character: The savagery of a wild boar, terror, torment, and destruction combine with valor and virtue to provide storytellers with a hero who will be their meat and drink for centuries to come, and already it is clearly stated that he will not just free Britain from those who would oppress it, but he will reverse the power relation with Rome. The empire, which famously told the Britons to look to their own defenses, will soon have to defend itself against the Britons.

All, of course, occurs as Merlin has predicted. Aurelius and Uther arrive with an army from Brittany, and Vortigern is burned alive when the castle in which he seeks refuge, on the banks of the River Wye, goes up in flames. The brothers go on to defeat the Saxons, the first defeat of the white at the hands of the red dragon. Hengest, their leader, is captured and executed by beheading outside Conisbrough Castle and buried in an earthen barrow, according to the custom of his people.

Octa, Hengest's son, surrenders to Aurelius and agrees to convert to Christianity. He feels let down by his pagan deities, who include, along with goddesses such as Tervagant and Frea, the unlikely figure of Dido (*Brut*, l.8381), who is well known as the Queen of Carthage loved, and forsaken, by Aeneas (the ancestor of both the Romans and Britons). According to the legend, retold by Virgil in Book One of the *Aeneid,* Dido flees from her native land when her brother murders her husband. Arriving on the Libyan coast of North Africa, she asks the local inhabitants for a small area of land, no more than can be encompassed by an ox-hide. Cutting the hide into strips, she is able to cover a hill, and on this she builds the foundations of what will become a great civilization.

Curiously, the same story is told of Hengest, who initially, in return for his help in defeating the Picts, asked Vortigern for as much land as could be encircled by a single thong from a bull's hide (ll.7079f). The king agreed, not realizing that, by cutting a bull's hide into the thinnest of thongs, in a continuous strip, Hengest could mark out for himself a sizeable area (ll.7095–8). Having solved the "Dido Problem," as mathematicians refer to it, to his own satisfaction—perhaps guided by the deity his people worship—he selected a rocky spot and began work on building a castle there. As soon as he had built it, Hengest sent for eighteen shiploads of his relatives to come over, thus starting the first mass immigration since the arrival of the Trojans. But with the surrender of Octa, Hengest's son, the threat of the Saxons is, for now, over.

King Aurelius begins the reconstruction of the desolated land: he rebuilds the churches and monasteries that were destroyed by the pagans and restores the houses and towers in the cities. At last he comes to Amesbury, the site of the infamous Night of the Long Knives, where so many British noblemen were treacherously slain. He decides he must build there a fitting monument to the massacre, and on the advice of the Archbishop of Caerleon-on-Usk, he sends messengers to find the prophet Merlin. For Merlin, says the cleric, can impart to the king secret knowledge that will enable him to build a monument so sturdy and enduring that it will last as long as the human race itself!

The messengers eventually locate Merlin at the Spring of Alaban in Wales, and he presents himself willingly before the king, refusing offers of payment. Aurelius asks him to foretell the future ("about the world's circuit,/And about all the years which were still to come here"), but Merlin will not perform party tricks. The spirit that is within him, he proclaims, would abandon him if he misused its powers by treating them as entertainment or as an amusing attraction (220). The prophetic spirit can be "baleful" (*bælwes*), but if people approach him with humility when the nation is troubled, then, he says: "If I by my own intent may remain silent,/Then I can pronounce on how things will come to pass" (221).

We are used in the late twentieth and early twenty-first centuries to seeing divination reduced to a parlor game. Astrology especially has become an entertainment, an amusing attraction featured in tabloid newspapers. But the widespread use of the *I Ching* and the Tarot, along with other "New Age" oracles, also extends far beyond their possibilities for psychological therapy or spiritual transformation.

We would expect materialistic scientists to dismiss the effectiveness of divination and representatives of the Church to warn of its spiritual dangers, but Merlin, today an iconic figure for Neo-Pagans, also has a warning about the baleful effects of misusing the inner spirit for personal gain or cheap entertainment. The prophetic spirit, he appears to be saying, can only pronounce when the conscious intention of the diviner is silenced, and out of that silence will come truth, as in meditation or Quaker worship.

It is important that we distinguish here between prophecy and divination, on one hand, and the art of fortune-telling or the science of predicting the future, on the other. Merlin knows what is going to happen because he is a *diviner,* one who speaks with divine inspiration: A prophet is literally one who "speaks on behalf of" a god, who can walk, at least in vision, in their timeless world, and whose speech therefore transcends the limits of linear time.

Prophecy, according to the French philosopher Henry Corbin (1903–78), is, like prayer, an act of the creative imagination, but, as in Blake's poetry, "imagination" must here be understood in an esoteric sense, which Corbin dedicated his life's work to expounding. It would be worth pausing our narrative at this point to examine what we mean by this esoteric understanding of the imagination; since Corbin's model, I believe, helps us to understand how we can see Faerie and the otherworldly domains of the Arthurian legends, not just as leftovers from an old paganism, but as representatives of a model of reality that we need to reconnect with if, as Blake envisioned, we are to restore the "British antiquities" as a "source of learning and inspiration."

## An Excursion into the Imaginal World

We are used, at least in the modern western world, to seeing reality in terms of dualities: as divided between matter and spirit or body and soul (to use "religious" language), between mind and matter, or between the abstract and the concrete (to use "scientific" language) and, indeed, to see religion and science in terms of yet another duality. Materialist science has attempted to deny this duality in our experience by arguing that the material is in fact the only reality and that consciousness is merely an epiphenomenon of the brain. Visionaries, mystics, and inspired poets have, however, always advocated a third way between the extremes of dualistic thinking, on one hand, and scientific reductionism on the other.

This third way is rooted in ancient soil, for in antiquity, reality was seen as having a threefold structure. This traditional model was expounded by the Greek philosopher Plato. It was adopted by the Neo-Platonists and Gnostic Christians in the first centuries of the pagan Roman Empire, but it was abandoned in the West with, according to Corbin, catastrophic consequences.

In the threefold model, the human being is seen as composed of body, soul, and spirit. The soul has a mediating function, holding the tension of the opposites, acting as a bridge between body and spirit, linking them and enabling us to overcome a destructive matter/mind dualism.

What is true in the microcosm of the human being is also true in the macrocosm: As above, so below. On the macrocosmic level, the threefold model posits three interlocking worlds or universes in which we exist. The first of these three universes is the physical, sensory world, the universe of matter (corresponding to the body in the individual human being); this is the only world that materialist science recognizes, for it is the world that we all perceive through our five senses or that can be observed using the inventions of the human mind. This is a world that can be examined with a microscope or a telescope, just as the body can be dissected on a laboratory table.

But this world is not all there is, according to the traditional model. There is another, spiritual world which is, in many ways, opposite to (and in some cultures seen as *opposed to*) the material world. This is the *archetypal* world, in which exist those ideal forms of which physical objects and material beings are reflections—some would say shadows. Hence Blake could write: "There Exist in that Eternal World the Permanent Realities of Every Thing which we see reflected in this Vegetable Glass of Nature" (*BCW*, 605). This Eternal World is sometimes called the *intelligible* universe, since it can only be perceived by the intuitive intellect. This is the world of whose existence the religions teach and in which many people believe.

These are the two worlds over which religion and science now fight. But there is, in the traditional model, a third world between the sensory and the intelligible, between the physical and the archetypal—a world whose existence has been all but forgotten in the West, squeezed out, as it were, by the opposition between spirit and matter, which constitutes the destructive dualism of the modern world. This third world is the universe of psychic images (corresponding to the human soul in the microcosm), and just as matter is the domain of science and spirit the domain of religion, so is the psyche the domain of psychology, which is arguably neither a science nor a religion, although it has frequently been accused of being both!

This third world is itself traditionally seen as having a dual aspect: Some psychic images are drawn from—and attached to—the material world and the physical body; others, what the Swiss psychiatrist Carl Jung (1875–1961) calls *archetypal images,* have a "psychoid" or transcendent aspect (1946, 424), although as a scientist Jung avoided spelling out what the ancients believed: that they reflect spiritual realities that we can perceive in the soul, even if only *as through a glass, darkly.* Because it is a world of images, this universe has also been called the *imaginal* world (or, in Latin, *mundus imaginalis*), although, as Corbin uses the term, it applies only to the "higher" plane of spiritually oriented, archetypal images and not to the "lower" plane of sensory-bound imagery (the contents of what we might call the Freudian subconscious).

Corbin coined the term "the imaginal world" precisely in order to avoid its being confused with the *imaginary* worlds of popular culture and to prevent its being dismissed as in some way *unreal.* The *mundus imaginalis* is situated on the threshold of the soul. It is an intermediate universe, or "interworld," positioned between Heaven and Earth; it bridges the opposites in the traditional threefold model of being, but (despite the work of psychologists such as Jung, exploring the disputed borderland between science and religion) it has been effectively banished from our modern, dualistic mindset.

As a result, science and religion become what William Blake calls *negations,* as opposed to the contraries needed for harmonious progress. Thus, in Blake's *Milton,* the eponymous poet declares: "The Negation must be destroy'd to redeem the Contraries./The Negation is the Spectre, the Reasoning Power in Man." The "filthy garments" of a rationalism that denies faith must be cast aside in order to clothe Albion with Imagination (*BCW*, 533), and we can then rediscover the ancient wisdom: that faith and knowledge (what Blake calls "sweet Science" [301]) are not negations of each other, but contraries that we must redeem.

With the banished *mundus imaginalis,* Corbin argues, has also gone our understanding of the ability of the imagination to transform consciousness. For if we use our physical senses to perceive the material world and our intellect to understand the spiritual world, so we require the imagination to perceive this third order of reality. But we are not talking here about imagination in the everyday sense, such as when we think of the crafters of fictional works as being very imaginative, or describe someone who fantasizes a lot as having an overly developed imagination. On the contrary, what Corbin (1995, 2) calls "the imaginative consciousness, or *cognitive* Imagination" (sometimes also the "spiritual" or, following Jung, the "active" imagination) is a faculty that enables us to perceive, not the products of fiction or fantasy, but an *objective* universe that transcends everyday reality: "a world as ontologically real as the world of the senses and the world of the intellect" (9).

This world, the imaginal world, is the *place* of prophetic inspiration; *within it* we can experience on a symbolic level the truth of prophetic revelations, which would otherwise be merely taken literally—as fortune-telling, from the perspective of a superstitious materialism, or as the announcing of divine commandments, from the perspective of legalistic religion—exemplified by Blake as a chapel built on the green where he played ("And 'Thou shalt not' writ over the door" [*BCW*, 215]). As Blake's writings testify, prophecy is an act of the spiritual imagination.

The loss of this world (which Corbin characterizes as a "metaphysical tragedy") can be traced through various Church councils in which the status of sacred images as revealing spiritual realities was downgraded to that of merely being allegorical of official doctrine and in which, at the same time, the traditional threefold model of the human being was replaced by a dualism of body and soul. Blake, on the other hand, like all true poets, knows that "Man has no Body distinct from his Soul" (149), but his poetry is mocked "with the aspersion of Madness/Cast on the Inspired" (533) in the soulless, mechanistic universe of the rationalists that was created in the vacuum left by the disappearance of the Imaginal World.

By the twelfth century, a rationalist philosophy seemed to have triumphed over the prophetic imagination, but it was precisely at this point that the Prophet Merlin makes his appearance in Arthurian literature, as if sprung fully formed from that imaginal reality which exists between the transcendent world of the spirit and the earthbound world of matter. The *mundus imaginalis* is, one can say, the place where the two worlds of spirit and matter meet and cross over. For, in the imaginal world, matter becomes spiritualized and spirit becomes "corporealized," is made flesh; it is therefore the place of incarnation, where divine immortality and human mortality are united.

As Jesus is the son of a divine Father and a human mother (Mary), so Merlin has his own nativity myth, a miraculous birth as the son of an immortal incubus and a mortal but holy woman; hence later French versions of his story, with a more theological agenda, will explore his relationship with the figure of the Antichrist. In the version of the chroniclers, however, it is easier to see him as personifying the imagination itself: in his preternatural wisdom; in his knowledge of what lies beneath the surface of the everyday; in his ability to appear when most needed, while resisting bribes or compulsion; in his magical ability to overcome physical limitations; and, as we will see, in his shape-shifting and in his ability to fulfill desires and make dreams come true; but, above all, in his ability to perceive the divine pattern reflected in earthly events and help to engineer its working out in history.

For, whether or not we understand Arthur to have been a historical figure, *his story* has undeniably *made* history, and Merlin's appearance in the legendary chronicles acts as a prelude to the appearance of Arthur himself. In the earliest versions, Merlin is not so much an Antichrist *manqué* as a John the Baptist to the British Messiah, prophesying his appearance on earth. But he does not just limit himself to prophesying the coming of the king; he actively engineers Arthur's conception, as we will see.

Further, the prophetic inspiration of Merlin acts as a prelude to the development of Arthurian storytelling. Geoffrey of Monmouth published his *Prophecies of Merlin* in the 1130s, while he was still working on his *History of the Kings of Britain*, and later incorporated them into the larger work. Once his account of Arthur's life was translated into French, a creative dam was unblocked. A flood of stories flowed freely, focusing on the heroes who gravitated around the king and drawing often on Celtic stories that used elements of pagan mythology. One of these elements is what is known as the Otherworld, which must not be confused with the afterlife or the land of the dead.

We are more familiar with the classical and Christian concept of *another* world which is an eternal afterlife of light (Heaven or Elysium) or darkness (Hades or Hell). We are also familiar with the stories of the hero who descends into the Underworld, like Aeneas, the ancestor of Brutus, who goes down into Avernus, armed with the Golden Bough, or like Christ, who harrows Hell on Holy Saturday. In Welsh poetry, Arthur crosses the sea to reach Annwfn, which is sometimes described as an infernal region. But in the Celtic tradition, the Otherworld is not just underground or overseas, but all about us; it is frequently approached by crossing a stream (hence the common theme of the Perilous Ford) or fordless river, but often we stumble upon it just beyond the fields we know.

The Otherworld is not an eternal afterlife, but an eternal reality (what Eliot called *the intersection of the timeless moment*) ever present in the world of time, if only we know how to contact it or have the vision to see it all about us. It is the inner landscape, the soul of the land. What happens in one world has an effect in the other, and sometimes, in order to resolve a crisis in this world, it is necessary to cross over into the other.

The young Arthur, as we will see, sets off intentionally to seek this realm, but just as often the hero crosses an invisible boundary without knowing he has done so. He finds himself somewhere *other*.

One sets out; at a given moment, there is a break with the geographical coordinates that can be located on our maps. But the "traveler" is not conscious of the precise moment; he does not realize it, with disquiet or wonder, until later. If he were aware of it, he could change his path at will, or he could indicate it to others. But he can only describe where he was; he cannot show the way to anyone [Corbin 1995, 14].

The above is not, however, intended to be a description of the path that takes us from Logris to the Otherworld, but of the passage from the sensory to the imaginal world as it is described in many accounts, according to Henry Corbin. But clearly, the description is equally applicable, for what is the Arthurian Otherworld but a vividly realized region of the *mundus imaginalis?*

By incorporating the Otherworld into the Arthurian universe, the early poets effectively countered the dualism of body and soul that had developed by the twelfth century. For, in addition to the earthly Kingdom of Logris and the spiritual Kingdom of the Grail, we find an imaginal "interworld" of fays, of giants, of sorcerers and enchantresses. This intermediate world reflects and restores the ancient, threefold balance of body, soul, and spirit, and, as such, was a challenge to the dominant philosophy which opposed reason to imagination.

Thus it is that, as I have shown in a previous work,[1] the creativity of the poets was undermined in the thirteenth century by the triumph, in the Vulgate prose romances, of a dualistic theology that was uncomfortable with an imagination that could not be constrained by doctrine, with images that tried to burst the bounds of allegory.

Nevertheless the creative imagination, like an underground stream, will always find a way to resurface. Thus it is that we find an alternative vision of the figure of Arthur presented in the poetry of Layamon, of Edmund Spenser, and of William Blake. Layamon, as we will see, places fays at the beginning and at the ending of Arthur's life. In Spenser, Arthur dwells in the imaginal realm of Faerie, chasing a dream. In Blake he is, as the Spectre of Albion, clothed in "the rotten rags of Memory," which he must allow to be cast off by inspiration, for memory can produce only allegory, while inspiration produces imagination. "To take off his filthy garments & clothe him with Imagination" (*BCW*, 533): this is the task that Milton sets himself, in Blake's eponymous poem, but it is also the role of another seer, Merlin, in the destiny of the archetypal Eternal Man who, in his fallen form, is Arthur. Merlin can clothe Arthur with Imagination because he himself, like all prophetic seers, embodies "immortal Imagination" (663).

But before the birth of Arthur, Merlin must occupy himself with memory, in the shape of a stone memorial for the dead—a memorial that his own legend will do much to rescue from oblivion. Merlin will not just reconstruct Stonehenge on Salisbury Plain, but help to create its iconic status in the British imagination.

## The Giants' Ring

Merlin, we will recall, has been summoned by King Aurelius, but, of course, he already knows what the king wants. The king requires, states Merlin, to build at Amesbury a "memorial to the dead,/Which there will stand till the world's end." There is, he says, in Ireland "a structure surrounded with mystery," a stone monument brought by giants from Africa and known, therefore, as the Giants' Ring; there is nothing like it throughout the world's realm. It is a place of healing: People who are sick go to the stones, wash them, and bathe themselves with the water, which is now imbued with the stones' virtue. "Within a little while they're completely whole" (*LB*, 221). Though the stones are so massive that none but giants could carry them, yet Merlin will achieve this feat by cunning: He will bring them from Ireland and erect them in the same pattern as before, and King Aurelius himself, when it is his time to die, will be buried among them.

Accordingly, Merlin goes to Ireland with an army led by Uther, the king's brother. Prince Uther defeats the Irish king, Gillomar I, when he attempts to protect the Giants' Ring; meanwhile, after the British have struggled in vain to budge the stones, Merlin gives them a close examination:

> Three times he went round the ring, inside it and outside it,
> And was moving his lips like a man saying prayers [214].

Then he calls out to Uther to summon his men, who should now be able to move the stones as though they are made out of feathers. They pull down the stones with ease, and Merlin has them carried on board ships, whence he fetches them to Salisbury Plain. There he uses his artistry to put the stones back up in a circle, exactly as they had been in Ireland. This is the monument that is now known in England as Stonehenge.

Not surprisingly, Blake took an interest in the stones, given that scholarly speculation about the origins and purpose of the site had been going on since the middle of the seventeenth century. But for Blake the Giants' Dance was not a place of healing but of human sacrifice, a "serpent temple" erected as a symbol of the shrinking of vision. It is a stone circle like Stonehenge that presides over the slaughter of the Last Battle in Blake's missing picture. It represents an old dispensation, one that has been corrupted: the Age of the Druids that Abraham was called on to succeed. Blake's reading of Stonehenge may, indeed, have been influenced by the massacre that was believed to have occurred on the site and to which the erection of the Giants' Dance is a memorial (and to which Spenser refers when he says that we may view there "dolefull moniments" to the "eternall marks of treason" [*FQ,* II.x.66]).

While Merlin is building Stonehenge, however, Passent, the third son of Vortigern, who had survived his father's overthrow, has made common cause with the Irish, who wish to avenge themselves on Uther for the loss of their "magic stone-work" (*LB,* 226). He raises an army and lands at Menevia (now St. David's) in Pembrokeshire; Uther marches to meet them, while his brother lies ill. Shortly thereafter, Aurelius is poisoned by one of Passent's agents and killed, and at this very moment Uther sees a star, with a single beam of light shining from it, appear in the sky above Britain.

The beam of light culminates in a ball of fire in the shape of a dragon, and from the dragon's mouth issue two flaming rays, one of which stretches out over Gaul, the other to Ireland. The ray that stretches westwards is made up of seven beams that shine brightly over land and sea.

Uther asks Merlin the meaning of this extraordinary sight, and the prophet exclaims: "O wretched time in this world's realm:/Great is the sorrow which has settled on the land" (230). The significance of this phenomenon, Merlin explains, is manifold: The falling star signifies that his brother Aurelius is dead, struck down like Constans before him. As a consequence, Uther must lead his army against the enemy, but the victory will be his. Uther himself, therefore, is the fiery dragon who follows the star: "You are to have this land," Merlin tells him, "your power will be great and strong." As for the beam of light that stretches towards Gaul:

> This is a powerful son who from your body is to come,
> Who is to conquer by combat many a kingdom,
> And eventually he shall rule many a people [231].

Just as a star appeared above Bethlehem, announcing the birth of the Anointed King of the Jews, so a star appears to foretell the birth of the British Messiah. The beam that stretches to the West, on the other hand, signifies a daughter who will have seven sons; they will become kings in their own right, ruling over land and sea.

This, at least, is Layamon's version, but it is fair to say that there is a certain amount of confusion in our sources about this part of Merlin's prophecy. Geoffrey of Monmouth, for example, specifies that Uther's daughter's sons and grandsons will hold one after the other the kingship of Britain, but this does not seem to come true, which is disconcerting when it is supposed to be Merlin speaking! Both Wace and Layamon leave it vague as to where her descendants will rule, as though they had noticed the discrepancy in their source material. What the early sources do agree about is that Arthur's sister Anna will give birth to two sons: one of whom will be his greatest champion, but the other of whom will destroy both his brother and his uncle. But about this Merlin keeps uncharacteristically silent.

One possible explanation for this confusion is that our chroniclers are trying to historicize a mythical image, for, as the Arthurian scholar Thomas Green has pointed out, the sevenfold stellar ray may originally have signified the seven stars of the Plough, the polar constellation of the Great Bear (Ursa Major), which is also known in British folklore as Arthur's Wain, in part because the name Arthur derives from the Celtic *arth,* meaning "bear." Hence, in *The Lay of the Last Minstrel,* Blake's contemporary Sir Walter Scott can write of a starless night: "Arthur's slow wain his course doth roll/In utter darkness round the pole" (*SPW,* 5). While, in his poem "The Holy Grail," Tennyson's Percivale explains that the fellowship refer to the Bear as "The seven clear stars of Arthur's Table Round" (*PT,* 1680).

Green goes on to suggest that it may be more than just a coincidence that, shortly after describing Uther's vision of the sevenfold star, Geoffrey of Monmouth depicts a nocturnal assembly on Mount Damen (Dinian in Layamon's version). As the Bear (*Arctos*) revolves around the Pole, Uther and his nobles plan their strategy to crush the Saxons. Thus it may be the spirit of Arthur, the king who is to come, that lights the council of Mount Damen, presaging his own, even greater, victories over the Saxons (Green, 256*n*5).

But if the constellation of the Great Bear is Arthur's "wain," his farm wagon or chariot, the king himself may be Arcturus, the "Guardian of the Bear."

This of course is the identification made by Blake, which he derived from the Welsh scholar Owen Pughe, but *Arcturus* as a Latinization of Arthur's name goes back to Geoffrey of Monmouth and before (Green, 192). Arcturus, as the brightest star in the northern hemisphere, tended to become seen as a symbol of the northern celestial polar region generally (191f), so that Arthur's name already indicates what he is destined to become, the Lord of the North.

Behind the confused account given in the legendary chronicles, then, we may be looking at the remnants of a mythical image that could not be satisfactorily historicized. Uther, looking up to the sky, sees a vision that will give him his surname: his future son imaged as the bright star Arcturus, which guards the Pole as Arthur himself will guard Britain, and the seven-starred celestial North Pole enveloped in the flames of a dragon-shaped comet. This stellar myth of Arthur will be more fully developed in the story of the Dragon and the Bear, which we will encounter in Chapter Six.

Meanwhile, Uther marches on Menevia, where he defeats the combined army of Saxons and Irish. Aurelius is buried inside the Giants' Ring, as he had requested, and as he had no children, his younger brother Uther is crowned king. Uther celebrates his coronation by arranging for an artistic memento of the vision that heralded his accession to the throne. He has two golden dragons made, one of which he donates to Winchester Cathedral, where he was crowned, the other of which he carries with him in warfare, as a presage of victory. As a result he is forever after known as *Pendragon,* which, in the ancient British tongue, means "Dragonhead."

Thus is founded the dynasty of the Pendragons, whose fame is such that even Gibbon tried to rationalize the legend.

## Magicking Arthur

Almost immediately after he becomes king, Uther Pendragon is faced by another Saxon invasion led by Octa, the son of Hengest. Uther meets the invaders at York, but the British army is forced back to Mount Dinian, where it takes refuge for the night. The night turns into days of siege. King Uther consults his nobles: The first to speak is Gorlois, Earl of Cornwall, a hero of the wars against the Saxons, who advises the king to attack the pagans under cover of darkness. This they do, and the element of surprise is successful. The Saxons are routed and Octa imprisoned.

Uther Pendragon, having restored peace to his realm, holds a plenary court at London during Eastertide. And it is here, during the festivities, that he first sets eyes on Igerna, the wife of Gorlois.

The legendary chronicles tells us nothing about Igerna, except that she is the most beautiful woman in Britain. However, in the romances she brings with her "a train of pagan associations" (Darrah, 113). If the fact that her daughter Morgan is a fay does not necessarily make the mother one, we must also bear in mind her close association with Tintagel, a "fairy castle" (*chastel faéz*) built by giants, which has the habit of disappearing twice a year, once in summer and once in winter (Walter, 62f). In the first Grail poem, Igerna herself disappears, along with one of her daughters, only to reappear decades later, when everyone has assumed she was long dead, in an Otherworldly castle built by magic (*AR*, 489). Igerna's Otherworld associations may help to explain the fact that, when Uther Pendragon first encounters her, it is love (or lust) at first sight. Fays, the original *femmes fatales,* have this effect on men!

In seeking to win the love of Igerna, therefore, Uther may not just be pursuing an infatuation, but establishing a symbolic right to rule, by allying himself with an Otherworld figure who can confer sovereignty. This may also be indicated by the fact that he has brought the Giants' Dance, the "stones of sovereignty," from "Ireland," another name for the Otherworld. This is significant because it is the giants who represent the indigenous inhabitants of Albion, whom Brutus and Corineus had to overcome in order to create the human kingdoms of Britain and Cornwall.

Later we will see that Uther's son Arthur also wins the hand of an Otherworld bride, a giant's daughter, but he goes further than Uther, in that he also kills the King of the Giants in one-to-one combat on the sacred peak of Mount Snowdon.

The attentions that Uther lavishes on Igerna at the Easter festival infuriate her husband, who, without a by-your-leave, withdraws from the court, in turn infuriating the king. Gorlois takes refuge in one of his castles, leaving his wife in nearby Tintagel, the safest place he controls because of its restricted access. King Uther besieges Gorlois, but after a week his passion for Igerna becomes unbearable. He tells his faithful retainer, Ulfin, that he will die unless he can have her.

Ulfin replies that no earthly power can breach the impregnable fortress of Tintagel and suggests that they turn for help to Merlin, who has access to unearthly power. Unfortunately, no one has seen anything of the prophet since Uther's coronation, despite the king's offers of great wealth to anyone who can find him. At last, however, a hermit approaches Ulfin and tells him that he knows where Merlin sleeps each night: in a vast forest in the western wilderness, where they are wont to meet. In exchange for some land, the hermit agrees to bring Merlin to the king.

And so he meets the prophet at their accustomed spot. Merlin, of course, already knows what the hermit is going to ask him and explains that it is only through his magical ploys that the virtuous Igerna will be won by the king. She is destined to bear him a wondrous child who will grow up to rule the world. Not just the whole of Britain, but the rulers in Rome will bow to him. His glory will last as long as the world endures and he will never die.

> Of him shall poets sing their splendid praises:
> From his own breast noble bards shall partake;
> Great warriors shall upon his blood be drunk;
> From his eyes shall fly glowing coals of fire,
> Each finger on his hand a sharp sword of steel
> Ahead of him shall fall stone-constructed walls;
> Warriors will tremble, battle-ensigns will fall;
> In this way for a long time he shall march across lands,
> Conquer those who live there and impose his own laws [LB, 242].

When he arrives before the king, Merlin tells Uther to pay the hermit, but he himself, being rich in good advice, wants no reward, since if he coveted possessions it would be at the expense of his skills.

If the king is to obtain his desire, the prophet continues, he must make use of an exceptional medicine (*lechecraft* [*Brut*, l.9448]), which will make Uther look like the earl. Thus the king gets into Tintagel through a trick (*mid ginne* [l.9485]). The unsuspecting guards at Tintagel allow the man they believe to be their lord to enter, and the duchess allows the man she believes to be her husband to sneak into her arms. Uther takes full advantage of the situation. He makes love with the woman of his dreams; his desire is finally fulfilled and, that night, his son is conceived: the good king who will be called Arthur.

The next morning, however, things start to go awry, when news reaches Tintagel that Gorlois has been killed in battle. The king (who is still in the shape of Gorlois) reassures his men that news of his death has been somewhat exaggerated and sets off to rejoin his army. On the way, Merlin restores the king to his true likeness. After victory celebrations, Uther returns to Tintagel and marries Igerna without delay. The greatness of the son who is subsequently born is legendary.

As for Merlin, he disappears from Layamon's narrative; what remains of him are his prophecies and the prophesied king whose conception he has engendered through magic.

# Five

# *The Image of a Brave Knight*

Arthur, it could be said, is the greatest king we never had, for his earthly existence is as doubtful as his passing.

In this and the following chapters, I do not attempt to make a case, as so many other scholars have done, for the historicity of Arthur,[1] let alone whether he should be considered as a king and emperor rather than as a Romano-Celtic officer (*comes Britanniae*) or warlord (*dux bellorum*). It is *his story,* rather than mere *history,* which should concern us, for the stories we tell ourselves about our past define our present and herald our future in a way that the careful accumulation of facts can never do. It is the myths that have attached themselves to the figure of Arthur, if indeed he ever had an earthly existence, which speak to us most powerfully today.

Arthur exists in our national consciousness at the intersection of myth and history, and I have no desire to attempt to prise him away from either, for we need both. Where myth meets history, legend is born. It is therefore the legend of Arthur, which we do not know as well as we might, which I will now be exploring, revealing wherever possible the mythic structures embedded in the stories and where necessary clarifying the factual history with which the legend so often jostles.

The putative year of Arthur's birth can be established only by combining two sources. Geoffrey of Monmouth tells us that he passed to Avalon in the year 542 CE, and a later French romance tells us that he was at that time ninety-two (!) years old (*LG* 4, 144). Reading backwards, then, we have the year 450 for his birth—a date that is at least consistent with the tradition that he was the grandson of the Emperor Constantine III, who died in 411.

Equally, we do not know where Arthur was born, although later tradition identified his birthplace as the castle where he was conceived: Tintagel—a castle built by the primordial giants of Albion and existing under the spell of the Fates. It is haunted by elves (Walter, 62–4).

It is, however, only Layamon, among the chroniclers, who makes of Arthur's birth a magical event. When the moment arrives that destiny has chosen as his time to be born, he is received by fays (*aluen*) who enchant the child with the most potent of spells:

> They gave him the power to be the greatest of all soldiers;
> They gave him a second thing: that he would be a noble king;
> They gave him a third thing: that he should live long.
> They gave to him, the royal heir, the most excellent gifts:
> That he was the most generous of all living men.
> These the elves bestowed on him, and so the child throve [*LB*, 247].

The fairies who shower blessings on the newborn child are familiar to us from the folktale of Briar Rose, or the Sleeping Beauty; they can be traced back to the Fates of Greek Mythology, and indeed, as we have seen, it is from the Latin word *fata* that is derived the French word *fée*, which gives us "fay," Faerie, and "fairy," whence Morgan the Fay and the Faerie Queen. Tolkien preferred "elves" to "fairies," going back to the Anglo-Saxon *ælf*, which could also mean an incubus like the one who fathered Merlin, and it is this same Old English word that gives us Layamon's Middle English *aluen*.

The glamour of Faerie, which is cast upon Arthur at the beginning of his life, returns to him at its ending, when he goes to the realm of Morgan the Fay (or Argante, as Layamon calls her), Queen of Avalon: *to Argante þere quene, aluen swiðe sceone* (*Brut*, l.14278), "the most beautiful of elven women," to be healed of his wounds. He lives there still, with the fairest of the fays: *mid fairest alre aluen* (l.14291).

But in between, he has a lot to learn from Faerie, and our guide to the education he receives in this realm will be Edmund Spenser. The Elizabethan poet tells us that it is before he ascends to the throne that Arthur meets his first love, Gloriana, the Faerie Queen—or, at least, he sees her in a vision and thereafter searches for her. It is during this quest that he will encounter, first, St. George in the guise of the Red Cross Knight with his ladylove Una, and then Sir Guyon, the elven Knight of Temperance, in whose company he will read, in the stately turret of the Castle of Alma, an account of Britain's ancient glory from Brutus to the accession of Uther.

## The Changeling Prince

The version of the upbringing of Arthur with which we are most familiar is that given by Malory, based on French prose romances. Having promised

Merlin anything he wished for, in return for helping him to win the love of Igerna, Uther allows the boy she bears to be taken away by Merlin to be brought up, as so many mythical heroes are, in obscurity. In this version the young Arthur is fostered by a nobleman of the realm, Sir Ector, and his true identity is only revealed when he famously draws the Sword in the Stone, the sign that he is the divinely appointed King of Britain.

A rather different account of Arthur's fostering appears in *The Faerie Queene*, where the young prince himself recounts what he knows of his upbringing. The night of his birth, he says, he was taken from his mother's breast and delivered by Merlin, not to a mortal, but to a "Fary knight," "the wisest now on earth," whose "dwelling is low in a valley greene,/Vnder the foot of *Rauran*" in Merioneth, North Wales, at the source of the River Dee. There he is trained "in vertuous lore" and taught the arts of war and peace. There also he is visited by the great magician Merlin, who acts as his tutor, but will tell him only that he is "sonne and heire vnto a king/As time in her iust term the truth to light should bring" (*FQ*, I.ix.3–5).

As his pupil grows up, Merlin gives the young prince enchanted weapons, including a shield ("Hewen out of Adamant rocke with engines keene") that no spear or sword can pierce; resistant to sorcery ("No magicke arts hereof had any might,/Nor bloody wordes of bold Enchaunters call"), it dazzles all who behold it, exposes deception, and can turn men into stones, stones into dust and dust, into nothing at all. For this reason, it is not surprising that he must usually keep it covered up! And, if this stretches credulity, Spenser adds, we must remember that all this is the work of Merlin "which whylome did excell/All liuing wightes in might of magicke spell" (I.vii.33–6).

Well equipped for battle, Arthur grows up scornful of the ways of love, until one day he is riding in the forest and, overcome with weariness, lies down to sleep on the grass, using his helmet as a pillow. As Diana appeared to Brutus in a dream, promising him the land of Albion, so "a royall Mayd" appears to Arthur in his sleep, as he later recounts. She makes "most goodly glee and louely blandishment" to the man she claims to love, as will become apparent in "iust time"; and he must love her in return.

> But whether dreames delude, or true it were,
> Was neuer hart so rauisht with delight,
> Ne liuing man like wordes did euer heare,
> As she to me deliuered all that night;
> And at her parting said, She Queene of Faries hight.　　[= called

When he awakes to find her gone, Arthur weeps for sorrow: he knows that he loves "that face diuyne" and vows that he will not rest until he finds again the queen of his dreams (I.ix.13–5). He has been searching in vain for nine months when he encounters a "damsel in distress." This is Una, the Princess of Eden, whose true love, the Red Cross Knight (whom we know better as St. George), has been betrayed by a duplicitous woman called, appropriately enough, Duessa and imprisoned by the giant Orgoglio ("Pride").

Una is searching for her love when she first encounters Arthur, searching for his; the prince's armor is shining so brightly that it can be seen from afar. Spenser gives us a powerful description of the young knight on his first mission of mercy. He is protected from top to toe by glittering armor that shines abroad, like the glancing rays of Phoebus (the Sun); he wears on his breast a baldric that shines "like twinkling stars, with stones most pretious rare" (I.vii.29).

In the middle of this baldric there is set a jewel "Of wondrous worth, and eke of wondrous mights,/Shapt like a Ladies head"—this is presumably the image of the Blessed Virgin Mary (which gives both his shield and his ship their name in Welsh: *Pridwen*, meaning "sacred image") but which Spenser likens to Hesperus (Venus as the Evening Star), outshining "the lesser lights" in the night sky and dazzling those with weak vision. His "mortall blade" has a hilt of gold, a handle made of mother-of-pearl, and its scabbard, wrought with curious inscriptions ("ycaru'd with curious slights") is made of ivory (30).

Arthur may not know who his father is, but Merlin has given him a clue by placing on his helmet the sign of the Pendragons:

> His haughtie Helmet, horrid all with gold,
> Both glorious brightnesse, and great terrour bredd,
> For all the crest a Dragon did enfold
> With greedie pawes, and ouer all did spredd
> His golden winges: his dreadfull hideous hedd
> Close couched on the beuer, seemd to throw
> From flaming mouth bright sparckles fiery redd,
> That suddeine horrour to faint hartes did show;
> And scaly tayle was stretcht adowne his back full low [31].

Armed with his magic weapons, Prince Arthur is guided by Una to a castle where her love lies in the thrall of the proud giant. Finding the gates of the castle shut fast and no one to answer his summons, Arthur takes his golden horn, which is possessed of "great vertues": it can be heard from three miles away and, at its "shrilling sownd," locks break and gates burst open, even if they have been magically sealed:

> No false enchauntment, nor deceiptfull traine
> Might once abide the terror of that blast,
> But presently was void and wholly vaine [I.viii.3f].

Blowing his enchanted horn, Arthur causes the outer doors to fly open; and the giant rushes to meet the prince. A ferocious battle ensues, in the course of which Arthur strikes off the giant's right arm, but is himself thrown to the ground. As he falls, the veil that is covering his shield flies open:

> The light whereof, that heuens light did pas,
> Such blazing brightnesse through the ayer threw,
> That eye mote not the same endure to vew [19].

Dazzled by the supernatural light, the giant "has redd his end/In that bright shield." The prince, wielding his "sparkling blade" strikes off first the giant's right leg, then his head (21f).

Seizing the keys to the castle from the giant's aged foster father, Arthur lets himself into every room; he finds the floor stained with the blood of innocents and an altar on which human sacrifice has been performed. At last he comes to an iron door, from behind which he hears the "hollow, dreary, murmuring voyce" of one who lies "in balefull darknesse bound," longing for death (38).

But Arthur brings tidings of renewed life. Filled with pity and horror at the plight of the fallen warrior, he rends open the door, only to find "a deepe descent, as darke as hell,/That breathed euer forth a filthie banefull smell." Undaunted by the "darkenesse fowle," Arthur raises the prisoner up to the light (39f).

The duplicitous woman who had betrayed the Red Cross Knight to the giant flees. Sir George has been imprisoned for nine months, so his betrayal by a false love synchronizes with Arthur's discovery of true love; Arthur's part in bringing Una and her lover back together is the fruit, after nine months' gestation, of his vision. Seeing his friends united inspires Arthur anew to seek his own love, and after an exchange of gifts, he goes his separate way.

## Wonders of Antiquity

We next hear of Arthur in the Third Canto of Book Two of the *Faerie Queene,* where *Archimago,* an evil archmage or sorcerer, uses his supernatural powers to steal from the prince his flaming sword. This fiery weapon is not the famous Excalibur but another sword, "Which *Merlin* made by his almightie art" (II.viii.20). The steel is mixed with meadow-sweet, tempered in the flames of Etna, and dipped seven times in the waters of the Styx.

The now swordless Arthur comes across two brothers, pagan warriors, who are standing over the fallen body of an elven knight, Sir Guyon. The brothers attack the prince treacherously, one of them wielding Arthur's own sword, which the Archmage had given him, but that "vertuous steele" (22) cannot be used against its rightful owner and is cast aside. Arthur kills both warriors and, recovering his stolen sword, finds that Guyon is not dead, but in a trance.

The elven knight bears on his shield the image of the mighty Queen of Faerie, and the prince asks him why he does so. Guyon replies that it is because she is the flower of grace and chastity, whose glory shines as the Morning Star (II.ix.4), providing a fitting symmetry with the precious stone Arthur bears on his breast, which shines like the Evening Star. Seeing the image of his dream, the prince reveals:

> I God auow,
> That sith I armes and knighthood first did plight,     [sith = since
> My whole desire hath beene, and yet is now,
> To serue that Quene with al my powre and might.

But nowhere can he find "that Goddesse" (7). Sir Guyon tells Arthur to remain constant in his love; were he not otherwise engaged, he would guide his friend to the queen himself. As they are thus talking, they chance upon a castle that is under siege. It is the castle of Alma, the personification of the virginal soul, and after battling their way through the rabble which surrounds it, they are invited in by the lady of the castle.

The Lady Alma shows her guests round the castle and takes them up to a turret in which are several rooms, three of which are occupied by the three sages who counsel Alma. The first knows the future, while the second is expert on the present day. The third sage, Eumnestes, a "man of infinite remembraunce" (56), is surrounded by old books and parchments in his chamber. Prince Arthur lights upon

> An auncient book, hight *Briton moniments,*
> That of this lands first conquest did deuize,
> And old diuision into Regiments,
> Till it reduced was to one mans gouernements [59].

This man, of course, is (or will be) Arthur himself, who, as king, will unite the whole island under his sole rule, as well as subduing much of northwestern Europe and humbling the Roman Empire—but all that lies in the future of the young prince and is therefore the realm of the first sage.

We cannot know, but it is an intriguing speculation that the ancient book of Eumnestes, the sage of memory, may be intended to be the very book on which Geoffrey of Monmouth based his history, since it contains, as we are told in the "proem" (or verse summary) to Canto X: *A chronicle of Briton kings,/From Brute to Vthers rayne.* In the parallel universe of the reader, it is Geoffrey's prose work that provides the chief basis for Spenser's versification.

At the same time that Prince Arthur finds the book in which the history of his ancestors is written, the elven knight Sir Guyon finds a book containing the *Antiquity of Faerie Land*, and, with Alma's permission, they both satisfy their curiosity about their ancestors.

What Arthur reads is the chronicle of the founding of Britain by the Trojans. It takes us, in the elegant "Spenserian" stanzas that make even his heavily condensed summary of Geoffrey of Monmouth a pleasure to read, from the Brutine to the Molmutine dynasties, from the Roman conquest to the Saxon invasion, and, finally, to the death of King Aurelius Ambrosius.

But *Briton Moniments* comes to an abrupt end with the accession of Uther Pendragon. At this Arthur is half offended, half pleased, as though he half suspects that Uther is the king whose son and heir Merlin has assured him he is. For a long time he is speechless with "secret pleasure" and the "wonder of antiquity" (II.x.68). At last, "quite rauisht with delight," he cries out:

> Deare countrey, O how. dearely deare
> Ought thy remembraunce, and perpetual band
> Be to thy foster Childe, that from thy hand
> Did commun breath and nouriture receaue?      [nouriture = nourishment
> How brutish is it not to vnderstand,
> How much to her we owe, that all vs gaue,
> That gaue vnto vs all, what euer good we haue [69].

While Arthur has been discovering his glorious ancestry (understanding the story of Brutus means knowing what it is to be British in order not to be brutish), Sir Guyon has also been wondering at antiquity—not at that of Britain, but at that of Faerie which, like the Celtic Otherworld, exists as a sort of parallel universe or dream world, intersecting with our own. For, just as the legendary history of Britain begins where the historical Fall of Troy intersects with classical mythology, so that same mythology furnishes Spenser with the beginning of his fictional History of the Kings of Elfland, as Guyon discovers when he starts to read the "great/And ample volume" that is the *Antiquity of Faerie Land*.

It tells how the Titan Prometheus, brother of Atlas, was the first to create a man out of animal parts; in order to animate the creature, he stole fire from Heaven, for which he was punished by Jupiter (70). But his creation lives on:

> That man so made, he called Elfe, to weet
> Quick, the first author of all Elfin kynd:
> Who wandring through the world with wearie feet,
> Did in the gardins of *Adonis* fynd

> A goodly creature, whom he deemd in mynd
> To be no earthly wight, but either Spright,
> Or Angell, th'authour of all woman kynd;
> Therefore a Fay he her according hight,
> Of whom all *Faryes* spring, and fetch their lignage right [71].

Promethean man is "quick," i.e., "alive," as though "elf" has the same etymological root as "life," and the heavenly fire with which the Titan animates his creation is the counterpart to the breath of God that animates the first man in Genesis II: 7. Elf and Fay in the Gardens of Adonis are the counterparts of Adam and Eve in the Garden of Eden, but there is no equivalent fall of elven man, unless we consider the warlike ways of their descendants (they even go on to conquer America!) to be the wages of sin.

The *Antiquity of Faerie Land* continues down to the present queen, Tanaquil, whose people call her "Gloriana"; it is she who is the object of Arthur's visionary quest.

Having discovered the mythic histories of their respective races, the elven knight and the changeling prince go their separate ways. Arthur's first action is to defeat the warriors besieging the castle—an allegorical bunch (the Enemies of Temperance) who include the seven deadly sins and the five vices of the senses.

In the course of the succeeding four books of the *Faerie Queene* (Spenser must join the ranks of those, both named and unnamed, who left unfinished their Arthurian poems), the prince has many adventures; the intention of the whole, had it been completed, was, as he explained in his "Letter to Raleigh" (*FQ*, 715), *to pourtraict in Arthure, before he was king, the image of a braue knight, perfected in the twelue priuate morall vertues ...*

Each of these virtues would have been the subject of one of the twelve books that would have made up the whole; as it is, we only know the seven that Spenser lived to write about: holiness, temperance, chastity, friendship, justice, courtesy, and constancy. Of these, chastity and justice (the subjects of Spenser's Books III and V) are the most relevant from the point of view of the poet's development of the traditional story, for a female Knight of Chastity will meet justice personified in the form of Artegal, the son of Gorlois and Igerna (who is also, like his half-brother Arthur, a changeling prince), and from them will descend the heirs to Arthur's kingdom.

## The Heirs to the Kingdom

One of Arthur's greatest enemies is the giant King Rience, whom Arthur kills in single combat atop Mount Snowdon: a sacred site, where Vortigern built his ill-fated tower and where, for Blake, the Eternals gather in council. Spenser makes Rience the King of South Wales and gives him a daughter, Britomart, who will be both a woman warrior and the ancestress of a noble dynasty. This dynasty will unite the families of those two warring monarchs, Rience and Arthur, and also bring together at last the race of the giants and the race of humans, who have had to share the island, however unwillingly, since the Trojan conquest.

One day Britomart looks into a magic mirror that Merlin devised and gave to her father; it has the power to show to whoever looks into it any threats to the realm. What Britomart sees, when she looks therein, is a different sort of threat: It shows her the face of the man who will invade her solitude and steal her heart! Lovestruck for the first time in her life, Britomart is determined to find out the name of the man she has seen and can think of no better way than to ask the deviser of the mirror, Merlin himself.

She finds "the dreadfull Mage" in an underground grotto in his hometown of Carmarthen and is at first hesitant to enter when she sees him

> Deep busied bout worke of wondrous end,
> And writing straunge characters in the grownd,
> With which the stubborne feendes he to his seruice bownd [III.iii.14].

Merlin, of course, already knows why she has come and tells her not to be dismayed:

> For from thy wombe a famous Progenee
> Shall spring, out of the auncient Troian blood,
> Which shall reuiue the sleeping memoree
> Of those same antique Peres, the heuens brood,
> Which *Greeke* and *Asian* riuers stained with their blood [22].

Her "fruitfull Ofspring" will include kings of renown and "sacred Emperours," captains and warriors who will not only amend their own "decayed kingdomes" but go on to extend their conquests "through all lands" until the Britons, who have become enfeebled "with long warre," shall at last be able to defend themselves against foreign foes. Then "vniuersall peace" will supersede internal strife (23). Divine Providence is leading Britomart to fulfill her destiny through the love of a man of prowess.

Merlin now reveals that Gorlois and Igerna had two sons: One is Cador of Cornwall, whose relationship to Arthur is never made clear in the earlier sources; the other is a nobleman whom we know from the chronicles as the Earl of Warwick, and it is he whom the Princess of South Wales has seen in the mirror.

While his younger half-brother Arthur was handed over newborn to Merlin to be brought up in Faerie, the infant Artegal, we discover, was "by false *Faries* stolne away" (26) and does not realize he is human and of the distaff branch of the royal family. It is Britomart's task to bring him back to Logris, so that they can both aid their country against the pagan Saxons. In the end, though, Artegal will be destroyed (as was "the second Constantine" as well as his three sons Constans, Aurelius, and Uther, in what is an alarming family pattern!) "by practise criminall,/Of secrete foes" (28). Nevertheless, Merlin reassures Britomart:

> With thee yet shall he leaue for memory
> Of his late puissaunce, his ymage dead,
> That liuing him in all actiuity
> To thee shall represent.

This son, the image of his dead father, will grow up to seize by force the throne that he believes is rightfully his.

When Arthur goes to Avalon, he hands over the throne to Constantine of Cornwall, the son of his half-brother Cador. But if Artegal was the elder of the two brothers—and only denied his inheritance because he had been kidnapped by elves—then his son would have some justification in taking "the crowne, that was," as Spenser seems to believe, "his fathers right" (29). Arthur's nephew Aurelius Conanus, the son of Britomart and Artegal, unites in his person the human and giant races, and his descendants rule the kingdom until Cadwallader, the last native king, who has fled to Brittany, is prevented by a vision from returning to re-conquer his lost inheritance; for, as Merlin explains, Heaven has decreed that the sins of the Britons will cost them the government of Brutus's Promised Land (41).

Merlin predicts, however, that after several centuries have passed, a descendant of Cadwallader will be born in the Isle of Mona (Anglesey), where the Romans had once destroyed the Druidic resistance to their rule in an infamous massacre, and will unite the kingdoms of Wales and England, that is to say, of the ancient Britons and the Anglo-Saxon invaders. This heir to Cadwallader is Henry Tudor, who, eight hundred years after the death of the last indigenous British king, will defeat Richard III at the Battle of Bosworth Field in 1485.

Fittingly, this descendant of Britomart, the Knight of Chastity who will only give herself to the man whom Heaven has ordained, will be grandfather to "a royall Virgin": none other, of course, than Elizabeth I, the Virgin Queen, Spenser's patroness and the model for Gloriana. It is at this point that Merlin's predictions end:

As ouercomen of the spirites powre,
Or other ghastly spectacle dismayd,
That secretly he saw, yet note discoure [49f].     [note = might not

But the reader in the twenty-first century can fill in, from his own knowledge, some of the "ghastly" spectacles that humanity has witnessed in the centuries between the reigns of the first and the second Elizabeth.

## A British Hercules

Once Britomart knows who her destined husband is, she makes the journey from South Wales to Faerie. She eventually meets up with Artegal, and Arthur also has an encounter with his half-brother, although he knows nothing of their relationship. In fact, when the two sons of Igerna first meet each other, they come to blows.

By adventure, Artegal and Arthur have both strayed upon the scene of a damsel in distress, being chased by two men. Arthur defeats one of her attackers and rides hastily on to defeat the other, not noticing that Artegal has already done so; Artegal, in turn, seeing an armed knight charging towards him, makes against him.

The scene is familiar from countless medieval romances: Two heroes, not realizing the identity of the other, mistakenly fight. In this case, the mistake is even worse, since they are unwittingly brothers. But fortunately the damsel they have rescued puts them straight, pointing out that her pursuers are both now dead; her wrong has been redressed.

It is only now that the knights lift the ventails on their helmets to get a good look at each other. Artegal apologizes for his mistake, to which Arthur replies that the fault is more his, "As that I did mistake the liuing for the ded" (V.viii.13). But since no great damage has been done, they can put aside their mutual blame. Having fought and made up (but without, it would appear, noticing any family resemblance) the two warriors agree to team up against their common foe.

The damsel is seeking help for her mistress, Queen Mercilla, who is at the mercy of a pagan ruler whom Spenser refers to, anachronistically, as the Sultan. This is one of many instances (mosques in Camelot, pagans worshipping Mohammed) in which Arabic names and Muslim culture are prematurely transplanted to Romano-Celtic Britain, perhaps indicating, as Gibbon argued, an oriental influence on the Arthurian romances.

Arthur has already confused the living Artegal with a dead pagan; now Artegal will put on the dead man's armor, hoping the Sultan will make the same mistake. Thus disguised, he leads the damsel, as if she is his captive, to the Sultan's court, but refuses to hand her over. Arthur then arrives on the scene, demanding that the Sultan release her to his charge. The furious Sultan mounts a chariot drawn by horses fed on human flesh, and he and Arthur set to. The proud Sultan is motivated by a desire for revenge and a love of slaughter, but the "braue Prince" is equally fierce in his desire "for honour and for right." Setting his mind against the lawless abuse of power, he fights on behalf of "wronged weake"; he trusts more in "his causes truth" than in "might."

The Sultan foolishly imagines that he will tear the prince in pieces with the hooked wheels of his chariot, or else trample him under his horses' hooves.

> Like to the *Thracian* Tyrant, who they say
> Vnto his horses gaue his guests for meat,
> Till he himselfe was made their greedie pray,
> And torne in peeces by *Alcides* great [31].

In this extended simile, we have one of many references to Arthur as a British Hercules ("Alcides"); the "Thracian tyrant" is a king, whom Hercules feeds to his own man-eating horses in the course of his twelve labors.

Hercules's mother, like Arthur's, is tricked into fathering a son: Jupiter takes the form of her husband Amphitryon as Uther takes the form of Gorlois. Hercules has a half-brother whose father really is Amphitryon, just as Arthur has a half-brother (Artegal) whose father really is Gorlois. In the Vulgate Cycle, Arthur wins the Sword of Hercules, which had formerly been owned by King Rience, who is a descendant of Alcides; when drawn from its scabbard, the sword (like the shield that Merlin made for him) casts such a great light that it is a wonder to behold (*LG* 1, 296). Hercules used it to kill many giants, and Arthur later uses it to kill the Giant of Mont St. Michel, who, after King Rience, was his most powerful opponent.

Spenser pushes the analogy further: In Book II, he shows Arthur killing the Earth-born enemy of the Lady Alma by lifting him up from the ground, contact with which restores his strength; Hercules uses the same method to kill Antaeus, the son of Mother Earth.[2] But now, fighting the Sultan, Arthur unveils "his victorious shield" so that its "powerful light" dazzles the eyes of the tyrant's horses (V.viii.37), which bolt and throw their rider, who is torn to shreds by the iron wheels and grappling hooks of his chariot.

The damsel now takes Arthur and Artegal to the court of her mistress, Queen Mercilla, where a trial is underway: the trial of Duessa, who had been instrumental in the deception of the Red Cross Knight and of many others since.

Interestingly, Arthur, who, unlike his brother, has had direct experience of the consequences of her actions (having had to go to Hell and back to rescue the Red Cross Knight) shows himself to be more compassionate than the Knight of Justice; Arthur is moved to pity her ("Through the sad terror of so dreadfull fate,/And wretched ruine of so high estate" [V.ix.46])—the reader familiar with Arthurian legend will know, as the prince cannot, that his own fate will be equally dreadful—but he later repents, while Artegal is consistent and unbending "with constant firme intent,/For zeale of Iustice" (49). Duessa is executed. Arthur, it would appear, is learning a very important lesson about kingship: that justice must be tempered with mercy, but true mercy is not the same as pity. For Blake, Mercy and Pity are both divine attributes, but pity risks becoming hypocritical.

After Duessa's trial and execution, the two brothers go their separate ways. Artegal completes the quest on which the Faerie Queen, Gloriana, had originally dispatched him; the rescuing of another damsel in distress, but on his victorious return to the elven court, he encounters a creature that will cross the paths of many knights during Arthur's reign: the Blatant Beast.

This monstrous creature, which Spenser sees as embodying the vice of defamation, will be eventually mastered by the Knight of Temperance, although it will eventually escape its bonds and wreak mischief in the world, no longer able to be mastered. In the poignant stanzas that conclude the last completed book of his epic poem, Spenser expresses the hope that his verses will escape the beast's venom, and this author would like to express his hope that, through the selections he has presented here, he has gone a little way towards drawing the attention of those who love the Arthurian legends to a sadly neglected masterpiece of English literature.

Prince Arthur himself, meanwhile, must leave Faerie and return to the human realm of Logris, for, with his father's death, he must, at the tender age of fifteen, claim the throne of Britain. But he has not yet done with Faerie, nor have the fays yet done with him. In one form or another, they will be with him until he goes to live with the fairest of them all in Avalon.

# Six

# *The King of Two Worlds*

When Spenser died with his poem unfinished, he left Prince Arthur as he *went onward still/On his first quest, in which did him betide/A great adventure* (*FQ*, VI.viii.30), but we never discover what that adventure was, nor whether he ever saw, face to face, his Faerie Queen, who was the object of his first quest. As we will see later, he does eventually win an Otherworld bride, but not till after he has become what the magic of Merlin has devised for him to be, in fulfillment of divine providence: an anointed king.

The chronicles know nothing of the youth of Arthur. At fifteen years of age, while in Brittany, he hears of the death of his father, Uther Pendragon, after a protracted illness and returns home to take the throne. Uther is buried at Stonehenge, like his brother Aurelius before him, and Arthur is crowned king at the old Roman town of Silchester. He soon impresses everyone with his generosity of spirit, but before long, he will also have the opportunity to demonstrate his outstanding courage.

Arthur's first action as king is to take up the battle against the pagan Saxons who, under their leader Colgrim, have allied themselves with the Christian Scots and Picts in the north of the island. With the aid of his cousin Hoel (King of Brittany) and of Cador (who has succeeded his father Gorlois as Earl of Cornwall), Arthur routs his enemies at a series of bloody encounters, culminating with a battle at Bath, the city founded by Bladud and sacred to wise Minerva, where we first hear of the weaponry that will undergo so many metamorphoses in the romance literature.

First, Arthur dons his body armor, including a steel corslet made by an elven smith (*aluisc smið*) called Wygar (*Brut*, ll.10543–5)—the name may mean "lover of wisdom," from the Welsh *gwydd-gar* (*LA*, 267); Rosamund Allen translates the name as "Wiseman." It would seem that the elves, who

**115**

blessed his birth, are using their more-than-human wisdom to protect his life as an adult.

Arthur next girds on his sword Caliburn, better known as Excalibur, which has been forged in the Isle of Avalon using magic arts: *mid wiʒelefulle craften* (*Brut*, l.10548). He then places on his head a golden, jewel-encrusted helmet called Goose-White (*Goswhit,* l.10552). On it is painted a dragon, for it was his father's and therefore it bears the Sign of the Pendragons. Around his neck is his shield Pridwen, on which is depicted the image of the Virgin Mary, whose aid he invokes in battle. His spear the chroniclers call Ron, a contraction of the Welsh *Rhongomynyad,* "cutting spear."

The passage in Geoffrey of Monmouth's *Historia* where Arthur's weapons are first described constitutes the first known reference in literature both to the Isle of Avalon and to the sword that is forged there. The name "Avalon" appears to be Celtic in origin and has been related to the Welsh word for apples, *afallen.* "Caliburn," on the other hand, appears to be derived from the Latin *chalybs,* "steel" (*LG* 1, 219*n*16). In later literature the relationship between these two iconic symbols of sovereignty (the sword establishes Arthur's right to rule; the island is the place of exile from which he will one day return to rule again) is obscured, although the idea that some connection exists resurfaces in the accounts of his passing in the French romances and, famously, in Malory, where he must return the sword to whence it came before he can reach the sacred island.

Having defeated the Saxons at the Battle of Bath and finished them off at Thanet, King Arthur (whom Layamon frequently likens to a creature of prey, a wolf or a wild boar) turns his attention to the rebellious Caledonians, who seek refuge in the islands of Loch Lomond. This lake, we are told, is fed by sixty streams and contains sixty islands, on each of which is a crag containing an eagle's nest; whenever the kingdom is in danger, the birds start shrieking in concert. Layamon (*Brut*, ll.10851f) adds that the lake is a bathing-pool for water monsters (*nikeres,* "nixies") and a playground for the elves: *þer is æluene ploʒe in atteliche pole.*

It is here that the king's native enemies seek refuge. It is not clear from this episode whether the protection the lake offers is more than purely physical, but the presence of the prophetic eagles, nixies, and elves indicates that it is an ancient pagan sacred site, perhaps the Scottish equivalent of Annwfn, the Welsh Otherworld. This in turn suggests that the Caledonians may be seeking sanctuary there, reverting to the customs of their pagan forebears. Rather than violate that sanctuary, Arthur lays siege to the lake, and the refugees die in their thousands from famine.

But if Loch Lomond is, indeed, an entrance to Faerie, then we should not be surprised to see it protected by an Irish king, for, as we will see in the next section, Ireland is a country by which is frequently intended a rationalized Otherworld.

We have already seen how Gillomar I tried and failed to protect the Giants' Dance when Uther wanted to carry it off to Salisbury Plain. The King of Ireland was killed at the Battle of Menevia, but his successor, Gillomar II, arrives with a fleet of pagans and attempts to raise the siege of Loch Lomond. However, his army is driven off, and only a plea for mercy by the Caledonian bishops brings to an end the ensuing slaughter.

While he is at Loch Lomond, Arthur shows his cousin Hoel another pool nearby with miraculous properties, one which had been dug out by elves, and tells him about a third pool, near the Severn, which is equally extraordinary. Amazed by these wondrous things—and perhaps eager to dispel any lingering aura of Faerie—Hoel gives praise to the Lord who created such marvels.

Arthur celebrates the Feast of the Nativity at York, restores the churches, and reinstates the princes deposed by the Saxons. Principal among these are three brothers of royal lineage: Loth of Lothian, who is married to Arthur's sister, Anna; Urien of Moray, who is to father the great hero Ywain; and Augusel, King of Albany. These brothers, however, may not be all they seem. Urien and his son Owain (as he is called in Welsh literature) are, at least, historical figures, leaders of the northern British resistance to the Anglo-Saxon encroachment in the late sixth century and, as such, subjects of bardic praise from the historical Taliesin (*TYP*, 508–11), but in the romances, they will become embroiled with the machinations of Morgan the Fay, who is described as Urien's wife and Ywain's mother as well as Arthur's half-sister. Urien's brother Loth may be the eponym of Lothian, but the Welsh call him Lleu, a name which points towards an ancient pagan god of light (Green, 58f). Similarly, the third brother is called Arawn in Welsh, a name most familiar as that of the Lord of Annwfn (*TYP*, 279). Arthur, then, may not simply be establishing alliances with neighboring kings, but cementing that alliance with the Otherworld which began when his sister was married to a god.

## The Men Who Went to Ireland

We have seen, in Chapter Four, how Uther must win a victory in Ireland before gaining the Otherworldly Igerna as his bride; equally, Arthur gains his Otherworld bride, a giant's daughter, after winning his victory over the King of Ireland.

Having restored to Britain a state of peace and a sense of its own worth, free from foreign invasions and internal discord, the king decides that it is now time to marry. The woman he chooses is descended from a noble Roman family, but has been brought up in the court of Cador of Cornwall (Arthur's half-brother, according to Spenser). This is the most beautiful woman on the island, whom Layamon calls Wenhauer, but who is usually known today as Guinevere.

Arthur spends the winter in Cornwall with his new bride, but as the summer season commences, he determines to mount an expedition to Ireland, whose king had earlier intervened on the side of the northern rebels.

This journey to Ireland may be all that remains in the euhemerized world of the chronicles of a mythological tale, fragments of which survive elsewhere in Welsh literature, for Arthur undertakes a journey to Ireland in one of the earliest extant Welsh prose tales: the story of the quest of Culhwch for the hand of his cousin Olwen, the daughter of Hawthorn the Giant Lord. The giant imposes many conditions on the marriage, one of which is that Culhwch must win the cauldron belonging to the steward of the King of Ireland, something that Culhwch accomplishes with the aid of Arthur, who travels to Ireland in his ship Pridwen.

This story may in turn be derived from some suggestive verses in the poem *Preiddeu Annwn* ("The Spoils of Annwfn"), which possibly can be dated from as early as the eighth century (Green, 54f). This poem depicts a journey of Arthur with the bard Taliesin in the ship Pridwen (we can imagine that her figurehead is the "blessed form" of the Virgin Mary, an image that Arthur also bore on his similarly named shield) to Annwfn. This journey, from which only seven return, seems to be motivated in part by a desire to gain the cauldron of the king, a cauldron that will not boil the food of a coward and that is warmed by the breath of nine maidens. Annwfn is here called, among other symbolic names, Caer Sidi, the "Fortress of the Sídh," a name that immediately establishes an Irish connection, for the Sídh were originally the pagan gods of Ireland who, with the triumph of Christianity, were banished into the hills. They are now the "fairy" folk (Sims-Williams, 57). Annwfn is the Island of the Strong Door; it is also known as Caer Vedwit, "the Fortress of Carousal," and Caer Wydyr, "the Fortress of Glass."

The seven who return with Arthur from Annwfn can be compared with the seven who return with the head of Brân from Ireland in another Welsh tale ("The Men Who Went to Ireland") contained in the Second Branch of the Mabinogi, a collection of mythological stories. Here Brân the Blessed, the legendary King of Britain, who, as we have seen, is a euhemerized Celtic deity, invades Ireland and kills its king, who had married Brân's sister and to whom he had given the magical Cauldron of Rebirth as a dowry. As with the journey to Annwfn, the poet Taliesin is one of only seven survivors of the expedition.

After his death, Brân's severed head is buried on Tower Hill to guard the island from invasion (hence the sacred ravens that must never leave the tower!). But, according to the Triads, Arthur digs the head up because Britain needs no defender other than himself (*TYP*, 94f: This, along with Vortigern's exposing of the dragons concealed by King Lud, constitutes one of the Three Unfortunate Disclosures of the Island of Britain). He is therefore declaring that he, who has led his own expedition to Ireland, is the spiritual successor of Brân the Blessed as sacred king.

These three stories—Brân's expedition to Ireland, Arthur's to Ireland and Annwfn—are so closely aligned thematically that what we appear to have here is a mythological pattern, in which the sacred King of Britain (Uther or Arthur) must go on an armed expedition to the Otherworld ("Ireland"), thus reenacting the archetypal journey of the god-king Brân. The "spoils" of the raid include a treasure (the Giants' Dance or the Cauldron of Annwfn) that they must bring back.

## The Head of Annwfn

Another Welsh story about the journey of a British king to Annwfn suggests that such an expedition is one of the feats which establish British kings' worthiness to rule, and that, if successful, they win Otherworld brides. This is the Tale of Pwyll and Rhiannon, which constitutes the First Branch of the Mabinogi.

When the story opens, Pwyll, the King of Dyfed is as yet unmarried, and his chief love is hunting. On one occasion he encounters another hunter whom he unintentionally offends. The hunter turns out to be Arawn, the King of Annwfn (not yet Arthur's brother-in-law). Arawn offers Pwyll the opportunity to make reparation through some shape-shifting. Arawn will take on Pwyll's form and sit in his place on the throne of Dyfed, while Pwyll, transformed into the likeness of the King of Annwfn, will take Arawn's place in the Otherworld. Pwyll will have the good fortune of sleeping every night next to a beautiful Faerie Queen, but he will also be obliged to fight in Arawn's place against his old enemy, a rival king, in a year's time.

Accordingly, Pwyll spends a year as king in Arawn's place at court and in his bed, but he refrains from sexual relations with Arawn's wife, despite her beauty. (As we have seen, Merlin works a similar magic to that of Arawn when he effects the substitution of one lord for another and enables Uther to share a lady's bed, without her being able to tell the difference; in this case, however, the substitute lord consummates the relationship and the end result is Britain's greatest king.)

At the appointed day, Pwyll fights with and defeats the rival King of the Otherworld, who is carried away dying. The victor is acknowledged as the sole ruler over the twin realms of Annwfn, and the next day he returns to the place where he and Arawn first met. Both lords are restored to their true likenesses and return to their own lands. They continue to exchange gifts, and Pwyll is henceforth known as "the Head of Annwfn"; he is King in two worlds, this world and the Otherworld.

One way of reading this story is to see it as reflecting a ritual test in which the king must renew his rule. This appears to be the meaning of the substitution of the Lord of Dyfed by his Otherworld counterpart: Arawn, his "double," becomes king for a year, while Pwyll in Annwfn undergoes a test of his fitness to rule.

By overcoming the challenge of the Otherworld, Pwyll has discovered the "inner" aspect of kingship: his sacred relationship with the land. His rulership has been renewed, as is demonstrated by the comments his nobles make about the way he (or rather, Arawn, his sacred substitute) has ruled in the Year of Interregnum: Never has he been so wise in discernment, so generous in giving. Pwyll promises to maintain in future the new style of rulership that Arawn has introduced; henceforth, as the exchange of gifts between the two rulers suggests, the boundary between the two worlds is open.

Moreover, perhaps as a reward for his chastity in the bed of Arawn's wife, Pwyll himself wins an Otherworld bride, Rhiannon—whose name, meaning "Divine Queen" (Mac Cana, 80), suggests that she is in origin the Great Queen of Annwfn. Again, the yearlong abstinence of Pwyll can be seen as a ritual preparation for his sacred marriage to the goddess of the land, the Otherworld bride who personifies Sovereignty. This "goddess who rules" can be a monarch in her own right, or bestow her power on the man who wins her love, after proving his worthiness. She confers on him, through a sacred marriage, the right to rule; he becomes her champion, the guardian of the land and its treasures or sacred emblems.

The mythological journeys of Pwyll to Annwfn and of Brân to Ireland now become the prototypes for expeditions mounted by kings who are apparently historical. Just as Uther travels to Ireland, brings back to Britain its sacred treasure (the Giants' Dance), and gains an Otherworld bride (Igerna), so Arthur travels to Annwfn, brings back to Britain its sacred treasure (the Cauldron), and gains an Otherworld bride (Guinevere).

The account in the legendary chronicles of Arthur's early victories can now be seen as the euhemerization of a mythological pattern. By overcoming the threat from the Saxons and the Caledonians, Arthur has secured his kingdom against human threats. But the attempted invasion by the King of Ireland shows that Arthur must also be master of the Otherworld, the inner aspect of his realm. His victory over the Irish, like that of his father Uther before him, leads to his marriage to a noblewoman of supernatural ancestry.

The chroniclers tell us that Guinevere is descended from a Roman family—that is to say, she is one of those who ruled the island before the House of Constantine. They do not tell us the name of Guinevere's father, but in the Welsh Triads we are told that Arthur had three Great Queens, all called Gwenhwyfar, of whom the third is the daughter of Gogfran the Giant (*TYP*, 161).

But whether we follow the pseudo-historical tradition that makes Guinevere a Roman or the mythological tradition that makes her a giant's daughter—a child of the island's pre-human rulers—the stories about her are telling us the same thing: that she is an embodiment of the Sovereignty and that Arthur's marriage to her symbolizes both his marriage to the land and his connection with its history.

## The Princess of Faerie

The various names by which Arthur's bride is called in different texts are all ultimately derived from the Welsh "Gwenhwyfar," but this is itself a transliteration of the Irish Findhabair ("White Phantom"), the daughter of Medb (Maeve or Mab), a goddess whose name means "The Intoxicating One" (Mac Cana, 119).

In Irish mythology, Medb is the personification of the Sovereignty of the land; no man can become King of Ireland until he has slept with her, and she is described as being wife to nine kings. This nine-fold figure of Sovereignty also appears in the Otherworld of Welsh mythology, as the nine maidens whose breath warms the Cauldron of Annwfn, while nine sisters rule the Isle of Avalon.

As we have seen, the Welsh Triads give Gwenhwyfar as the name of three wives of Arthur, but it is easy to see these as the three persons of the one goddess of the moon, which moves across the night sky like a "white phantom." This meaning of her name has also led scholars to believe that Guinevere may have originally been a denizen of Faerie, for we know that pagan goddesses were frequently transformed into the fays of medieval literature. Thomas Green, in fact, calls her "Arthur's fairy wife" and translates her name as "sacred enchantress" (30).

There is, moreover, a literary tradition that links Guinevere directly with the Celtic Otherworld. This is the story of her abduction by Melwas, which was later taken up by the early Arthurian poet Chrétien de Troyes and reworked in the French prose Vulgate Cycle, appearing in its final version in

Malory. The earliest known account of the abduction, however, which will become such an important recurring feature of her career, appears in the Latin "Life of Gildas," which Caradoc of Llancarfan wrote for the monks of Glastonbury in the early twelfth century (*TYP*, 378).

Here we are told that the iniquitous Melwas, King of the Summer Country, has violated and carried off the wife of Arthur. Melwas brings her to Glastonbury, which Caradoc calls the Glass City (*Urbs Vitrea*). There continues to be much confusion about the etymology of the town's name (Ashe, 238), but the process of identifying Glastonbury with the mythical Glass Island, once begun, would lead to a revaluation of the importance of that town to the history of Christianity in Britain. By the end of the twelfth century it had been identified with that other mythical island, Avalon. In 1190, a few years after the Abbey was destroyed by fire, the monks discovered the tomb of Arthur and Guinevere in the cemetery of the Lady Chapel, which was convenient, as the money subsequently brought in by pilgrims helped to defray the costs of rebuilding. Where Glastonbury is concerned, God always works in mysterious ways!

In a medieval Welsh poem, "The Dialogue of Melwas and Gwenhwyfar," which may also predate Geoffrey of Monmouth, Melwas is described as the Lord of Ynys Wydrin ("Island of Glass"), a name which inevitably reminds us of Caer Wydyr, the Glass Castle of Annwfn (*TYP*, 380). Melwas is clearly the King of the Otherworld, and when he is transformed in the poetry of Chrétien de Troyes into the lord of a paradisiacal island, we know we are in the domain of myth rather than history.

But whatever the origins of the story in ancient paganism, Caradoc's account ends in a thoroughly Christian manner: The wise Gildas, one of the Glastonbury monks, intervenes when the armies of Arthur and Melwas are facing each other and persuades his king that he should return the abducted woman without any bloodshed. As a result (and here presumably is the moral of the story), Arthur and Guinevere are reunited, and both kings grant many lands to the abbot.

The original pagan myth may have had a very different ending, but we can only speculate as to its nature. Connections with the other tales of the journey to the Otherworld that we have mentioned do raise some interesting questions. Was Guinevere, for example, originally one of the nine maidens of the Cauldron, and was she one of the "spoils" with which Arthur returned from Annwfn? If this reading of Guinevere's story is correct, then her abduction by Melwas can be seen as an attempt by the King of the Otherworld to reclaim her. Further, was the Cauldron of Annwfn her dowry, as the Cauldron of Rebirth was the dowry of Brân's sister?

While it is unlikely that we can ever answer these questions definitively, there is some intriguing linguistic evidence to suggest that Guinevere did not just have a giant for a father, but also had a Queen of Faerie for a mother.

One of the names of the Queen of the Fays, made famous by Shakespeare and Shelley, is Mab. The name is, as I have said, an anglicization of the Irish Medb (related to the English word "mead") and has the same Celtic root as the Welsh word for drunkenness, *meddwdod*. But this root also gives us in Old Welsh *vedwit*, the name of one of the caers through which Arthur passed in his reiving of Annwfn. If Caer Vedwit is the Castle of Carousal, then Medb is the goddess of intoxication, and her daughter (Findhabair in Irish mythology, Gwenhwyfar in Welsh) is a princess of Faerie: Guinevere.

## The Kingdom of Marvels and Adventures

The chroniclers do not tell us at what point in his career Arthur was obliged to confront the giant King Rience. However, if we follow the chronology established in the later prose romances, we must place this titanic conflict very early in Arthur's kingship. After several earlier, inconclusive encounters, the final showdown occurs just after the marriage of Arthur and Guinevere.

Although we are not told that Rience is the descendant of the giants who ruled Albion before the Trojan conquest, this understanding is implicit in his confrontation with Arthur. The old, primordial, monstrous powers that ruled this island before it was civilized are rising up again, and Arthur knows that their defeat is essential if he is to rule. To show that he is the lord of the giants, Arthur must kill Rience. And so it is that, on the top of Mount Snowdon, in the shadow of Blake's Eternals, hero and monster fight to the death. There can only be one outcome: Rience is defeated, and only once more in his career would Arthur have to face such a monstrous foe in single combat. What will ultimately bring down the king will be a threat closer to home.

Having made his rule secure by his victory over the aboriginal forces represented by Rience, Arthur can turn his attention to another piece of unfinished business. So it is that, in the summer after his marriage to Guinevere, Arthur sets sail for Ireland, to put an end to the menace posed by its king once and for all.

Arthur is taking no chances: He threatens to castrate any knight (*his leomen he sculde leosen* [*Brut*, l.11131]) who will not support the war effort. In the event, his victory is definitive: Gillomar II surrenders, accepts Arthur as his overlord, agrees to pay him an annual tribute, and hands over his three sons and sixty noble hostages as a token of his good faith.

From there, Arthur makes his way to Iceland and receives the submission of its king, and while he is there, Arthur receives submission from the kings of other northern realms: the Orkney Islands; the Baltic isle of Gotland; and the kingdoms of Jutland and Wendland, on the Baltic coast. He then returns home to a hero's welcome.

Everyone who is anyone now wants to be part of Arthur's court; his renown exceeds that of the Roman emperor, and the stories of his deeds are meat and drink for many a minstrel. But inevitably, the close congregation of fame-seeking warriors leads to disputes over precedence, and, to avoid this, Arthur institutes the Fellowship of the Round Table, where all are equal.

This, at least, is Wace's version of events, and Layamon follows him by giving us a particularly bloody account of a fight that breaks out one Christmas, along with the even more savage retribution that the king wreaks, not just on the man who started it, but on his family: *pour encourager les autres,* one might say. It has the desired effect: Everyone present swears on holy relics that they will never start a fight among themselves, and it becomes a rule of the fellowship that the knights do not knowingly battle one another.

Arthur has made firm his position by defeating both the Saxon invaders and the indigenous, aboriginal giants, and he has won the Sovereignty by marrying a Princess of Faerie and vanquishing his Otherworld rival (Melwas) for her affections. He is now king both in this world and the other; and this dual role, both material and imaginal, is symbolized by the Round Table, around which, says Layamon (*Brut*, ll.11454f), the boastful Britons weave so many fables. But the adventures of the Round Table Knights cannot be reduced to boastful fables: At the heart of every great story is a myth, an archetypal truth. Myth is not mere fiction or fable, but metaphor; an image of a higher realm (as I try to show in Chapter Nine and the Appendix).

The stories that the minstrels sing about Arthur are neither wholly truthful nor wholly false, but unfortunately the British love their valiant king so much that they embroider the events of his reign with things that have never happened in *this* world. In fact, the simple truth about Arthur is marvelous enough for any poet (ll.11465–75).

Twelve years of peace ensue, and in this time, we must assume, befall the marvelous adventures of Logris for which Arthur's reign is renowned and which have become the stuff of legend. As Merlin himself prophesied even before Arthur was born, those who tell his story will be welcome everywhere and earn their food and drink till the world ends (ll.11491–9).

## The Lord of the North

The great peace ends when Arthur, at the urging of his barons but also through his own lust for glory, decides to extend his rule to the continent. First of all, however, there is a matter of family honor to settle.

During his father Uther's reign, Arthur's younger sister Anna had been married to Loth, King of Lothian, and she had borne him two sons, Gawain and Modred. The eldest of the sons had been sent, as a young boy, to be educated at Rome in the household of the Pope, whom Layamon calls Sulpicius; we must assume that the Pope who is meant here is St. Simplicius (468–483 CE). The Pope had knighted the young prince when he reached the age of twelve, but in the meantime, however, Gawain's father is embattled. The old King of Norway, before he died, being childless, had bequeathed his kingdom to his nephew Loth. The Norsemen, however, have refused to accept Loth as their king, raising one of their own nobles to the throne instead. Loth naturally turns to his brother-in-law to support his claim.

Arthur's first deed of war, therefore, after a long peace, is to invade Norway. The war is quickly won, the usurper killed, and Loth given the kingdom that was rightfully his. While they are in the area, as it were, the Britons subdue Denmark as well. Arthur is now the undisputed Lord of the North, but by now nothing less than total mastery of Europe will satisfy him. His armies prepare to embark for Gaul.

Returning to Britain from Rome at this time, Gawain encounters a happy court, and he is destined to add to its joy for, as Layamon tells us:

> Things were very well ordained that Gawain was created
> Because Gawain was most high-minded, and excelled in every virtue [*LB*, 297].

Generous, courageous, the best of knights, Layamon's Gawain bears no resemblance to the vengeful, murderous figure that we encounter in the later prose Grail romances and in Malory, a sort of anti–Galahad. As I have shown in a previous work, this downgrading of his character by writers with a more theological agenda can be attributed to his mythical origins in Celtic paganism (Dixon, 113–18).

Gawain will soon have an opportunity to show what he is made of, for the king now calls on warriors from every realm that owes him allegiance to assemble for the invasion of Gaul. A vast army is assembled, in which Norsemen, Danes, and Jutes join warriors from Orkney and Ireland. They all meet in Brittany, where Arthur's cousin, King Hoel, joins up with them. Together, they march on Gaul.

At this time, Layamon tells us, Gaul is ruled by King Frollo on behalf of the Roman Emperor, whom Geoffrey of Monmouth calls the Emperor Leo. Historically, this could only be the Eastern Roman Emperor Leo I (457–74 CE), during whose reign there was indeed an expedition of the Britons (probably consisting both of mainland British and continental Bretons) to Gaul in the year 470. But his imperial connections cannot save Frollo from the warrior king, who, in single combat on the Isle of Paris, cleaves him from the head to the chest with one blow of Excalibur, exclaiming to Gawain, his dear nephew, that he will soon be speaking to Frollo's kinsfolk in the eternal city:

> Rome's walls I shall break
> And remind them how King Belin there led his Britons in,
> And conquered all the lands which belong to Rome [*LB*, 307].

Meanwhile, however, he contents himself with bringing the whole of Gaul under his jurisdiction and distributing castles and lands to his nobles. Arthur stays in Gaul for nine years; in that time, says Layamon, many wondrous things befall (*Brut*, l.12045). It is during this period, then, that we must situate so many of the famous adventures of the Knights of the Round Table.

Having established his rule over northern Europe, Arthur is at the height of his powers. He determines to return to Britain to hold a plenary court at Whitsuntide, where he will wear his crown in state and receive homage from all his subject kings. It is to be held at Caerleon-on-Usk, the city originally founded by Belin, the first British king to conquer Rome.

The gathering of kings and nobles is unique in Britain's history. There are the four principal rulers of the island: the Kings of North and South Wales and Cador of Cornwall and Augusel of Albany. Alongside Augusel are his brothers Loth and Urien (father to that other great Arthurian hero, Gawain's cousin Ywain). The leading nobles from the principal cities are also in attendance, including Artegal, the Earl of Warwick (l.12150), who, as we have seen, is married to the daughter of (the late) giant-king Rience.

And, of course, there are the Knights of the Round Table. The role-calls of knights that appear in some of the verse romances can be interesting insofar as they contain elements of forgotten legendary lore, and lists of warriors in Welsh tales often include mythological figures. By contrast, the chroniclers' list of names of famous men who attend Arthur's plenary court at Caerleon is tedious because they are not historical characters, nor do they have any back-story in romance, despite being "the highest born and worthiest leaders in all this land" apart from those who eat at Arthur's table (*LB*, 311).

But what distinguishes the Caerleon gathering from every similar state occasion, before or since, is the number of crowned heads of Europe who come to Wales to pay homage to the High King as their overlord. Thus, from the north, come the kings of Iceland, Ireland, Orkney, Norway, Jutland, Friesland, Denmark, and Gotland; from the south comes Hoel, King of Brittany, accompanied by the twelve peers of Gaul.

The proceedings begin with mass: King Arthur is escorted to the south entrance of the church by two archbishops, and he is preceded by the four insular kings (of Albany, North and South Wales, and an upgraded Cador representing Cornwall) bearing swords; at the same time, Guinevere is escorted to the north entrance, preceded by four queens bearing doves.

After mass, the feasting begins. In honor of a tradition that dates back to the first Trojan settlement of this island, the men eat with the king in one palace, the women with the queen in another, and after food, games—and so on for three days. On the fourth day, King Arthur gets down to the serious business of state, distributing castles and lands and making clerical appointments, and it is while he is attending to this business that he receives an embassy from Rome.

History tells us that the Roman Empire was divided into east and west, for once and for all, on the death of Theodosius the Great in 395 CE. It was under his son Honorius that Britannia ceased to be a province of the western empire, and in 476 the last Emperor of the West, Romulus Augustulus, abdicated his throne, after being made an offer he couldn't refuse by Odoacer, King of the Visigoths.

Odoacer became King of Italy under imperial mandate; that is to say, he ruled the country, in theory at least, on behalf of the Emperor of the East in Constantinople. The Byzantine Empire, as it later became known, lasted a thousand years, and several attempts were made to regain its western provinces, most successfully under Justinian. But in the alternative history of the West presented in the Arthurian legends, an early attempt to reassert imperial rule leads, conversely, to the greatest triumph of our greatest king, the restoration of our ancient glory, and the vindication of Albion as the Promised Land of Brutus.

## The Empire Strikes Back

At the height of the festivities during Arthur's plenary court at Caerleon-on-Usk, twelve white-haired old men enter the hall, wearing bands of gold on their heads, and present to the king a communication from the Emperor Lucius.

Lucius, sometimes surnamed Hiberius ("the Iberian"), is a figure whose identity is much disputed. Geoffrey of Monmouth calls him "procurator," a position that would mean he was second-in-command to the emperor, and says that he is acting on behalf of the Roman Senate (an institution that did indeed survive the barbarian conquest and, although it eventually fell into decline, was revived under Justinian in the sixth century). Wace, however, says that Lucius is *l'empereür de Rome* (*RB*, l.10637). Layamon agrees: Lucius is the *kaisere, hexst of quicke monnen* (*Brut*, l.12370), the Caesar who lords it over all who live, and all our sources agree that it is from the time that the first Cae-sar invaded Britain and exacted tribute from the natives that the empire dates its claim to sovereignty.

Rome is demanding the restoration of that tribute, which was first imposed after the invasion by Julius Caesar and which was apparently still being paid by Arthur's father Uther Pendragon, as well as recompense for the death of Frollo. Arthur is ordered to present himself in Rome by the middle of August to account for his actions; failing this, Lucius will march against him.

A fourteenth-century English poem, known as the Alliterative *Morte Arthure*,[1] gives a colorful portrait of the king's reaction to this embassy. Here Arthur is a lion of a man before whose majesty the ambassadors cower. As for the British nobles, they are furious at this insult to their king, and Arthur is obliged to intervene to protect the safety of the ambassadors. He then calls a secret conclave of his leading nobles to decide their response, and they retire to a chamber in the Giants' Tower. This stone tower (which is not referred to elsewhere) may date, like Tintagel, to the days when giants ruled Albion. It adds to the mystique of Caerleon-on-Usk, which the chroniclers describe as a center for astronomy, but which, after the death of Arthur, was, according to Layamon (*Brut*, ll.12111–5) accursed (*biwucched*, "bewitched").

When the conclave begins, the first to speak is Cador, King of Cornwall, who says that the Britons need a good war to wake them up; peace means idle-ness, and idleness breeds weakness. Gawain, by contrast, points out that the land loves peace, which breeds good deeds.

King Arthur states that if the Romans believe that the Britons should pay them tribute, just because Julius Caesar once exacted it, then they have even more reason to pay tribute to Britain. For Belin and Brennus, two kings of Britain, had earlier conquered Rome and exacted tribute from the Senate, and Constantine the Great, the son of Helena, inherited the throne of Britain through his mother, before going on to overthrow the emperor. Likewise, Mag-nus Maximus was both King of Britain and Emperor of the West.

> And these were my ancestors, my esteemed predecessors,
> And they owned all the territories which were tributary to Rome,
> And through such example, I ought to possess Rome [*LB*, 320].

As for Gaul, the Romans made no effort to defend it, so they deserved to lose it.

Arthur's cousin Hoel of Brittany is the next to speak, pointing out that the Sibyl of Rome herself had prophesied that three Kings of Britain would also rule in Rome. Two of Arthur's forebears, Belin and Constantine the Great, had ruled in the Eternal City, and when Arthur himself reached Rome, the Sibyl's prophecy would be fulfilled.

Augusel of Albany backs them up and adds that, once they have conquered Rome, they should seize Germany as well. The *Morte Arthure* typically embellishes: Arthur's nephew Ywain promises to seize the imperial banner; Lancelot (here presented, not as the Queen's lover, but simply as a loyal knight), to knock the emperor off his horse; King Loth, to cut a swath through the enemy's ranks. Egged on by his nobles, King Arthur tells the ambassadors that they will have safe conduct out of Britain in order to deliver this message to their emperor: that Arthur will arrive in Rome to take tribute, not to render it!

The gloves are off. Arthur assembles his armies, summoning the forces of all his subject nations. The Emperor does likewise, but Lucius Hiberius is able to call on forces far greater than had ever before been at the call of a Roman Emperor of East or West.

We are not surprised that he is able to summon to his aid the rulers of Greece, Africa, Libya, Egypt, Bithynia, Phrygia, Syria, and Crete, since these were all provinces of the Eastern Empire. He also has the support of the neighboring Medes and Babylonians. But it is somewhat more surprising that he can call on the aid of the Parthians (*HKB*, 222), the traditional rivals of Rome in the East. Layamon informs us that he also had help from the Turks (*Brut*, l.12659), a nomadic people from Central Asia, while, according to the *Morte Arthure*, Lucius's influence stretches as far north as Prussia and Lithuania; as far east as Tartary and India; and into such indeterminate locations as the country of the Amazons and Prester John's Land.

Nor are all his allies human, as we discover when the imperial subjects assemble in Rome before their fully-armed liege.

> In front were sixty giants, fathered by fiends,
> With witches and warlocks to watch his tents
> Wherever he went, in winter or any season.
> No battle-horse could bear them, those barbarous creatures,
> Only camels with mail-clad castles for saddles [*MA*, 52].

With such formidable forces at his disposal, Lucius marches into what is now the British province of Gaul, and Arthur, in response, prepares to embark for the continent. Before doing so, he entrusts his realm and his queen to his nephew, Modred, of whom he is clearly very fond: "You are my dearest nephew," he tells him, "my nursling of old,/The child of my chamber whom I have cherished and praised" (54f).

The tragic irony of this love of an uncle for his nephew is heightened by Layamon, who tells us that Modred is secretly in love with the queen. The poet compares the dishonorable Modred with his brother Gawain ("the most loyal of men who ever came to court") and suggests that the younger benefited vicariously from the older brother's popularity. Layamon also implicates Guinevere in Modred's treachery, declaring that it was an evil day when they were born:

> They betrayed this country with unmeasured miseries,
> And in the end the Evil One brought them to destruction
> In which they forfeited their lives and their souls ... [*LB*, 325].

Unaware of her impending treachery, Arthur's final act is to say goodbye to his queen; he will never see her again.

## How the Dragon Became the Bear

The British fleet sets sail across the channel. En route, Arthur tries to catch up on some sleep, but his rest is disturbed by a vivid and frightening nightmare in which a dragon that flies from out of the West fights and eventually kills a monstrous bear that comes from the East. Awakening, Arthur tells his dream to his wise men. They suggest that he is the Dragon of the West and that the bear betokens a bestial giant that he will have to fight; no one dares to suggest that the prognosis is anything but favorable.

Consequently, when the king lands on the coast of Gaul and is told that a man-eating giant has been terrorizing the neighborhood for the last seven years, he is shocked but not surprised. To add insult to injury, the giant has carried off the daughter of Hoel of Brittany to his lair on Mont St. Michel, some sixty miles up the coast. Undaunted, the king races off to save her, accompanied only by his faithful companions Kay and Bedivere, but he is too late. He finds an old woman, grieving over a freshly dug grave, who cries out to him that her mistress has been raped and murdered.

The cannibal rapist giant has been collecting the beards of kings to make into his tunic (a detail that is sometimes attributed to Rience before him), but he never gets the chance to add Arthur's to his collection. The king makes the punishment fit the crime and cuts off the fiend's genitals, but even so, the giant nearly succeeds in crushing Arthur to death as he dies.

The king tells Bedivere to cut off the fiend's head and carry it to Hoel, the bereft relative; he himself will keep the giant's club and tunic.

Arthur the Dragon has defeated the bear of his prophetic dream, and one could say that, by taking the bear's tunic, he has symbolically become the Bear (Walter, 82).

Now, "bear" is precisely the meaning of Arthur's name in its Celtic roots, so we may have here an aetiological myth: a story that purports to explain a name. Arthur has inherited the title of "Chief Dragon" from his father, Uther

Pendragon: The Red Dragon will remain his emblem, as leader of the indigenous Britons (as it will become the emblem of their heirs, the modern Welsh). But "bear" is a name that he must earn; he was given it by Merlin, who would have known that Arthur would overcome a bear-like giant and thus gave him a name that revealed his destiny.

But there may be a deeper meaning to the story of how the Dragon became the Bear, for this is one way of describing the consequences for our polar alignment of a phenomenon that is known to astronomers as the Precession of the Equinoxes, a natural phenomenon that has found its way into many myths. Put simply, "precession" is caused by the wobble in the Earth's orbit. It means that the position of the stars in the heavens alters in relation to the Earth. The stars appear to move, in fact, in a cycle, coming back to their original position after 25, 920 years, and this period is divided by astrologers into twelve equal segments of 2160 years. Each of these is named after a Sign of the Zodiac, corresponding approximately to the constellation in which the Sun rises at the Spring Equinox: thus the Age of Pisces (the two Christian millennia which followed the Age of Aries) will be followed in turn by the Age of Aquarius (Godwin, 23).

Most importantly for our purposes, precession means that the Pole Star, the star that is most closely aligned with the rotational axis of the Earth, also changes over the millennia. The current Pole Star (or North Star, since it is the visible star that is closest to the northernmost point of the axial line), is, of course, Polaris—technically, *alpha Ursae Minoris:* that is, the brightest star in the constellation of the Little Bear.

But around five thousand years ago, due to precession, the North Star was Thuban ("snake"), or *alpha Draconis,* the brightest star in the constellation of Draco. Over the millennia, the Bear has supplanted the Dragon as the locus of the Pole Star, and is this not precisely what happens in Arthur's dream, where the dragon, having overcome the bear, *becomes what he has overcome?* The bear supplants the dragon.

We may, then, have in this episode a precessional myth, in which the transition from Thuban (in the Constellation of the Dragon) to Polaris (in the Constellation of the Bear) as the North Star, is depicted as a battle between the dragon and the bear. We may also have an aetiological myth of the origin of Arthur's name, which Blake derives from Arcturus, the stellar Guardian of the Bear.

If Arthur's dream is of War in Heaven, that war is reflected on Earth: As above, so below. The sovereignty of Europe is at stake, for it is worth remembering that, according to Spenser, Albion was ruled by giants when it was still connected to the continental mainland. Layamon says that the monster of

Mont St. Michel hailed originally from Spain. So it may be that the giants once held the sovereignty, not just of Britain, but of continental Europe. To destroy such a fiend is, therefore, not just a humanitarian act, but a means to establish, in the present, hegemony over the primordial past and create a legend that will be remembered in the future: to become, in effect, a once and future hero.

Whether we see in it a precessional or an aetiological myth, the defeat of the Giant of Mont St. Michel is a symbolic watershed. The defeat of the giants of Albion by Brutus was a necessary prelude to the founding of Britain; the defeat of Rience marked Arthur's conquest of all his insular foes; and now the death of the monster of Mont St. Michel is the prelude to Arthur's conquest of continental Europe, symbolized by his defeat of the Roman emperor.

# Seven

# *The Sun of Britain Sets*

For William Blake, Arthur's triumph over the Romans constitutes the last battle he ever fought and took place in the shadow of Stonehenge, or at least in the shadow of one of those ancient megalithic constructions that Blake saw as Druid temples, places of human sacrifice that reflected the degradation of the Eternal Gospel of the Imagination. In all the medieval sources, however, the Last Battle took place after Arthur had been obliged to return from continental Europe following his victory over the Romans. Arthur's defeat of the massed forces of the Roman Empire constitutes, not his last battle, but his last great victory.

Before he went abroad, Arthur's triumphs had been against internal enemies, foreign invaders, and indigenous giants, who threatened the peace and stability of his kingdom. But thereafter he seems to have been lured by the glory of war into foreign adventures and, ultimately, to have over-reached himself. After hubris there will come nemesis.

## The Overlord of Earth

First blood in the Roman campaign is usually claimed by the king's nephew Gawain, who, although no stranger to the delights of peace, does not shirk when warfare is required. When he is sent to deliver an ultimatum to the emperor (having been brought up in Rome, he is fluent in Latin), he responds to a Roman insult by splitting the man's head in half with his sword.

Thenceforth the casualties come thick and fast: Ywain, Lancelot, and King Loth all fulfill the pledges they made before leaving Britain, Lancelot going even further by wounding the emperor himself. Arthur single-handedly chops off the legs of Golopas, the most formidable of the giants, before decapitating him.

> Sternly in that assault he struck another,
> And set on seven more with his stalwart knights:
> Till sixty giants had been so served, they never ceased.
> So this assay saw the destruction of the giants [*MA*, 98–100].

Adding to his defeat of Rience and the monster of Mont St Michel, Arthur's reputation as a giant-killer—and hence his claim to the Sovereignty of the West—cannot be doubted.

But before the war is over, King Arthur will lose some of his most trusted, most faithful followers: Bedivere is killed by the King of the Medes, although his death is avenged by his nephew, and Sir Kay is fatally wounded by the King of Libya.

But there is no time as yet to mourn the dead. The Emperor Lucius engages in single combat with Gawain, whose fame is so great that the emperor intends to boast of their battle in days to come, but he will not have the opportunity. Although he and Gawain are separated in the mêlée, the emperor must face the wrath of King Arthur, who is determined to avenge the death of his beloved Kay.

According to the chroniclers, Lucius is killed by a spear wielded by an unknown hand, but the *Morte Arthure* allows us a more satisfying final confrontation between the two arch-enemies. The emperor draws first blood, striking a "bitter backward blow" that breaks Arthur's visor and cuts his nose, splattering blood on his shield and mail-coat. But now the king has his opportunity. Turning his horse, he strikes hard, "hitting through hauberk and chest/Slantwise from the slot of the throat, slitting him open" (*MA*, 103f).

To the great affright of the Romans, the emperor is dead. It is at this point, Layamon tells us, that one of Merlin's prophecies is fulfilled, for even before Arthur was born, Merlin predicted that Rome should be filled with fear at his coming[1] and its stone walls would quake and fall (*Brut*, ll.13531–8, 13964–8). The "walls" of the prophecy are Lucius and his nobles who have, indeed, fallen before Arthur, and the city itself will be next (*Brut*, ll.13952–4). Before sending his body back to Rome, Arthur has the emperor shaved, for, as his encounters with giants have taught him, to take a ruler's beard is to take his sovereignty.

Having defeated the imperial armies, Arthur subdues Germany, as the King of Albany had recommended, before entering Italy and laying waste to the north of the country. The Pope sends an embassy to Arthur, suing for peace and offering to crown him Emperor of the West. When he receives this proposal, in the ancient city of Viterbo in central Italy, the king predicts:

> As Emperor of Germany and all the eastern marches,
> We shall be overlord of everything on earth.

Ascension Day shall see us sovereign of these lands,
And come Christmas Day, we shall be crowned thereafter
And rule in royal style, keeping my Round Table,
With revenues from Rome, as is right and proper

and he even threatens to take his armies afterwards on a crusade to Jerusalem (*MA*, 133f), which, at that time, would have been part of the Eastern Roman Empire. But, if Arthur intends to take on the Byzantines in their back garden, his lust for conquest may be becoming overweening.

According to Layamon (*Brut*, l.13632), King Arthur is already the master of thirty-three kingdoms—a number with important symbolic resonance, for it was traditionally considered to be the age of Jesus when he died. This may, therefore, be an attempt on the poet's part to identify Arthur as the British Messiah. But Jesus's kingdom was not of this Earth, while Arthur, it appears, wants to be the lord of the known world. We will discover that fate has another destiny in store for Arthur. Such hubris will not go unpunished.

A messenger (Sir Craddock, whose mantle at Dover Castle will later be taken as evidence for the historicity of Arthur) arrives from Britain, intending to warn the king about events back home, but he cannot bring himself to break the bad news and, instead, stays up all night chatting with his monarch. That night, however, Arthur has an extraordinary dream, although our sources do not agree about its contents.

In Layamon's version, the king recounts the next day how disturbed he is by a nightmare in which the hall he sits in with his nephew Gawain, high up, the lord of all he surveys, is cut down by Modred and Guinevere, whom he then kills. He wanders alone on the moors, beset by griffins and grisly birds (*gripes and grisliche fuȝeles* [*Brut*, l.14006]) until carried off by a lion into the sea. The waves part them, but a fish brings him to dry land.

The first part of the dream seems like a straightforward transposition of later events; the second half is more mysterious. Rosamund Allen suggests that the lion may really be a lioness, signifying Argante (*LB*, 460). We can imagine that Arthur might have sorely missed the counsel of Merlin at the point when, not surprisingly after such a nightmare, he wakes up, shivering and feverish, only to learn that the treachery he dreamed about is a reality.

In the *Morte Arthure*, however, the king's dream is very different. He flees from wild beasts into a beautiful meadow where he sees the goddess Fortune spinning her wheel. Atop it have already climbed six kings, only to be dashed down again. Two more will also be raised up in the future, but for now, it is Arthur's turn. He is enthroned on the summit of the wheel as Sovereign of the World and given the goddess's own Sword of Victory. She bids him:

Brandish this blade! The sword is my own;
Many have lost their life-blood with the slash of it,
And while you work with this weapon it will never fail you [*MA*, 138].

The sword is thus reminiscent of Excalibur, forged in Avalon. Is the dreaming Arthur already in the Fortunate Isle with its "fairy queen" Argante?

She tells him to toast her in wine, and thus the morning passes. But at midday exactly, the goddess's mood becomes menacing, as she cries: "King, you can claim nothing, by Christ who made me!"—and here we can see how the old pagan Goddess of Fate has been downgraded to an agent of Divine Providence. "For you shall lose this pleasure, and your life later:/You have delighted long enough in lands and lordliness!"

With that, Fortune whirls her wheel, casting Arthur down from off his throne so that he is smashed to pieces by his fall. He wakes up shivering.

When the king, the next day, consults his wise men, he is told that he has reached the height of his prowess. From now on, Fortune is his enemy; there is nowhere to go but down. This is because Arthur has over-reached himself. His early battles were in defense of his land and his people against invaders. But Layamon exposed his savage streak, and his adventures in northern Europe have revealed a lust for glory that has, in the end, undone him. As the sage admonishes him: "You have destroyed sinless men and spilled much blood/In vainglory in your victories in various kings' lands" (*MA*, 139).

As for the six kings who preceded him on the wheel, they explain: the first is Alexander the Great, who conquered the known world; the second Hector of Troy, whose fall presaged that of his city, which would lead in turn to the foundation of Britain and Rome by Trojan exiles; the third, Julius Caesar, whose invasion of Britain began to reverse the achievement of Brennus and Belin; the fourth, Judas Maccabaeus, who won Israel's independence from the successors of Alexander; the fifth, Joshua, who led the Israelites into the Promised Land; and the sixth, King David, who was, like Arthur, a giant-killer.

With regard to the two kings who will come after Arthur, the first is Charlemagne, who will become the ruler of a group of heroic paladins comparable to the Round Table Knights; the second is Godfrey of Bouillon, who will recapture Jerusalem from the Turks, thus fulfilling an ambition that Arthur has failed to achieve: to rule in the city of the Holy Sepulcher.

Arthur is, the sage announces, in good company. He has been chosen by Fortune to make up the number of those noble conquerors who surpass all others; his deeds will be read by knights in books of romance and, at the Last Judgment, he will be accounted

One of the worthiest warriors ever to dwell on earth.
Accordingly many clerics and kings shall recount your exploits
And keep your conquests in the chronicles for ever [*MA*, 140f].

But the Nine Worthies must all fall after their rise; accordingly, Arthur should prepare himself for some bad news.

The king walks to the top of a nearby hill just as the sun is rising and sees a knight riding posthaste towards him. It is, it transpires, the British knight Craddock, to whom he had given custody of Caerleon, but who has been driven out of his homeland by recent events. He then recounts to Arthur the treachery of Modred, who has allied himself with "legions of loathsome foreigners" (142), notably the king's old enemies: the Irish, Picts and Saxons. But this is not the worst: He has married Guinevere and got her with child. They are living together "in the wild parts of the western marches" (143).

For the chroniclers, the tragedy of Arthur's reign is that his wife is unable to bear him any children; for her to become pregnant by the king's nephew adds insult to injury. Arthur has been betrayed by the wife he loved and the man he most trusted; it is as though his life's work has been wasted.

But King Arthur is not a man to be ground down by sorrow. He will act decisively. His plans to march on Rome are indefinitely suspended; appointing Hoel of Brittany to administer the lands he has conquered (giving him strict instructions to hang the one hundred and sixty Roman children he has taken hostage should the Senate refuse to pay the tribute he will be exacting—an echo of the war crimes of Belin and Brennus), he sets off for home, declaring that he will kill Modred and have the queen burned at the stake for adultery (*Brut*, l.14605). Once this has been accomplished, he will return to take the city of Rome, but this time it is to Gawain that he will entrust his land. Gawain himself is furious at the news, disowning his brother and threatening to have the queen torn apart by horses.

Before they can reach the shores of Logris, Arthur and Gawain encounter the enemy.

## The Last Battle

Arthur's forces engage with Modred's mercenaries before they even reach dry land. Slaughtering the enemy in their ships, Gawain, incensed by the sight of the traitor, jumps onto the shore with a small troop following.

Gawain is in a berserker fury as he lays into his opponents, desperate to grapple with the man he can no longer acknowledge as his brother. At last they fight hand-to-hand, but it is Modred who is triumphant. Watching his brother die on the sand, the traitor is honorable enough to grant him an encomium: Gawain the Good will be deeply mourned by all those who knew him, and even his killer sheds tears for him, bemoaning "his knighthood, his noble acts and wisdom,/His manners, his might and his marvellous deeds in war" (*MA*, 154).

Arthur, disembarking too late, mourns all of the warriors he has lost, including his brother-in-law Augusel, King of Albany. But it is his nephew's death that he regrets the most, as he cradles Gawain's blood-spattered body in his arms. The king in his grief regrets that he was ever born: '*wa is me þat ich was mon iboren!*' (*Brut*, l.14147). Gawain dies as the sun sinks to rest, and we may think that with his death the sun has set on the Arthurian Empire.

Unwilling to face his uncle, Modred flees to Winchester, sending word to Guinevere that everything has now changed with the return of the king. The queen is devastated, for, like Modred, she did not believe that Arthur would ever return alive from Rome. Layamon is in no doubt about her guilt: He tells us that Modred was the dearest of all men to her (l.14101). Now the usurper sends word to his queen that she should cross the sea to Ireland, but she flees to Caerleon instead and takes the veil. Her end is obscure.

Meanwhile, Arthur has laid siege to Winchester, where Modred is holed up. Terrified for his life, the traitor tells his men to take the field against the king while he himself secretly escapes to Cornwall. King Arthur destroys his army, then sacks the city. He slaughters its inhabitants, young and old, sets fire to the buildings, and tears down the walls. Thus is fulfilled the prophecy of Merlin,[2] foreseeing the anger of the king (ll.14195–202).

Layamon's tying of events in Arthur's life to the prophecies of Merlin made before the king was born goes farther than that of the other chroniclers and provokes comparison with the tying of events in the life of Jesus to Biblical prophecies made in anticipation of the coming of the Messiah. But if Layamon is implying that we should see Arthur as the British Messiah (a theme that we will develop more fully in the next chapter), we must also contrast the actions of this "king in wrath" with those of his Savior. For Arthur, far from turning the other cheek, is incensed beyond measure that his nephew has once more eluded him, hastens on to Cornwall, and finally catches up with Modred where he is encamped on the banks of the River Tamar.

The end of the battle is as inevitable as it is tragic, for the wheel of fate has turned full circle. Logris, the kingdom founded by the son of Brutus, is torn apart; Arthur's continental empire, the restoration of our ancient glory, will die with him, and the hegemony of the native Britons, the remnant of Troy, will not long outlast the catastrophe.

Arthur, wielding Excalibur, fights Modred, who, according to the *Morte*

*Arthure,* has stolen Uther Pendragon's sword Clarent, perhaps believing thereby to confer a dubious legitimacy on his usurpation. Modred gives the true king his death wound, but Arthur hacks off his nephew's sword hand and runs him through, leaving the traitor squirming on Excalibur in his final agony.

The battle is over, but King Arthur is consumed with grief when he sees the bodies of some of his greatest Knights of the Round Table lying in the field: his nephew Ywain; Cador of Cornwall; King Loth, the traitor's father, who has not only witnessed Modred's treachery but also, albeit briefly, outlived his eldest son, Gawain; also Sir Lancelot and many others, leading the king to exclaim: "Here the blood of the Britons is borne out of life,/Here all my happiness ends today" (*MA,* 166).

The remaining Knights of the Round Table carry him to the "Isle of Avalon" in Glastonbury—a rare example in Arthurian literature of a clear identification being made between an earthly location in Somerset and what, as we will see in the next chapter, is often presented as a mythical or Otherworldly island.

In Avalon, Arthur hopes to be healed, but the surgeons are powerless. Realizing that the end is nigh, the dying king proclaims his kinsman Constantine his heir while insisting that Modred's children should be "secretly slain and slung into the sea" (167). Here, at Glastonbury, he dies and is buried.

## To Avalon

The version of the death of Arthur found in the *Morte Arthure* is considerably more down-to-earth and realistic than that found in the poet's sources.

Geoffrey of Monmouth, in his *History of the Kings of Britain,* merely says that Arthur was carried to the Isle of Avalon to heal his wounds, without specifying a geographical locale for the island. In a poem he wrote later, however, a Latin "Life of Merlin" (the *Vita Merlini,* written around the middle of the twelfth century), Avalon, or the "Island of Apples," is a paradisiacal region, called the Fortunate Isle because it produces all manner of plants spontaneously. It is ruled by nine sisters, who can fly and are shape-shifters, chief of whom is Morgen (later known as Morgan the Fay, presumably the same as Layamon's elven queen Argante) who taught her sisters the science of astrology. Morgen is also a great healer, and it is into her care that Arthur is entrusted. She says that she can heal him, but he must stay with her a long time.

To this Wace adds that, in his day (i.e., in the twelfth century), the Britons believe that Arthur is still there and that he will one day return. As to the veracity of this claim, the poet will only commit himself so far as to reiterate a prophecy of Merlin: that Arthur's death would be doubtful. Since he had no children of his own, he committed his kingdom to Constantine's steward-ship, asking him to safeguard it until his return (*RB*, ll.13279–98).

In Layamon's version, Arthur addresses Constantine of Cornwall as fol-lows: He should safeguard the Britons and protect the kingdom with the laws that he and his father Uther had established.

> And I shall voyage to Avalon, to the fairest of all maidens,
> To the Queen Argante, a very radiant elf,
> And she will make quite sound every one of my wounds,
> Will make me completely whole with her health-giving potions.
> And then I shall come back to my own kingdom
> And dwell among the Britons with surpassing delight [*LB*, 364f].

As he began his life so he ends it: touched with the glamour of Faerie. The gifts of the fays who appeared at his birth—gifts of strength of body, generosity of spirit, a long and kingly life—have all been spent. And now the fays ("two women in remarkable attire") return to transport him to that realm that has always been so close to his own earthly kingdom. They arrive from the sea in a boat driven by the waves and carry him off, thus fulfilling Merlin's prophecy: "That the grief would be incalculable at the passing of King Arthur" (365).

His kingdom is no longer of this world.

## Froward Fortune

We are familiar with the process whereby certain historical figures, due to their great achievements for good or ill, take on heroic status and, after their deaths, develop a legendary "afterlife": They accrue to themselves various apocryphal stories that reveal archetypal mythic patterns and take them out of the limits of time. In the case of Arthur and Merlin, however, for whose lives there is no solid historical evidence, we find that their afterlife consists of a gradual materialization from the realm of myth into that of literary history. By the twelfth century, we can begin to date their fictional existence, that being the time when Geoffrey of Monmouth wrote a chronicle of both their lives.

Geoffrey, however, gives only three dates in the whole of his "history," all relating to the deaths of significant kings. The first is 156 CE, the date he gives for the death of King Lucius, in whose reign Britain first became a Chris-tian country; the last is 689, the date of the death of the blessed Cadwallader, the last King of the Britons. In between comes 542 CE, which Geoffrey gives as the date of Arthur's passing to Avalon and the handing over of the crown of Britain to his nephew Constantine of Cornwall: the last Briton who could conceivably lay claim to the Empire of the West.

But the "third" British Constantine does not follow the "second" in leading his armies to the continent to establish his title, nor is he a Pendragon. His grandmother, Igerna, was Arthur's mother; but his grandfather, Gorlois, was the rebellious ruler of Cornwall slain by Uther Pendragon. Modred, on the other hand, was Arthur's sister's son and, in the absence of any direct offspring of the king, could be considered the rightful heir to the throne of the red dragon.

Modred's own sons might believe that their father should have inherited the kingdom, but when they attempt, with Saxon help, to seize the throne, they are killed without mercy. King Constantine hunts them down and kills them while they are seeking sanctuary, one in a monastery, the other in a church: a crime against the Molmutine laws, for which God will punish him. Consequently, his reign is a short one. Within four years he has been killed by his enemies and buried, like his illustrious forebears Aurelius Ambrosius and Uther Pendragon, at Stonehenge.

The death of Constantine is followed by a dispute over the succession, a dispute which is resolved when Constantine's cousin, Aurelius Conanus (the son of Britomart and Arthur's half-brother Artegal, according to Spenser), kills all other contenders for the throne and then proceeds to "issew forth with dreadfull might,/Against his Saxon foes in bloody field to fight" (*FQ*, III.iii.29). All this, of course, has been predicted by Merlin, as we saw in Chapter Five, when he told Britomart about the deeds of the dynasty she will mother.

Layamon tells us that Aurelius Conanus dies after falling off his horse in the sixth or seventh year of his reign. He is succeeded by his son Vortipor, who continues his father's wars against the Angles and Saxons, until at the last he is forced to yield "to th'importunity/Of froward fortune." Vortipor is succeeded by his son Malgo, who is, by all accounts, a "goodly creature" whose looks certainly impress Merlin, who sees him as resembling the giants or heroes of old (31f). In fact, such is Malgo's beauty that men as well as women fall in love with him and he causes a wave of homosexuality to break out in court. Thousands of women emigrate in disgust (*Brut*, ll.14392–7).

But Malgo is not just a pretty face. He is an astute politician who reestablishes Arthur's northern empire by making himself overlord of "the six Islands" that were once British provinces (*FQ*, III.iii.32), to wit: Iceland, Ireland, Orkney, Norway, Denmark, and Gotland. But he does not attempt to regain control over Gaul, which is now the Kingdom of the Franks, and there will not be another Emperor of the West until the Pope crowns Charlemagne on Christmas Day 800, nearly three hundred years after Arthur threatened to win that title.

## The African Invasion and Its Aftermath

The northern empire that Malgo bequeathes to his son Careticus soon falls to "a straunger king from vnknowne soyle." This is Gurmund the Great, who, "hauing with huge mightinesse/Ireland subdewd, and therein fixt his throne" (33), crosses the sea with his Norwegian allies to assist the Britons' foes, the Angles and Saxons, in their conquest of the island.

According to the chroniclers, Gurmund is the rightful King of the Africans, but he gave up the kingdom he inherited in favor of his brother, in order to conquer a kingdom for himself by force of arms. Gathering together young pagan warriors from Nubia, Arabia, Babylonia, Persia, Turkestan, and Macedonia, he embarks with an army of one hundred and sixty thousand to conquer all the islands of the sea (*Brut*, ll.14428–56).

According to Wace, this was in fulfillment of the destiny that Merlin had once prophesied for him, that he would become a pirate. But Merlin had also prophesied to Britomart about the effect that this pagan invasion would have on the kingdom her descendants would rule. Not only does he sack and raze to the ground the cities that, in his fury, he over-runs; he also defaces the churches "with faithlesse handes," and even lays waste the land, burning the grass so that even wild animals starve and the people are forced to flee to the mountains:

> Was neuer so great waste in any place,
> Nor so fowle outrage doen by liuing men [*FQ*, III.iii.34].

Gurmund, having come, seen and conquered, like Julius Caesar, moves on, leaving power in the hands of a small group of kings (historians refer to them as the Anglo-Saxon Heptarchy, or "Rule of Seven," although Layamon reduces them to five). It is from this time forth that the south and east of the island becomes known as "England," and Careticus, who flees to Wales, becomes known as the king without a kingdom.

For the first time since the arrival of Brutus the Trojan, his Promised Land is no longer in the hands of the Britons, and also, for the first time since the days of good King Lucius, it is no longer in the hands of the Christians, many of whom have fled to Wales, Cornwall and Brittany.

Wordsworth laments this unhappy exodus, the exile of the Christian faith, in "Saxon Conquest," the eleventh of his *Ecclesiastical Sonnets:*

> Heaven's high will
> Permits a second and a darker shade
> Of Pagan night. Afflicted and dismayed,
> The Relics of the sword flee to the mountains:
> O wretched Land! [*WPW*, 331].

The conversion of the English Heptarchy did not begin until the arrival on these shores of St. Augustine, a missionary sent by Pope Gregory (590–604 CE).

Ethelbert, King of Kent and acknowledged *bretwalda* or "overlord" of the Heptarchs, was the first to convert, and he arranged for Augustine to meet with the bishops of the Britons. The meeting did not go well, as Augustine attempted to persuade the Britons to abandon their local traditions and to conform to standard Roman practices. According to Layamon, they reply that, unlike the English converts, "we come of Christian stock,/And our ancestors were also, for the last three hundred years" (*LB*, 380). Not only will they not adopt the Roman method of baptism or of calculating the date of Easter (after all, they might have added, Arthur threw off the Roman yoke! Should they allow the Pope to achieve what the emperor could not?), but also, they will not join with Augustine in converting the English. They hate him and "those hounds of heathens" equally (379).

It is this unchristian attitude, some believed, which invited divine retribution, in the form of the massacre of the monks of Bangor at the hands of Ethelfrith, the pagan King of Northumbria. But Merlin sees that the king is "Serving th'ambitious will of *Augustine*" (*FQ*, III.iii.35). Wordsworth describes the shocking event, at which some believe the ubiquitous bard Taliesin was present, in his twelfth Ecclesiastical Sonnet, entitled "Monastery of Old Bangor":

> *The oppression of the tumult—wrath and scorn—*
> *The tribulation—and the gleaming blades—*
> Such is the impetuous spirit that pervades
> The song of Taliesin;

Wordsworth's song, by contrast, will mourn the unarmed monks who try to preserve its treasure—"the store/ Of Aboriginal and Roman lore,/And Christian monuments,"—which will now be burned away, representing in microcosm what will happen throughout the island: the destruction of the British language along with its ancient, glorious heritage.

> Mark! how all things swerve
> From their known course, or vanish like a dream;
> Another language spreads from coast to coast;
> Only perchance some melancholy Stream
> And some indignant Hills old names preserve,
> When laws, and creeds, and people all are lost! [*WPW* 331].

We do not know whether it is Taliesin's song—an eyewitness account of the massacre, in the best bardic tradition—that provokes the shame and awakes the pride of the Britons, but they decide to fight back and elect Cadwan, King of North Wales, to be their overlord.

"Cadwan" appears to be based on the historical Cadfan ap Iago, who was King of Gwynedd (Venedotia) in the early seventh century. Cadfan was the great-great-grandson of Maelgwn Gwynedd, on whom the legendary Malgo is loosely based (although there is no historical evidence for his allegedly sodomitical tendencies), so it would appear that through him the dynasty founded by Britomart continues.

Cadwan halts the English advance in the North, but it is his son Cadwallon who takes the offensive, just as Merlin predicted:

> Then shall the Britons, late dismayd and weake,
> From their long vassallage gin to respire,
> And on their Paynim foes auenge their ranckled ire [*FQ*, III.iii.36].

Cadwallon's greatest victory is over Edwin, King of Northumbria, whom he defeats and kills at the Battle of Hatfield. And here the chronicles do reflect known history: The Battle of Hatfield Chase in October 633 was one of the last great victories of the indigenous Britons over the English, but Cadwallon was decisively beaten and killed a year later at the Battle of Heavenfield.

This, of course, had been foreseen by Merlin, who knew that the British success could not be sustained. With Cadwallon will die the rule of the Britons over their ancestral island, for his son Cadwallader will be helpless to prevent disaster "When the full time prefixt by destiny,/Shalbe expird." As the people are destroyed by pestilence, Cadwallader will flee to Brittany, intending from there to launch a counter-offensive to re-take the island, but he will be prevented from doing so by a vision. For the heavens, as if envious of the Britons' long years of success, have decreed that they must now ("for their sinnes dew punishment") yield sovereignty to the Saxons (40f).

> Then woe, and woe, and euerlasting woe,
> Be to the Briton babe, that shalbe borne,
> To liue in thraldome of his fathers foe;
> Late king, now captiue, late lord, now forlorne,
> The worlds reproch, the cruell victors scorne,
> Banisht from princely bowre to wasteful wood:
> O who shal helpe me to lament, and mourne
> The royall seed, the antique *Troian* blood,
> Whose empire lenger here, than euer any stood [42].

Merlin further predicted[3] that the Britons will not regain their island until the bones of Cadwallader the Blessed are brought from Rome to Britain; it is to Rome, therefore, that he must take himself, and it is in Rome that he dies.

> His bones are securely encased in a golden coffin,
> And there they shall still remain until the days have arrived
> Which Merlin in days of yore determined with his words [*LB*, 410].

We are still awaiting the arrival of those days.

## The Warlord and His Spoils

Cadwallader the Blessed makes the journey to Rome that Arthur never quite managed, but not, as his predecessor had hoped, as a conquering hero. Arthur had defeated the might of Rome, but was never crowned in the city. In fact, his proclamation that he intended to march on Rome and be crowned emperor there on Christmas Day by the Pope immediately preceded the prophetic nightmare that announced his downfall.

But as the Goddess of Fortune showed him in his dream, another king would follow him in the ranks of Christian worthies and would take up the position of Emperor of the West that Arthur's passing had left vacant. This is the King of the Franks, known as Charles the Great, or Charlemagne. Where Arthur is a legendary figure, Charlemagne is historical, but he nevertheless took on legendary attributes, as so many great historical figures do.

Charlemagne achieved what had eluded Arthur: in the Eternal city, at Christmas, in the last year of the eighth century, Charlemagne was crowned by the Pope as Emperor of the Romans. Arthur had vowed to go overseas to mount what would have been the first crusade: to avenge the death of Jesus on the cross. Charlemagne will continue the legacy of the legendary British emperor by combining military conquest with the quest for sacred relics. For, as the sage who interprets Arthur's dream about Charlemagne predicts:

> He will capture the crown that Christ himself wore,
> And the very same spear that struck to his heart
> When He was crucified on the Cross; and all the cruel nails
> He will recover with courage for Christian men to keep [*MA*, 140].

There are also legends that Charlemagne, like Arthur, will come again.

When Charlemagne died, in 814 CE, it was believed (there being uncertainty about his year of birth) that he was in his seventy-second year (*TLC*, 84)—but this is a precessional number that may indicate that he has a mythical as well as a historical status. For, as I have said in Chapter Six, the time it takes for the heavens to make a complete revolution in the Precession of the Equinoxes is traditionally 25,960 years. This "Great Year" can, if seen as the circling of the heavens, be divided into three hundred and sixty degrees, and each degree would therefore correspond to 72 years. To put it another way, the traditional lifespan of Charlemagne represents one degree of the circle of the Great Year.

That both emperors should be associated with cosmic myths of precession reinforces their messianic status. Arthur does not die, but lives on in Avalon, whence he will return to restore Britain's ancient glory; Charlemagne also does not die, but lives on in a German mountain, whence he will reappear to bring back the western empire to its former glory.

Given these parallels between the lives and afterlives of the two emperors, it is interesting that it is within about twenty years of the death of Charlemagne that the first account of the great military deeds of Arthur is written as part of an early "History of the Britons." The Latin prose *Historia Brittonum* is attributed to a Welsh monk called Nennius, the pupil of a Welsh bishop (*BH*, 9), and it is generally accepted that it was written in the first third of the ninth century.

Nennius described Arthur as the warlord (*dux bellorum*) who led the British kings in twelve great battles against the Saxons. The eighth battle was the one where he carried the image of the Virgin Mary on his shield; the twelfth battle was on Badon Hill, where Arthur himself struck down nine hundred and sixty men in one charge. Arthur was victorious, and the pagans were put to flight in each battle (35). Allowing for some heroic exaggeration, so far, so apparently historical.

But even allowing for the conventional symbolism of the number twelve, scholars have found in the names of some of the battles evidence for mythology rather than history. Thus Thomas Green (207f) sees Nennius's accounts of battles in the Caledonian Forest, the River Tribruit, and Guinnon Castle as, in origin, mythical battles against supernatural opponents.

Also, Nennius cannot resist mentioning a couple of what by then must have been a burgeoning corpus of oral legends: the stone bearing the footprint of Arthur's dog (called, presumably because of its giant size, "Horse") at Carn Cabal (modern Carn Gafallt) near Builth Wells in Powys, and the grave of Amr, Arthur's son, whose size cannot be measured (*BH*, 42). These distortions in the normal experience of space suggest a mythical Arthur already, by the ninth century, existing side by side with the Arthur of history, but it is not until the twelfth century that we have a clear statement of the belief in Arthur's return, involving a distortion in the normal experience of time.

In between we have the evidence of Welsh poetry, which is unfortunately very hard to date accurately, a fact which has led to much scholarly dispute. But it seems fitting that poems about a legendary king should be as hard to pin down to time and place as the king himself.

The most important of the early medieval Welsh poems about Arthur is the "Spoils of Annwfn," which we have already referred to in relation to the theme of the Otherworldly bride. A date of around 900 is often quoted for this poem, but some scholars argue for it being much older (Green, 54f). For Green, the earliest stratum of the Arthurian legend predates Nennius and portrays the king as "a monster-slaying and peerless Protector of Britain against all supernatural threats, a thoroughly mythical and folkloric creature who is intimately associated with the Otherworld" (91f). In the end, although we cannot be certain whether or not "The Spoils" was written before the *Historia Brittonum,* we can nevertheless be sure that, if the poet (whom we may refer to as the pseudo–Taliesin, to differentiate him from the historical sixth-century bard) knew of the *dux bellorum* of Nennius, it was not Arthur's military exploits against human foes that interested him.

*Preiddeu Annwn,* which survives in a fourteenth-century manuscript, has been the subject of numerous studies and several attempts to translate it into English, but it remains elusive.[4] It describes a voyage by Arthur in his ship Pridwen to Annwfn, where he passes through eight caers ("castles" or "fortresses") before returning. But, of those who went with him, only seven return.

Along the way, Arthur encounters marvelous treasures such as the Cauldron of the Head of Annwfn—a title of Pwyll, King of Dyfed, who is the pagan prototype of Arthur as the King of Two Worlds. Also, like Pwyll, Arthur may have brought back an Otherworld bride, the Maiden of the Cauldron.

But if these elements in the poem suggest the pagan myth of a quest for the Lady Sovereignty and her magical treasures, it has clearly been reworked for a Christian audience, for the Otherworld is also referred to as *Uffern*, "the infernal region." In which case, if we see the caers as stations of descent into the lowest level of the Underworld, then Arthur's journey becomes a Harrowing of Hell, equivalent to the mythological theme, popular in the Middle Ages, of the descent of Jesus into Hell on Easter Saturday to redeem the souls of the just—a comparison that is strengthened by the fact that Arthur also appears to be intent on releasing a prisoner.

The eight caers may also point us towards the Christian symbolism of baptism, a sacrament that, through the symbolism of immersion in water, is equated with the voyage of Noah.[5] Eight people survive the Deluge: Noah and his wife, their three sons, and their wives. Noah is therefore the *ogdoon* ("the eighth man"), as he is called in the Second Epistle of Peter (II: 5), and all Christians, through the mystery of baptism, can be saved, like the eight souls in the ark, by water.

This only comes about, however, through the resurrection of Jesus Christ, who, having died in the flesh, first descends in spirit (1 Peter, III: 18) to Tartarus, where he proclaims his redeeming action to the fallen angels (2 Peter,

II: 4) and to the godless antediluvians who are imprisoned there (1 Peter, III: 19f). After his Harrowing of Hell on Easter Saturday, medieval Catholics believed,[6] Jesus Christ emerges from the tomb in his "resurrection body" on Easter Sunday: a day that has a symbolic resonance with the eighth day of creation, the first Sunday. For, bearing in mind that the Sun is created by God on the fourth day of the first week (Genesis I: 14–19), then it follows that the first Sunday is the first day of the second week of creation, i.e., the eighth day.

This same symbolism also surrounds Arthur in the Welsh poem, for he makes a descent into Hell (*Uffern*) to redeem a prisoner, and as the leader of a group of seven survivors who travel in Pridwen to safety, he is also, like Noah in the ark, "the eighth man." The baptism of Jesus is a regal anointing that makes of him the messianic King of Israel, in fulfillment of Biblical prophecy, but when the Holy Spirit descends upon him in the Jordan, the true meaning of this anointing is unveiled, for Jesus is now revealed as the incarnate Word, "the Son of God" who baptizes with the Holy Spirit (John I: 33f) and whose true kingdom is not of this earth (XVIII: 36).

Similarly, Arthur's "crossing of the waters" can be seen as an initiation ritual which makes of him an anointed king, not just of the earthly realm of Logris, but also of the Otherworld. The Jordan is, in Biblical symbolism, the river that separates the Chosen People from the Promised Land, and perhaps, in the Arthurian mythos, the "infernal" waters that separate our world from Annwfn must be crossed by the true king in order for Albion to reconnect with its destiny as a Promised Land. Arthur's Harrowing of Hell is an *imitatio Christi* that makes of the king, after his baptism in the waters of Uffern, the British Messiah—as we will see in the next chapter.

# Eight

# *The British Messiah*

Arthur Pendragon is famous as "the once and future king," and this paradox suggests that he cannot be located in time but exists in an eternal present.

As a historical figure, he remains elusive; as a mythical hero, he is stamped on the landscape. His story—from his mysterious birth, his heroic deeds, his marriage to a noblewoman (which, as we have seen, can be interpreted as a "sacred marriage" to the goddess of the land), his betrayal, and his mysterious death—establishes him as the archetypal image of the pagan divine king.

But despite his mythical origins, he is also specifically a Christian king, who, according to his medieval chroniclers, tries to preserve the remnants of Romano-British civilization against the encroachments of the pagan barbarians. He becomes the first of the three Christian worthies, along with Charlemagne and Godfrey de Bouillon.

But if Arthur is a champion of Christ, his birth, life, and doubtful death also echo curiously the fate of his model, Jesus. Arthur's supernatural conception and his escaping death by passing into an unearthly realm reflect the manner in which Jesus transcends the normal limitations of human existence. Arthur's betrayal by his trusted nephew Modred echoes the betrayal of Jesus by his disciple Judas.

Even Arthur's marriage to a noblewoman, not matched in orthodox accounts of the life of Jesus, finds its counterpart in apocryphal legends of the marriage of Jesus to Mary Magdalene, legends that are finding a renewed popularity in the twenty-first century as fundamentalist religious belief wages a renewed assault on the imagination. For, according to Welsh mythology, Arthur has three wives, all called Gwenhwyfar, while according to early Christian mythology, Jesus has three women in his life, all called Mary: his mother, his sister, and a "companion" (*NHL*, 145). This latter term (*koinonos* in Greek) has been taken to mean "partner" in the modern sense of long-term lover, while the Cathars, those medieval heretics who flourished in southern Europe at the same time as the Arthurian literature was developing, believed that Jesus married Mary Magdalene (Stoyanov, 222f).

The depressingly literal-minded account of Jesus's fathering on Mary of a child who founds a continuing dynasty of messianic lost kings is not, however, matched in the legends of Arthur's progeny. The various accounts in Welsh, French, German, and English sources of the fate of Arthur's sons are contradictory, although all at least agree that no son of his survived the king's own death. According to a German tradition, Arthur's son Loholt rides away with his father to the land whence their return is expected. It is this belief in Arthur's "second coming" that establishes him as the British Messiah.

## Arthurian Afterlife

Between the ninth and the twelfth centuries, between the "History of the Britons" of Nennius and the pseudo-history of their kings by Geoffrey of Monmouth, we have little apart from the poems of pseudo–Taliesin to suggest that the *dux bellorum* of Nennius was evolving, in the popular imagination, into the mythical once and future king that he was destined to become.

Our main native prose source for this period is "Culhwch and Olwen," a Welsh tale dating from around the eleventh century, in which the eponymous hero goes to the court of his cousin the king to ask for help to win the hand of Olwen, the giant's daughter. Arthur is here presented as a lord of lavish hospitality, whose court attracts a multitude of visitors, including those who have travelled from far-off lands.

But the king himself has travelled far beyond the fields we know—for, as Arthur's gatekeeper tells Culhwch, the king has been not just to the Near and Far East, but to places that are clearly Otherworld castles, like the ones that Arthur traversed in Pridwen on his way to Annwfn.

Culhwch hails his cousin as chief of the nobles of this island, not just as "duke of battles." The nobles he commands include not just familiar names such as Cei and Bedwyr (Kay and Bedivere) and Taliesin the Bard (who went with him a-reiving), but men who come from the borderlands of Hell (where the raid took place): a certain Teyrnon, who is in origin none other than *Tigernonos,* the "Great King" of the Underword (Mac Cana, 81); Teyrnon's adopted son, Guri Golden Hair; Guri's uncle Manawydan who, like Taliesin, was one of the seven who returned with Brân from Ireland; Gwyn, the King of Faerie; the three warriors who would survive the Last Battle (the ugly Morfran, the beautiful Sanddef, and the saintly Cynwyl); and various other heroes from Welsh mythology, with superhuman powers and magical or accursed weapons.

Culhwch must pass a series of tests in order to win his bride. Among them is the hunting of a boar that was once a man, whom God transformed into a swine because of his sinfulness. This task can only be accomplished by Arthur himself. In the event, the king leads his warriors in the quest.

After settling a matter that has been troubling Britain since the days of King Lear—the strife between Gwyn and his rival for the hand of (the apparently immortal) Cordelia—Arthur embarks in Pridwen for Ireland, where he wins the magical cauldron that appears to be the double of that possessed by the Head of Annwfn. Then, after receiving the blessing of the Irish saints, he begins the hunt for the great boar. Arthur assembles all the warriors of the six islands, as well as from his subject realm of Gaul, and leads them in the boar hunt to end all boar hunts. It concludes with the boar being driven into the sea.

The final task is accomplished by Arthur himself: the gaining of a witch's blood from the infernal regions. Being familiar with the territory, he makes straight for the witch's cave and dispatches her with his knife.

Having apparently accomplished all the tasks set by the giant lord, Arthur sends his cousin off to claim his bride. Culhwch, it seems, can rest on the laurels of his illustrious relative.

Arthur also appears in other Welsh tales, but although the dates are much disputed, we cannot be sure that the main ones ("The Countess of the Fountain," "Peredur," and "Geraint") are any earlier than the French verse romances of Chrétien de Troyes that they resemble, although they undoubtedly contain archaic remnants. One story, "The Dream of Rhonabwy," contains tantalizing echoes of a myth of a raven goddess (Loomis 1956, 96f), but was probably written around 1200. None of these Welsh Arthurian prose romances, therefore, can have anything to do with the source material, the supposed ancient book written in the British language, that Geoffrey of Monmouth drew on to write his *Historia*.

Geoffrey's work seems, if anything, to be an act of euhemerization on an epic scale. Figures from Celtic mythology such as Beli and Brân (Belin and Brennus), Llŷr and Creiddylad (Lear and Cordelia), Lleu (King Loth), having been metamorphosed into kings, queens, and heroes, act out their parts in a drama that is part history, part legend, part fiction. But if the "British book," turns out, as some believe, to be mere fiction, Geoffrey's own book appears to use old myths as the raw material for the creation of new ones. The euhemerist becomes the myth-maker, substituting new gods for old.

Thus the figure of Gawain, whom Geoffrey seems to have drawn in part from Welsh heroes such as Guri Golden Hair and Gwalchmai, develops into a literary character with a life of his own, but this life, which is larger than life, takes on a powerful mythic resonance which cannot be limited to the fictional creation of any author. It is as though Gawain, once he has been written into the story, has his own destiny to follow: as though the myth, regardless of the intentions of authors, writes itself.

Very much the same can be said of Merlin, who demands of his creator two additional works (the Prophecies and the Life) when his brief appearance in the *Historia* cannot do credit to his creative potential. Merlin casts a spell on his inventor and walks out of the pages of fiction into literary history. Morgan the Fay, who is now so famous, only appears briefly in the "Life of Merlin"; we cannot know whether the nine sisters of Avalon were inspired by the nine maidens of the Cauldron of Annwfn, but we can be sure that once Morgan was let loose in Britain, she let flow the waters of poetic utterance. Enchantment followed. Arthur himself now has a beginning, middle, and end; he has a sword to accomplish his heroic deeds, and the place where his sword was forged becomes his final destination.

## The Second Coming of Arthur

In Geoffrey's "History," Arthur's end is shrouded in mystery, but he revisited the story of the death of Arthur in his *Vita Merlini,* which was written in Latin verse towards the middle of the twelfth century, beginning a tradition of Arthurian poetical composition in various languages that would dominate the Western European literary world for a hundred years.

In the *Vita* we are told that Merlin and the bard Taliesin sail with the mortally wounded king over the water and come to the Palace of the Nymphs on the Island of Apples: the home of Morgen the Healer, better known as Morgan the Fay, who says that she can cure the king if he stays with her long enough (*VM*, 103).

Reassured by her words, Merlin and Taliesin happily commit the king to her care and return to the mainland, but after five years of civil strife and Saxon encroachment, Taliesin thinks it is time to send for Arthur to return and reestablish peace in the nation.

But Merlin puts him straight: though Arthur is still alive, he is not the destined savior of the indigenous Britons. That role, in accordance with Welsh prophetic convention, is reserved for Conan Meriadoc, the founder of the Breton Kingdom in Armorica, and for Cadwallader the Blessed (105), the last British king, who, according to legend, would die in Rome towards the end of the seventh century. It is only when Cadwallader's bones are brought home that the native Britons will once more have sovereignty over the island that they have ruled since the coming of Brutus.

In fact, it is not until Geoffrey's Latin prose History was translated into French verse by the Anglo-Norman Wace, a native of the island of Jersey, that we find a literary reference to the belief, apparently already widespread since at least the beginning of the century, in Arthur's destined return from Avalon. In 1113, clerical visitors to Bodmin nearly caused a riot when they questioned the assertion by a Cornishman that Arthur still lived (Green, 73). Anyone in Brittany at that time who openly doubted Arthur's survival would be lucky to escape stoning, according to one contemporary commentator (Loomis 1959, 54).

Wace is therefore contributing to the written record of an oral tradition when he states that Arthur is still in Avalon, according to the Britons, who believe that he is still alive and await his return. Merlin had prophesied that Arthur would have a doubtful death, and the truth is that there will always be doubt about whether the king is still alive (*RB*, ll.13279–90).

So we know that the myth of Arthur's second coming was already developing in Western Europe when Wace dedicated his poem to Eleanor of Aquitaine in 1155. Wace is continuing a theme that we have already found in early Welsh literature, in which the battle chief has become the British Messiah. By the time that Layamon made the first translation of Wace into English, the doubt had become certainty.

Thus, in addition to the other marvels that Merlin prophesies of Arthur, Layamon tells us that this is the greatest: that there would be overwhelming grief at the king's departure, but that no Briton would believe that the king would ever truly die until the world's end at the Last Judgment. Arthur himself told his British subjects that he was to voyage to Avalon and would return when he was fully healed.

> The Britons believe this: that he will come like this,
> And they are always looking for his coming to his land,
> Just as he promised them before he went away [*LB*, 295].

Thus the wounded Arthur himself, at the end of his final battle, tells his heir, Constantine of Cornwall, that he will be made whole in Avalon: "And then I shall come back to my own kingdom/And dwell among the Britons with surpassing delight." To this Layamon adds:

> The Britons even now believe that he is alive
> And living in Avalon with the fairest of the elf-folk,
> And the Britons are still always looking for when Arthur comes returning.

No man alive can add any more to what we know about Arthur's fate, but the soothsayer Merlin, whose words were true (*soðe*), prophesied that "an Arthur once again would come to aid the English" (365).

We can see here how the hero of the Celtic resistance against the Anglo-Saxons is already being transformed into the future savior of England, and the metamorphosis of Arthur into an *English* king is something that we will explore in the final chapter.

But if Layamon expresses a certainty that Arthur will return (after all, Merlin has predicted it and Merlin's prophecies always come true), the doubt expressed by Wace remains characteristic of the French romances that followed in his wake. Wace's verse *roman* was to inspire not just a series of literary masterpieces, but a whole genre that seized the imagination of Western Europe, and the Arthurian verse romance itself would quickly metamorphose into another genre: the Grail romance.

The early Grail poems, with their mysterious imagery suffused with pagan mythology, were however soon replaced by prose compilations that attempted to tie the life and adventures of Arthur and his knights into a spiritual quest that reinforced the medieval dualism that pits this life against the afterlife. The first prose "cycle" was in fact begun in verse by a Burgundian knight called Robert de Boron, but the poetry was turned into prose and completed by an unknown redactor, to form a trilogy combining the life and death of Arthur with the Grail legends.

In the "De Boron Cycle," we find a reference to the *belief* that Arthur would recover from his wounds and one day return, but without any commitment on the part of the author to its authenticity. In the final part of the trilogy, a seriously wounded Arthur tells his warriors to stop grieving: He will not die, but will be carried to Avalon, where his wounds will be tended by his sister Morgan, and he will then return. The Britons wait for more than forty years for Arthur to return, but, when he fails to do so, they appoint a new king. Nevertheless, the hope that he will return has not died, for he is sometimes heard in the forests, hunting with his hounds (*MG*, 171).

The expectation of Arthur's imminent return may refer back to the discussion between Merlin and Taliesin in Geoffrey's *Vita Merlini,* but it also reminds us of the apostles' expectation of the imminent return of Christ after his Ascension. In both cases, the return does not occur in the lifetime of those who witnessed the death of their Messiah.

The author is also referencing the folk legends of the Wild Hunt, which the Saxons associated with their god Woden but which, in Wales, was led by Gwyn, the King of Faerie. He leads the Hounds of Annwfn, with their characteristic white bodies and red ears, who hunt the souls of the living through the air. The association of Arthur with Gwyn, who is supposed to live inside Glastonbury Tor, is particularly interesting in the light of the belief that developed at the end of the twelfth century—that the Avalon whither the dying Arthur was carried was another name for Glastonbury, of which more anon.

Shortly after Layamon wrote his English version of Arthur's passing, the De Boron Cycle was reworked and developed into a vast anonymous ensemble known (thanks to its popularity in continental Europe) as "the Vulgate Cycle."

The final part of this Cycle is *La Mort le Roi Artu,* a work whose very name, like Malory's *Le Morte Darthur,* suggests that the king must, after all, die. In this account, which gives us the first version of the famous episode in which Arthur asks his last surviving follower (Girflet, in this case) to cast his sword into a nearby lake, there is no longer any suggestion of his return.

When, after twice prevaricating, Girflet eventually carries out his lord's command, Arthur sends him away, telling him twice that he will never see him again. What Girflet does see is a ship filled with women taking his lord away and sailing out of sight. Three days later he finds a tomb in a chapel on which is written: HERE LIES KING ARTHUR .... When Girflet asks the hermit of the chapel if this is true, the hermit tells Girflet that Arthur does really lie there in the tomb; his body was brought there by some ladies whom the hermit did not know. Girflet immediately thinks that they must be the same ladies that had taken his lord aboard ship (*LG* 4, 155f).

Even here, though, there is room for ambiguity: Girflet does not actually see Arthur die, nor does he see his body in the tomb; he simply accepts the word of the hermit that the tomb contains the king and likewise assumes that the ladies the hermit refers to are the ones he saw receive his lord.

It is precisely this open-endedness that is used by a later redactor, who reworked parts of the Vulgate Cycle as *The High Scripture of the Holy Grail,* sometimes known as the Post-Vulgate Cycle, to reintroduce the suggestion of Arthur's survival. Here, in an echo of Wace, his death once more becomes doubtful: Arthur insists that no one will ever be able to boast that he knows for certain the truth about his ending.

Girflet watches the king depart across the sea in a barque full of ladies, but no one can ever say with certainty that he has seen Arthur afterwards. When Girflet himself finds the chapel that contains the tombstone bearing Arthur's name, he is told that some ladies had brought the body of a knight there and put it in the tomb. Amid much lamentation, they stated that it was the body of King Arthur; but after that they went away and never returned.

But when Girflet checks the tomb, in order to be sure in his own mind that it is indeed Arthur who is buried there, he finds it empty—except for the helmet that the king had worn in the Last Battle. Girflet concludes that Arthur's death will remain as mysterious as his birth (*LG* 5, 306f).

The empty tomb inevitably reminds us of the sepulcher of Jesus, which Arthur had once threatened to reclaim from the Romans. It is as if the author of the Post-Vulgate accepts the authority of the earlier Vulgate version and concedes that Arthur has, in the event, died—but then reasserts the element of uncertainty by implying that Arthur may have risen from the dead.

The mystery remains, to furnish the legend.

## Hic Iacet

It is this legend that inspires the best-known English language versions of the passing of Arthur: those of Sir Thomas Malory, who wrote, in the fifteenth century, one of the greatest works of English prose, and of Alfred, Lord Tennyson, the Poet Laureate who wrote, in the Victorian age, "The Passing of Arthur," which became the conclusion to his cycle of poems known as the *Idylls of the King*.

Malory's version was based in part on the Vulgate *Mort* but also on an English-language reworking of it called *Le Morte Arthur,* which turned the French prose of the Vulgate into stanzas of eight rhyming lines. The stanzaic *Morte Arthur* was actually written earlier than the alliterative *Morte Arthure,* which Malory primarily relied on for his account of the war with Rome, but whereas the alliterative poem continued the heroic tradition of Layamon, presenting Arthur as a great conqueror tragically betrayed, the stanzaic poem continues the alternative French tradition, in which the Grail Quest has revealed the futility of earthly glory, and Arthur's court will tear itself apart well before Modred's revolt delivers the *coup de grâce.*

The stanzaic *Morte Arthur* also introduces two elements that are not found in the French sources, but will become part of the evolving legend: Firstly, Bedivere replaces Girflet as the knight who will throw Excalibur into the lake and witness Arthur's passing (hence Tennyson calls him the "the latest left of all the knights" [*PT*, 1743]); secondly, Guinevere will be buried with her husband at Glastonbury. The alliterative *Morte Arthure* also clearly states that Arthur dies and is buried at Glastonbury.

In his version, Malory, drawing on the earlier English writers as well as the French *Mort Artu,* describes Arthur being carried by his sister Morgan in a barge to Avalon, where he *hopes* to be cured of his wounds, but later we find Bedivere discovering the tomb in a chapel, which the hermit *claims* contains a body brought there by a group of women. On the basis of this, Bedivere *assumes* that the tomb in the hermitage now contains the dead body of King Arthur.

Malory does not shy away from the ambiguity about what has really happened, when he comments on the tale:

> Thus of Arthur I fynde no more wrytten in bokis that bene auctorysed, nothir more of the verry sertaynté of hys dethe harde I never rede, but thus was he lad away in a shyp ...
>
> Now more of the deth of kynge Arthur coude I never fynde, but that thes ladyes brought him to hys grave, and such one was entyred there whych the ermyte bare wytnes .... But yet the ermyte knew nat in sertayne that he was veryly the body of kynge Arthur; for thys tale sir Bedwere, a knyght of the Table Rounde, made hit to be wrytten.
>
> Yet som men say in many partys of Inglonde that kynge Arthur ys nat dede, but had by the wyll of our Lorde Jesu into another place; and men say that he shall com agayne, and he shall wynne the Holy Crosse. Yet I woll not say that hit shall be so, but rather I wolde sey: here in thys worlde he chaunged hys lyff. And many men say that there ys wrytten uppon the tumbe thys:
>
> HIC IACET ARTHURUS, REX QUONDAM REXQUE FUTURUS [*MCW*, 717].

Interestingly, however, Malory does not end the story there. As if uncomfortable with the ambiguity about whether or not Arthur is really dead and buried, he adds an episode that is not found in any of the known sources.

Lancelot, here in his familiar role as the queen's lover, has a vision that compels him to fetch Guinevere's body from the abbey where she died and bury it by the side of her husband in the hermitage, which, Malory now reveals, is in Glastonbury. When he sees the bodies of Guinevere and Arthur lying side by side in the earth, Lancelot faints, later explaining, "My sorow may never have ende. For ... whan I sawe his corps and hir corps so lye togyders, truly myn herte wold not serve to susteyne my careful body." At the end of this speech Malory adds: "So the Frensshe book maketh mencyon" (723).

This is in fact the first definite mention of someone seeing Arthur's dead body. Despite Malory's reference to the "French book," neither the Vulgate nor Post-Vulgate cycles, which are his best known French-language sources, contain this passage, nor do they ever refer to Glastonbury by name. The stanzaic *Morte Arthur* simply says that Guinevere is buried at Arthur's side in Glastonbury.

Malory seems possibly to have been influenced by this indigenous British tradition of the identification of Avalon with Glastonbury and by the legend of the discovery of Arthur's bones there. In the Preface to his printed edition of Malory (published in 1485), Caxton says that, first among the many evidences to the historical existence of Arthur, is the fact that one may see his sepulcher in the Monastery of Glastonbury (*MCW*, xiv).

The claim that Glastonbury was the last earthly resting place of King Arthur cannot be documented before 1191, when the monks at the Abbey made an extraordinary discovery: the gigantic, battle-scarred bones of a man, apparently killed by a blow to the head, beneath a leaden cross on which was a Latin inscription: HIC IACET SEPULTUS INCLITUS REX ARTURIUS IN INSULA AVALONIA, "Here lies buried the renowned King Arthur in the Isle of Avalon" (Ashe, 240f).

But not everyone was convinced.

•••

## No Grave for Arthur

The Welsh, for whom Arthur is a national hero and one of their great leaders in the resistance against the *Saesneg,* are unequivocal.

According to the "Stanzas of the Graves," there is a grave for March (King Mark of Cornwall); a grave for Gwythyr (who fought the King of Faerie, Gwyn, for the hand of Cordelia); and a grave for the hero Gogaun of the Red Sword. But a grave for Arthur is "the wonder of the world": *anoeth bid bet y Arthur* (Green, 72). This wondrous place is also named as one of three prisons where Arthur spent three nights: One of the Triads calls it Caer Oeth and Anoeth, the "Fortress of Wonders" (*TYP*, 146–8). There is, then, no earthly grave for Arthur; he rests, sleeps, or is imprisoned in the wondrous Otherworld. His grave is, literally, "nowhere"—a concept that we might tend to associate with an unreal "utopia," but which, as Henry Corbin (1995, 4–6) has shown, is also a description of the *mundus imaginalis*—a spiritual place that is nowhere in relation to a physical somewhere; that is, at the same time, everywhere and nowhere.

Arthur has crossed over an invisible threshold to an imaginal kingdom that is not of this Earth, but since everything that can be imagined is an image of the truth, the British continued to put their faith in the literal truth of their hero's returning in tenfold splendor.

The early twelfth-century historian William, a monk in the Benedictine Abbey of Malmesbury, in his *Gesta Regum Anglorum,* "Acts of the English Kings," written in 1125, confirmed what appears to have been a tenacious oral tradition when he wrote that the sepulcher of Arthur was nowhere to be seen, whence ancient ballads fable that he is still to come (Green, 73). By the middle of the century, it was being reported that the Welsh were threatening their Norman overlords with the possibility that Arthur would return to lead them to drive out the invaders and reestablish Celtic Britain. There is then a certain irony in the fact that it was a nationalist cleric, Gerald of Wales, who first reported the story of the discovery of Arthur's grave.

Gerald, otherwise known as Giraldus Cambrensis, who was born in Pembrokeshire and nearly became Bishop of St. David's, visited the site a year or two after the discovery. He recounts how it was King Henry II himself (to whose wife, Eleanor of Aquitaine, Wace had dedicated his *Roman de Brut*) who, before his death in 1189, instructed the monks to dig at least sixteen feet beneath the ground, where they would find the body, not in a tomb of stone, but in a hollow oak. This had been revealed to Henry, apparently, by "an ancient Welsh bard, a singer of the past."

Gerald recounts that, after the Last Battle, Arthur had been carried away to the island that is now called Glaston, but which, in "the British tongue," was called Inis Avallon, "the apple-bearing isle." The ruler of the island, Morgannis, was not an airborne shape-shifter, like Geoffrey's Morgen, but "a noble matron," kin by blood to Arthur, who had tried to heal his wounds—unsuccessfully, it would appear. The reason that the body was buried so deep underground was in order that it should not be found by the Saxons, who were only able to occupy the island after his death: the very people over whom he had achieved such spectacular victories and whom he had come close to utterly destroying (*AGW*, 120).

Gerald, in his account, is at pains to rid the story of Arthur's death of its supernatural and messianic accretions. The only thing out of the ordinary is the manner in which the truth about Arthur's death itself is revealed:

> Now the body of King Arthur, which legend has feigned to have been transferred at his passing, as it were in ghostly form, by spirits to a distant place and to have been exempt from death, was found in these our days at Glastonbury deep down in earth and encoffined in a hollow oak between two stone pyramids erected long ago in the consecrated graveyard, the site being revealed by strange and almost miraculous signs; and it was afterwards transported with honour to the Church and decently consigned to a marble tomb [119].

There does indeed seem to be something miraculous about the way in which the tomb was discovered only seven years after most of the abbey, including the wattle Old Church, had burned down. Tourism, following the discovery, might be expected to supply the funds needed for rebuilding, when royal largesse was lacking.

Regal, rather than divine, intervention might also be suspected in the attempt to lay to rest, not just the king himself, but the myth of his return.

Geoffrey and Wace were writing at a time when the descendants of the

Norman conquerors were transforming themselves into islanders, and the Plantagenets were keen to reinvent themselves as British kings, transcending the historical division between Celt and Saxon, at best, or, at worst, ruling by division. If they were happy to consider themselves the true heirs of the Emperor Arthur (Hutton 2003, 68), they were not so keen to foster the belief that the original Arthur might return to drive all invaders out of the British homeland.

It is significant in this regard that Henry's grandson (born 1187), the posthumous son of Geoffrey, Duke of Brittany, should have been christened Arthur. Richard the Lion Heart, who succeeded Henry II—and whose failure to maintain the donations to the abbey restoration project may have precipitated the search for Arthur's grave in the place that his father had predicted—declared that his nephew Arthur of Brittany should be heir to the throne of England if the king himself died without issue. However, when Richard died in battle in 1199, his brother John Lackland seized the throne and, when much of the French nobility supported Prince Arthur's claim, invaded France.

Arthur was captured, imprisoned, and mysteriously vanished in 1203. According to some he was murdered by John's own hand, in a curious inversion of the struggle between king and nephew that led to the disappearance of the first Arthur; so it is possible that it is Arthur of Brittany, rather than Arthur of Logris, who is the true subject of Layamon's reference (*Brut*, l.14297) to the prophecy of Merlin *þat an Arður sculde зete cum Anglen to fulste:* "that an Arthur should yet come to aid the English."

## The Island of Glass

The legend of the burial of Arthur and Guinevere at Glastonbury first finds its way into romance literature in a prose work written in Old French, probably around the first decade of the thirteenth century. This is an anonymous work known as *Perlesvaus,* or *The High Book of the Grail*, which features a rare appearance by Loholt, who is sometimes depicted as the illegitimate child of Arthur, but is here actually the son of the royal couple. This is a rare instance of Arthur and Guinevere being seen as having conceived a child together; for Wace (*RB*, ll.9656–8), their inability to do so was an important element in the tragedy of their marriage.

The parents do not escape tragedy, however, for Loholt has been murdered and Arthur has had his head carried to the Chapel of Our Lady in the Isle of Avalon. It is here that Lancelot later comes, after discovering that the queen herself has died of grief for her son. He sees a newly built chapel atop a mountain that is so steep that he must dismount in order to climb up it.

Inside the chapel he sees two tombs, and the three hermits who live there tell him that the tombs were made for the king and queen. When Lancelot objects that the king is not yet dead, one of the hermits tells him that this is so. In one tomb lies the body of the queen, in the other the head of her son, but the queen has requested that, when he dies, her husband should be laid next to her. She has also left instructions that the chapel and site be restored (*HBG*, 204f).

The text does seem to be at pains, not only to identify the Avalonian chapel with the Lady Chapel at Glastonbury, but also to suggest that there was a tradition that the renovation of the chapel should be accomplished by royal largesse. All this may lead us to suspect that the Romance of Perlesvaus is in some way an "official" Grail legend, commissioned by the Glastonbury monks themselves. This is, in fact, precisely what is suggested at the very end of the romance, where we are told that it had been translated into French from a Latin original composed in a religious house on the Isle of Avalon, where Arthur and his queen lie buried (265).

But however much the monks may have had financial reasons for promoting this legend—and however much the monarchy may have wished to dismiss the possibility that Arthur might return to lead a Welsh rebellion— it is still possible that the story that Arthur and his queen lie buried at Glastonbury took root, at least in part, because of the spiritual traditions already associated with the area.

The Tor, the steep mountain that Lancelot climbed on foot in order to find his queen's tomb, was believed to be hollow; inside it dwelled Gwyn ap Nudd, the King of Faeric, in whom, according to Welsh tradition, God had set the energy of the demons of Annwfn (*MMWT*, 142f). Both Gwyn and Arthur, as I mentioned earlier, are associated with the spectral Wild Hunt of European folklore, but these pagan associations were transformed into Christian ones at a very early date.

There is no historical evidence to support the legend that the first Christian community was started at Glastonbury, nor that its founder was Joseph of Arimathea, the uncle of the Virgin Mary, while the story that he brought the Grail vessel there seems to have been established by the popularity of Tennyson's *Idylls of the King*. In the poem "The Holy Grail" that forms part of this cycle, Percivale exclaims that the Grail is the cup from which Our Lord drank at the Last Supper and which Joseph brought to Glastonbury (*PT*, 1663).

William of Malmesbury merely notes a belief that the old wattle church at Glastonbury was built by disciples of Christ. However, by the time a new edition of his work (*De Antiquitate Glastoniensis Ecclesiae*) had been produced at Glastonbury Abbey, towards the middle of the thirteenth century, it contained an interpolation, possibly influenced by the continental Grail romances, in which Joseph, at the head of twelve missionaries, comes to Glastonbury, where a barbarian king, later identified as Arviragus, grants them a plot of land. In honor of the Virgin Mary, they build the *vetusta ecclesia,* or Old Church, where the Lady Chapel now stands (Ashe, 239).

We saw in Chapter Six, in the context of a discussion of Guinevere as Arthur's Otherworld bride, that the Welshman Caradoc of Llancarfan, who was a contemporary of William of Malmesbury, gives us an early version of what will become a familiar trope: the queen's abduction. According to Caradoc, Melwas, King of Somerset, abducts Arthur's wife and keeps her in a stronghold at Glastonbury.

This story, which provides us with the first direct association of Glastonbury with Arthur himself, eventually finds its way into a verse romance of Chrétien de Troyes ("The Knight of the Cart"), where Melwas becomes Meleagant and his realm becomes the Kingdom of Gorre, an Otherworld realm from which none can return, until the spell is broken by Lancelot, replacing Arthur as the conquering hero.[1]

However, by then, Melwas has already appeared in an earlier romance (*Erec and Enide,* Chrétien's first surviving Arthurian poem), in which he is called Maheloas and described as the Lord of the Isle of Glass (*l'Isle de Voirre*), a paradisiacal realm where nature is uniformly benign, unmarred by storms or other extremes of weather (*AR*, 26). This Isle of Glass, whose miraculous qualities entitle it to be called a Fortunate Isle, is like Geoffrey's Island of Apples, which spontaneously produces crops in abundance (*VM*, 101). This association between the realm of Melwas/Maheloas and Avalon is carried forward into Tennyson's "Passing of Arthur," where the king believes he is going to a place "Where falls not hail, or rain, or any snow,/Nor ever wind blows loudly ..." (*PT*, 1753).

But this Otherworldly Glass Island is not just another name for Avalon; it is also the mythic substratum of the "Isle" of Glastonbury. Gerald of Wales tells us, in his autobiography:

> It was also once called "Inis Gutrin" in the British tongue, that is, the glassy isle, wherefore when the Saxons afterwards came thither they call that place Glastingeburi. For "Glas" in their language has the same meaning as *uitrum,* while "buri" means *castrum* or *ciuitas* [*AGW*, 120f].

We see here the same process of rationalization that transformed Morgen the Flying Healer, a shape-shifting astrologer in Geoffrey's account, into the noble matron Morgannis. The miraculous Isle of Glass has been buried beneath the medieval penchant for false etymology.

Eschewing the reason why the area should once have been known as "the glassy isle," Gerald attempts to explain the name as a simple translation by Christian Saxons (they had been converted from their pagan ways by the time they reached the southwest of Britain towards the end of the seventh century) of the local name for the area, but in doing so he inadvertently establishes its connection with a mythical topography. For there is little evidence that Glastonbury was ever known as the Isle of Glass before the Saxon conquest; Gerald, or his sources, may simply have misread the syllable *glas* as the English word "glass" and made an unintentional connection with "the glassy isle" of pagan Celtic mythology (Ashe, 238f).

This Celtic Isle of Glass appears, as we have seen, in the ancient poem known as "The Spoils of Annwfn," where the Otherworld is described as a place that can be reached by ship, and one of its titles is Caer Wydyr, "the glass fortress." This mythic image may have also been the inspiration for an episode in the pseudo-history of Nennius, who describes a magical glass tower on a western island near Ireland (*BH*, 20): a country which itself is frequently confounded with the Otherworld in British stories.

We can only guess at the pagan rituals that were once associated with Glastonbury and that led to its also becoming identified with the Otherworld. We do know that the southwest of Britain was particularly rich in such associations. It is easy to see then that what Gerald of Wales reports as a straightforward discovery of the tomb of a king turns out to contain within it the myth of an island of the dead where the sacred king, at the end of his earthly reign, passes through a portal to the Otherworld, where he reigns eternally as the Lord of Annwfn, or of Faerie.

And Gerald of Wales, it must be acknowledged, in his earlier account of the history and landscape of Ireland, the *Topographica Hibernica,* made exactly the same confusion between ritual and myth. In this case the ritual was not the burial of a king, but his coronation: Gerald described a "sacred marriage" in which the king mated with a mare—a scene familiar to students of Hindu mythology but which, he claimed, was still taking place in parts of Ireland in the twelfth century (Hutton 1991, 172). This reveals a view of medieval Irish Christian culture that, it needs hardly to be said, cannot be independently corroborated!

Despite those sources that attempt to portray Arthur as a dead king buried at Glastonbury, it is as a King of Faerie that he lives on in the popular imagination. The idea that he has gone to live with the fays, described in the poems of Geoffrey of Monmouth and Wace, was already so persistent by 1170 that it could be mocked, for political reasons, by the Norman poet Etienne de Rouen. He describes Arthur living in the Antipodes, made eternal by the law of the Fates (*LAL*, 236–9). And it is this same idea, though taken quite seriously, that we find in Layamon, who describes Arthur as going to live among the fays.

And here we must note a very important difference between the British Messiah and Jesus Christ. Jesus, after his Ascension, lives with his divine Father in Heaven, while Arthur lives in Faerie, which is not a spiritual eternity but a part of that intermediate world that we know as the *mundus imaginalis*. The Otherworld is not the celestial afterlife, but something much closer to home: an inter-world that is found just beyond the fields we know. This is an imaginal world that we can see now, today, while we are alive on this earth, if we look with the eyes of the imagination. In this respect the British Messiah is closer to the Jesus of early Christian texts such as the Gospel of Thomas, in which the Savior tells his disciples that the Kingdom of Heaven is all about us, but we do not see it (*NHL*, 138).

According to Layamon, Arthur dwells in Avalon with Argante, the Faerie Queen, and when she has made him whole, he will return to his earthly kingdom. But Layamon is already hinting that this kingdom is no longer the Celtic realm of Logris, but what we now call England.

# Nine

# *The Couch of Albion*

It is one of the prime errors of historical and rational analysis to suppose that the "truth" and "original form" of a legend can be separated from its miraculous elements. It is in the marvels themselves that the truth inheres .... Myth embodies the nearest approach to absolute truth that can be stated in words.[1]
— Ananda K Coomaraswamy (1943)

We have seen, in the last chapter, that the legendary figure of Arthur was eventually subsumed into the myth of the British Messiah and that his last resting place, the Isle of Avalon, was claimed by Glastonbury, which also recuperated as its own the legend of the Holy Grail. But what of the land itself, the land of which the king is the embodiment, the land promised to Brutus, the land in the West where the remnant of Troy took refuge, that land whose ancient glory matched that of Rome itself and that alone on this earth was worthy to be a home, for hundreds of years, to the Sangreal? This also was recuperated by a new concept, that of "England."

At the time of the Norman Conquest, the land of Brutus was clearly and irrevocably divided between the kingdom of the English and the Celtic "fringe." One of the political aims of the Plantagenet monarchs, when they promoted the writing of the story of Arthur, was to "divide and rule." Thus Gibbon tells us that, in order to encourage the indigenous Celts to see themselves as the last of the Trojans, the heirs of Brutus, the Norman conquerors "eagerly applauded the merit of a prince, who had triumphed over the Saxons, their common enemies" (*DF* 2, 500).

At the same time, the new kings did not want to encourage the belief that Arthur Pendragon would return any time soon to restore the native monarchy. The discovery of Arthur's tomb at Glastonbury, while it would not have deterred true believers, nevertheless pushed the messianic hope of his Second Coming, like that of Christ, into the furthest reaches of an indeterminate future. It was the Norman kingdom itself that could be presented as the heir of Camelot. Thus, when Layamon wrote that Merlin prophesied that an Arthur would come again to help the English, he may have been understood to be referring to Arthur of Brittany, who, as I have said, was the grandson of Eleanor of Aquitaine and who had been designated by his uncle Richard the Lion Heart, the hero of the Third Crusade, as Richard's successor (*LA*, 280).

What is perhaps more significant than the recuperation of the myth of Arthur by the Norman monarchy is the identification of the British Messiah with the English—the descendants of those very invaders that the Arthur of the chronicles resisted so long and with such great ferocity. This change is recorded in the literary record when Layamon becomes the first Arthurian poet to write in the English language and originates the English-language Arthurian epic that would find its greatest exponents in Thomas Malory and Edmund Spenser.

Wace had already noted the change of language in the island. The Trojan language spoken by Brutus had gradually become known as the "British" tongue, but it did not survive the African conquest led by Gurmund. With the invading Angles came the English (*Angleis*) language, and Arthur's Logris (the British *Lloegr*) became England (*Engletere, Englelande*) when the Britons were driven into exile, never to gain redress (*RB*, ll.1199f). It is thanks to Gurmund that what is now England gained its name, along with a new people to inhabit it, and new kings and lords to rule it (ll.13657f).

Henceforth, the English will rule Britain, and the native Britons will never recover it until the time comes when Merlin's prophecy is fulfilled (ll.14792–4). Wace neglects to give us the details of this prophecy, but Layamon (who reprises Wace's explanation of how Gurmund handed Britain over to the English [*Brut*, ll.14668–803]) explains, through a dream vision, what it was that Merlin said. According to the prophet, the native British would never again possess the island until the bones of Cadwallader were carried from Rome to Britain, but once this happened, the newly emboldened British would achieve their desires:

> Then within Britain bliss will be abundant,
> With fruits and fine weather, exactly as men want [*LB*, 409].

We are already moving away from political fortune-telling into eschatological prophecy: When the bones of the last true king are brought home, the Golden Age will return. Britain will become the Fortunate Isle.

Until that day arrives, the ancient Trojans maintain their laws and customs in what is now called "Wales." They will do so forever more, but not as kings, having lost the rulership of the land to the English. Sovereignty has passed from the ancient Britons, but can it be restored? "So far it hasn't come, that actual day, let future things be as they may" (410).

As for Arthur, when he returns, it will not be to restore the hegemony of the ancient Britons but rather, according to Merlin, to aid the English: *cum Anglen to fulste* (*Brut*, l.14297).

## An English Tragedy

After Layamon, there are no surviving Arthurian poems written in English for about a hundred and fifty years! This is not necessarily to say that they were not being composed—only that there were no patrons to pay for the expense of writing them down (O'Loughlin, 520).

There is, however, a profusion of written poems dating from the late fourteenth to the early fifteenth centuries—and, by this time, the Kings of England were adopting Arthur as their illustrious predecessor and his court and Round Table as models of chivalry.

At the end of the thirteenth century, Edward I "played the Arthurian card" when faced with a rebellion of the Welsh, who were prophesying the return of the Sleeping Lord. In Easter 1278, Edward and his queen paid a state visit to Glastonbury Abbey and took the opportunity to dig up the remains of our most illustrious royal couple, reinterring them with an inscription that places Edward's name next to that of Arthur's, as though he were the Pendragon reborn. The comparison is magnified both by the numerous "Round Tables" and tournaments he held and by his presentation to the Shrine of St. Edward the Confessor at Westminster Abbey in 1284 of the Welsh "crown of Arthur" and the Scottish Stone of Scone. Edward claimed that just as Augusel held Albany as Arthur's gift and carried the Pendragon's sword before him at the plenary court at Caerleon, so all Kings of Scotland ever after must acknowledge the King of England as their overlord (Carley, 50–2).

This Arthurian identification was continued by his grandson, Edward III, who went as far as to declare his plan to reestablish the Order of the Round Table in 1344. The foundational date was to be the Feast of Pentecost, hallowed in Arthurian tradition. In the event, Edward founded the Order of the Garter instead, reflecting a shift towards St. George rather than Arthur as the patron of Englishness, but Edward continued to be inspired by Arthurian concepts of chivalry (53f).

This is reflected to some extent in the literature that developed in such profusion in the late fourteenth century. Most of the poems from this period feature the adventures of individual knights, notably Sir Gawain, who in English literature maintains the supremacy Chrétien accorded him right up to the time of Malory, even though in French literature there had been a steady degeneration of his character through the prose cycles of the early to mid-thirteenth century.

Gawain is the hero of many original English poems, in which we find his uncle invoked as an *English* king who is overlord of the whole island, just as the early kings of Loegria were High Kings of Britain. In one of the best known of these poems, *The Wedding of Sir Gawain,* we find the hero, who is called "the best of Englond" (*WSG*, l.695) marrying a Sovereignty figure who transforms herself from the Loathly Lady to "the fayrest lady of ale Englond" (l.826).

In this poem, King Arthur firsts encounters Lady Sovereignty in her most threatening guise: as a Hideous Maiden. Her giant brother will kill the king unless he can discover the secret of what women desire above all other things. Ragnell knows the answer, but will only reveal it if the king agrees to arrange for her to marry Gawain. The knight is only too willing to sacrifice himself for his uncle's life, and Arthur is able to dispatch the giant with the knowledge that what women want above all else is sovereignty!

And the marriage turns out to be not such a great sacrifice on Gawain's part, for once they are in bed together, the Loathly Lady transforms herself into a beautiful woman. Gawain, she says, can chose whether to have her beautiful when they are alone together, at night, but ugly during the day, when they are in public, or vice versa. Gawain lets her choose for herself, and, in doing so, he has said the magic word. From now on, Ragnell will always be beautiful. Gawain has proved his worth by saving the life of his king; as a reward, he wins the hand of Lady Sovereignty. By acknowledging her ancient mythic power, Gawain gains the Sovereignty of England.

Sadly, as we know, divine providence has other plans. Gawain will never live to inherit the throne from his uncle, dying in battle against his treacherous brother even before the Last Battle. And the tragedy of the passing of Arthur is, in the poems from the turn of the fourteenth/fifteenth centuries, above all, England's tragedy.

In Malory's prose retelling it is clear, right from the beginning, that Arthur, like his father before him, is an English king. Where the French poets set the adventures of the Round Table Knights in an amorphous medieval realm, Malory is at pains to make Arthur's kingdom an England recognizable to his readers by, for example, identifying Camelot with Winchester (*MCW*, 58), where Edward I had set up his own replica of the Round Table, and Astolat, the home of the "Lady of Shalott," with Guildford (622). Lancelot's castle of Joyous Guard, whither he takes Guinevere, is situated in Alnwick or Bamborough, in Northumberland (724).

Caxton, in his Preface to the printed edition, extends this process when he offers the following "evidences" to the historicity of Arthur:

> Fyrst, ye may see his sepulture in the monasterye of Glastyngburye .... And in dyvers places of Englond many remembraunces ben yet of hym and shall remayne perpetuelly, and also of his knyghtes: fyrst, in the abbey of Westmestre, at Saynt Edwardes shryne, remayneth the prynte of his seal in reed waxe, closed in beryll ... ; item, in the castel of Dover ye may see Gauwayns skulle and Cradoks mantle; at Wynchester, the Rounde Table; in other places Launcelottes swerde and many other thynges [xiv].

Caxton had already printed a book about Godfrey of Bouillon, one of the Nine Worthies, and claims that it was pointed out to him that of all the Worthies it was Arthur whose history most deserved to be put into print, "consyderyng that he was a man borne wythin this royame and kyng and emperour of the same" (xiii).

If Malory's is an English book about an English king, the tragedy, when it comes, is an English tragedy. When Arthur hears of Modred's treachery and returns from the continent to fight him on home territory, he finds that many of his people ("the moste party of all Inglonde") have turned against him, as a warmonger. "Lo ye all Englysshhemen, se ye nat what a myschyff here was?" asks Malory.

> For he that was the moste kynge and nobelyst knyght of the worlde, and moste loved the felyship of noble knightes, and by hym they all were upholdyn, and yet myght nat these Englyshemen holde them contente with hym. Lo thus was the olde custom and usayges of thys londe, and men say that we of thys londe have nat yet loste that custom. Alas! thys ys a greate defaughte of us Englysshemen, for there may no thynge us please no terme [708].

Writing at the time of the Wars of the Roses, Malory had good reason to lament the tendency of his fellow countrymen to switch their allegiance: a tendency that he could see went back nearly a thousand years, at least, to a time when England was Logris.

## Eternal Union

Malory finished the whole book of King Arthur and of his noble Knights of the Round Table in the ninth year of the reign of King Edward the Fourth (726), that is to say, between 1469 and 1470, and it was printed by Caxton in 1485, a couple of months before Henry Tudor defeated Richard III at the Battle of Bosworth Field and effectively brought the Wars of the Roses to an end. Henry claimed his right to the throne, not just through his descent from John of Gaunt (*time-honoured Lancaster* in Shakespeare's phrase), but all the way back to Cadwallader the Blessed, the last King of the Britons, who had died eight hundred years earlier.

Cadwallader was the grandson of Cadfan, who was in turn the great-great-grandson of Maelgwn Gwynedd. In the legendary history of Britain, Maelgwn, the King of North Wales, becomes Malgo, the King of the Britons. Edmund Spenser, writing in the reign of Henry VII's granddaughter Elizabeth, makes Malgo the great-great-grandson of Igerna (King Arthur's mother). Since Arthur's sons died before him and his heir Constantine of Cornwall died without issue, the descendants of Cadwallader the Blessed can lay claim to be the heirs of Arthur and, beyond Arthur, the heirs of Brutus.

And this is precisely what is prophesied by Merlin, when Britomart (the female Knight of Chastity whom we encountered in Chapter Five) consults him about the future of her progeny. She discovers that Artegal, the half-brother of Arthur, will father on her a son, Aurelius Conanus, who will seize the throne after Constantine, and that his descendants will rule until the death in Rome of Cadwallader the Blessed.

Thenceforth, as a result of "heuens fury" the Britons will give over the governance of the island to the English. Britomart asks Merlin: "But shall their name for euer be defaste,/And quite from off the earth their memory be raste?" (*FQ*, III.iii.43).

No, the soothsayer replies, the time that they shall spend "in this thraldome," where they are strangers in their own land, is limited: After eight hundred years they will be restored to "their former rule," as "their importune fates" are transformed in "the iust reuolution" of destiny.

> Yet during this their most obscuritee,
> Their beames shall ofte breake forth, that men then faire may see [44].

Merlin specifies three Welsh kings who will maintain the honor of their race: Rhodri Mawr (Roderick the Great, who died in 878 CE); Rhodri's grandson Hywel Dda (Howell the Good, the legal reformer, who died in 950); and Gruffudd ap Cynan (Griffith son of Conan, who died in 1137), in whom *the old sparkes renew/Of natiue corage* (45).

When the term of thraldom is ended, one such spark, kindled in exile in the Isle of Mona (Anglesey), will break into flame

> And reach into the house, that beares the stile
> Of roiall maiesty and souerine name;

So shall the Briton blood their crowne agayn reclame.
Thenceforth eternall vnion shall be made
Betweene the nations different afore,
And sacred Peace shall louingly persuade
The warlike minds, to learne her goodly lore,
And ciuile armes to exercise no more [48f].

Thus shall the House of Tudor found a dynasty in which Wales and England can be united, both politically (as was done through the Act of Union of 1536) and through the historical symbolism implicit in placing on the throne of England the heirs of the Pendragons. This is represented in the iconic Tudor Rose, which combines the red rose of the House of Lancaster and the white rose of the House of York, but whose colors also recall the red dragon and the white, once locked in combat beneath Vortigern's tower, but now locked in alliance.

When Henry Tudor of Mona's son, Henry VIII (the younger brother of another ill-fated Prince Arthur), had Edward I's Round Table at Winchester repainted, it was done in the colors of the Tudor livery, with the image of Arthur reworked to look like the Tudor monarch (Starkey, 194).

## Albion's Bosom

Spenser's Arthurian epic turned out to be a literary dead end; it spawned no successors of equal worth. John Milton considered using Arthur as the subject of a great epic, but he had doubts about whether King Arthur really existed, writing in the Third Book of his *History of Britain* that he had become a figure of fable rather than history. These doubts, combined with his rejection on political grounds of a legend that was associated with "the mystique of divine kingship" led him to turn to King Alfred (Brooks and Bryden, 248) and, finally, to Adam (or rather, as some, including Blake, would argue, to Satan!) as his hero. By the eighteenth century the usefulness of Arthur for political allegory or heroic fantasy had been rejected by a cultural spirit of rational inquiry that would eventually lead to the historicity of Adam also being questioned; many would eventually conclude that Milton had rejected a legendary hero in favor of a purely mythical one.

That great Enlightenment rationalist, Edward Gibbon, might have been expected to cast doubt on the historicity of Arthur, but in fact he seems to have felt that his age had gone too far in this respect. He accepted that Arthur was the hero of twelve battles against the Angles and Saxons, but believed that the traditions preserved by the Welsh and Breton bards and taken up by the Norman courts in the twelfth century were enriched by the "fancy" of the

time and embellished by oriental elements brought to the West during the
Crusades:

> Fairies and giants, flying dragons, and enchanted palaces, were blended with
> the more simple fictions of the West; and the fate of Britain depended on the
> art, or the predictions, of Merlin .... At length the light of science and reason
> was rekindled; the talisman was broken; the visionary fabric melted into air;
> and by a natural, though unjust, reverse of the public opinion, the severity of
> the present age is inclined to question the *existence* of Arthur [*DF* 2, 500f].

William Blake, as we have seen, had no time for Gibbon. He saw himself rather
as the prophetic heir of Milton, who, he famously claimed, was of the Devil's
party without knowing it (*BCW*, 150). That is to say that if, as readers of *Paradise Lost* have often claimed, he gives the Devil the best tunes, this is because
the poet in Milton cannot be constrained by the theologian. Milton famously
tried to "justify the ways of God to men" (*PL*, Book I, l.26), but many people
have felt that he unintentionally went some considerable way towards justifying
Satan's rebellion!

Blake attempts to resolve this paradox in his own homage to the earlier
poet, his epic entitled *Milton*. Blake felt that Milton embodied energy as Satan
and reason as Christ and tried to justify the enslavement of energy by reason.
Blake believed that this enslavement was itself what was truly satanic and that
energy and reason are rather contraries that need each other, for without their
opposition (which is "true friendship") there can be no progress.

Blake's Paradise is the state of primordial unity; for him, Paradise is lost
before Eve ever tempts Adam. The division into the sexes is itself the loss of
Eden. He therefore wrote his own poem about Milton's personal journey from
self-division to wholeness, which is the journey of each of us to overcome,
through imagination, the negation of our sense of eternity. Along the way, he
wrote a partial version of the myth that he developed more fully in *Jerusalem*.

In *Milton: A Poem in Two Books* (the twofold structure representing two
paths, that of Milton and of his female Emanation, to the overcoming of the
dualism that is embodied in their separation) we are told that Albion has been
slain "thro' envy of Living Form, even of the Divine Vision" (*BCW*, 482). As
a result of his murder, "Jerusalem's foundations," which were in Albion
(Jerusalem *was* built here) are "laid in ruins from every Nation, & Oak Groves
rooted" (485) as the primordial religion is replaced by the Druidic cult.

> Thence stony Druid Temples overspread the Island white,
> And thence from Jerusalem's ruins, from her walls of salvation
> And praise, thro' the whole Earth were reared ... till Babel
> The Spectre of Albion frown'd over the Nations in glory & war.

All things begin & end in Albion's ancient Druid rocky shore:
But now the Starry Heavens are fled from the mighty limbs of Albion [485f].

Just as Albion was once spread across the Earth, for all things begin in him, so, after the Fall, which is his separation from Jerusalem, the Druidic temples spread across the whole Earth. The original Druids are indistinguishable from the Biblical patriarchs as heirs of the primordial revelation, but with the fall of Albion their religion degenerates into a cult that practices human sacrifice ("Satan's Druid Sons/ Offer the Human Victims throughout all the Earth" [491]). Albion's murder is in itself a form of human sacrifice that reduces him from a cosmic to a purely material being: the starry heavens having fled from his limbs, Albion's land is merely "this earth of vegetation" (496).

As a result, it is his Spectre which dominates the nations, substituting for vision and imagination (the attributes of the eternal Albion) the spectral qualities of glory and war. These are precisely the attributes of Arthur, as the king is represented by Nennius and the chroniclers, but in this poem, Blake names the Spectre Babel— that is, Babylon, the ancient adversary of Jerusalem, the place whither she is exiled and where she is enslaved.

As his Spectre spreads over the Earth, frowning over the nations, so Albion himself is reduced to the island that bears his name: London, Bath, Caerleon (the "bewitched" City of Legions) and Edinburgh are "the four pillars of his Throne"; his feet are in the south of England; his bosom "involves" the cathedral cities, including Bath where the pagan Bladud fell and Arthur won his greatest victory over the heathen invaders; "his right hand covers lofty Wales,/His left Scotland; ... his right elbow/Leans on the Rocks of Erin's land, Ireland, ancient nation./His head bends over London ..."

Although the spiritual Albion has been "slain" as far as the rationalists and materialists are concerned, "the visionary eye" can see that he has merely "changed his life," to use Malory's evocative phrase. Looking eastwards towards his beloved Jerusalem in exile, Albion groans and, as his tears flow down, he tries to rise up from "his Couch/Of dread repose," but his strength fails him and he sinks back "down with dreadful groans" (531).

All is not lost, however. At the end of the poem, Blake shows Jesus (whose divine body is "the Human Imagination" [482]) walking forth "to enter into/Albion's Bosom, the bosom of death" (534). When the divine imagination is rekindled in the heart of Albion, the giant will awake.

## All the Fables of Arthur ...

*Milton* was written in 1804 but not printed until around 1809, when Blake held his one-man show at which he exhibited his Arthurian painting, the now-lost "Ancient Britons," and it was Blake who eventually wrote the epic of Arthur that Milton rejected in favor of *Paradise Lost*. For it is in *Jerusalem,* which he worked on over the next twenty years, that Arthur is identified as the Spectre of Albion.

Thus the story of Albion can be read as a prehistory of Arthur, and the story of Arthur as the acts of Albion once he has fallen into time and space. For Blake, Arthur is one of the "kings in wrath" who represent historical incarnations of the Spectre, following after Belin, who, like Arthur, crossed the channel to humble Rome. In Blake's lost painting, however, it is not military conquest, "glory & war," that is celebrated, but "the last battle that Arthur fought," which is conflated with his victory over the Romans. From the perspective of earthly glory, it is a hollow victory, however, because only three of Arthur's warriors survive the battle.

As Blake tells us in his *Descriptive Catalogue,* they march through the field *unsubdued, as Gods,* rolling the enemy soldiers before them like a whirl-wind. As the last of the warrior-bards sings his death-song, the setting sun, blood-red like the field of dead and dying, disappears behind the mountains, where stand Druid temples: stone circles like the one at Stonehenge. These Druid temples take on a symbolic importance here, because the human sacrifice Blake associates with Stonehenge and other megalithic monuments is the religion of the Spectre that grows up when Albion is separated from Jerusalem. They are the temples of a religion of blood—symbolic of the literalist approach to the sacred—that must also fall on the day of battle.

With Arthur's death, the Sun of Britain sets, *but shall arise again with tenfold splendor when Arthur shall awake from sleep and resume his dominion over earth and ocean.* Arthur's awakening will not be the return of the Spectre, but that of Albion, who will once more encompass the whole world. This awakening will not be celebrated by warrior-bards, the last of whom died with Arthur, but by poet-prophets such as Blake, for whom our ancient glory is not exemplified by the conquests of "the warlike naked Britons" but by "his own country" being again, as it once was, "the source of learning and inspiration" (*DC*, 68).

Blake describes "all the fables" of Arthur and his Round Table as having been "written in Eden." In other words, Blake's "visionary contemplations" are able to discern the archetypal reality that is the eternal truth behind the stories "of Arthur's conquest of the whole world; of his death, or sleep, and promise to return again"; and it is this Edenic version that Blake gives us in *Jerusalem,* where his "Artist's hands" rework the "British Antiquities" (68f).

But in his use of the word "fables," Blake must remind us of the concerns of Wace and Layamon that the historical reality of Arthur was becoming obscured by all the fabulous stories that, even in the twelfth century, were being told about him. In *Jerusalem,* Blake gives us a list of the spectral "kings in wrath" who rule on earth in the absence of the sleeping Albion:

Satan, Cain, Tubal, Nimrod, Pharaoh, Priam, Bladud, Belin,
Arthur, Alfred, the Norman Conqueror, Richard, John ...
And all the Kings & Nobles of the Earth & all their Glories [*BCW,* 713].

For Blake, this is a list of real characters. The first five names are found in the Bible; Priam is the last King of Troy, the fall of whose city starts the exodus that culminates in the founding of Britain; Bladud, Belin, Arthur, and Alfred are all names in Milton's *History of Britain* (which continues up to the Norman Conquest).

For us today, by contrast, it is only the last four names—Alfred, William the Norman Conqueror, and the Plantagenet brothers, Richard and John—who are undeniably historical kings and therefore "real" in the modern sense of the word, within the framework of a materialist philosophy. Some would argue that all the preceding names, including that of Arthur himself, are those of mythical beings. The existence of Satan, Cain, Tubal, and Nimrod is a question of religious belief; the Pharoahs of course were historical, but we cannot prove the historicity of *the* Pharoah referred to in Exodus. Troy existed, but we cannot prove the historicity of Priam; there is no evidence for Bladud or Belin being historical characters. As for Arthur, the jury is still out. Scholars such as Thomas Green have powerfully argued that Arthur was probably in origin a mythical being who was later historicized.[2]

But in suggesting that King Arthur may never have had a historical existence, however historically significant his story may be, I run the risk of encountering (or unintentionally creating) a misunderstanding as damaging as that which would reduce the *mundus imaginalis* to something merely imaginary. If Arthur is "just" a myth, does that in any way diminish his reality?

To the contrary, I would argue that the mythic is an order of reality in the imaginal world, just as the historic is an order of reality in the material world. Myth is just as real as history on its own plane of existence, and the mythic plane affects our lives today as much as, if not more than, the historic. Twentieth-century scholars have postulated the nature of myth to be the depiction of a symbolic truth as important to our understanding of ourselves as the literal truth of history. But to argue this point at length here would take us too far from our theme—so I refer to the Appendix the reader who is interested in the way myths continue to speak to the modern mentality.

For earlier scholars such as Gibbon, steeped in Enlightenment rationalism, the dualism was not between myth and history, but between fact and fable—stories were either literally true, or they were false. Even the poet Milton seems to have adopted such a test for the Arthurian stories, although he and Gibbon came out on different sides of the argument about the historicity of Arthur. They both dismissed as "fable" all that could not be consigned to "history."

For Blake, by contrast, the choice is not between fact and fable, but between fable and vision. Fables for Blake are stories based on allegory, which is quite distinct from vision ("Vision or Imagination is a Representation of what Eternally Exists, Really & Unchangeably"). They constitute an "inferior kind of Poetry" because they are "Form'd by the daughters of Memory," whereas the visionary imagination "is surrounded by the daughters of Inspiration." Nevertheless "Fable or Allegory is seldom without some Vision" (*BCW*, 604). The fables of King Arthur and his Round Table may likewise contain elements of imaginative vision, and it is precisely this eternal reality at their core that Blake attempts to reconstruct in his epic of Albion, which is nothing less than an imaginative mythos revealing the spiritual truth *within* British history.

Blake's Arthur stands at the midpoint of his mythos, at the intersection of myth and history, as Blake's England is situated at the intersection of Earth and Eternity. The spiritual Albion falls, becomes but a shadow of his former self, but will awake. The *space* where he sleeps is described by Blake as the Death Couch of Albion, "the Void Outside of Existence, which if enter'd into/Becomes a Womb" (534), which is to say, becomes a place of rebirth.

This womb-like place from which the Sleeping Lord will be reborn is Layamon's Avalon, the elf-realm of Argante, Queen of Faerie, but in the *Brut* it is not yet perceived as an existential void, because in the Middle Ages, before the Protestant Reformation, Faerie was still seen as a reality contiguous with our own, mortal realm. Arthur could sail there, in Pridwen, or be ferried there, after the Last Battle, to be healed of his wounds. Faerie was an intermediate world between Heaven and Earth, an imaginal interworld, a very British (and, as the centuries moved on, an increasingly *English*) landscape within the *mundus imaginalis*.

And it is precisely this world between the worlds that Blake revivifies when he bids us see through the Imaginative Eye, for the spiritual imagination is the faculty which we require in order to perceive this lost world on the threshold of the soul. In the Prefatory Poem to *Europe: A Prophecy* (1794), one of his earliest illuminated books, it is a "fairy" who appears to the poet to remind him of the existence of other worlds.

"Five windows light the cavern'd man," the fairy declares, reminding us that "man has closed himself up, till he sees all things thro' narrow chinks of his cavern" (120). Through one of these windows, the sense of sight, he "can look/And see small portions of the eternal world that ever groweth." The poet asks the fairy: "Then tell me, what is the material world, and is it dead?" To which the fairy replies that he will show Blake "all alive/The world, when every particle of dust breathes forth its joy." When the poet gathers wildflowers, the fairy shows him "each eternal flower" (237f).

To caverned man, whose vision has shrunk so that he can only perceive dead matter, the fairy appears as a messenger from another world, the imaginal world, to teach him to look at the world anew: not to believe the lie that rules our minds when we limit our perceptions to the physical senses ("This Life's dim Windows of the Soul") and see only with the eye,

> That was born in a night, to perish in a night,
> When the Soul slept in the beams of Light [753].

But if we see *through* the perishable eye (and not *with* it) we see with another eye: the Imaginative Eye, which shows us the world all alive, every particle of dust breathing, eternity in a flower. This is to see with the eyes of Faerie.

Layamon's fays come to bless Arthur at his birth and to welcome him at his passing into another universe. Spenser's Faerie Queen leads him in his youth to see that world, just beyond the fields we know, and Blake shows us what it is to encounter the world of Faerie, not as allegory, but as vision.

# Epilogue

## *Believing Vision*

... were it not better to believe Vision
With all our might & strength, tho' we are fallen & lost?[1]
—William Blake, 1822

The disappearance of Blake's painting "The Ancient Britons" is not just a loss to the world of art; it is also a symbol of what else has been lost in modern Britain. We know that beneath the fields and streets of England is buried a historical Celtic past, and beneath that, the prehistoric, aboriginal world of the people who built Stonehenge. And we know that beneath our modern Christian and post–Christian, secular culture there is a pagan antiquity, with its own religion and mythology.

Scholars such as Jung and Corbin have followed poets such as Blake and Yeats in postulating myths to be not merely fables, but rather the visionary truth of the imagination. They have shown how their symbolic language speaks more profoundly to our souls than do historical facts. In doing so, these poets and scholars have excavated a buried world of the imagination that has no place in the dualist paradigm which opposes spirit to matter, body to soul, and which opens the door to, on one hand, scientism and, on the other, religious fundamentalism. For the place of the imagination is rather as a bridge between Heaven and Earth; and once we restore the Human Imagination ("which is the Divine Vision & Fruition/In which Man liveth eternally" [*BCW*, 521]) to its rightful place, we rescue the soul from dualism and find again the lost continent that is the imaginal world.

With the rediscovery of the imaginal comes the restoration of the three-fold nature of being, the loss of which Corbin described as a metaphysical tragedy: a threefoldness that is fundamental to the Matter of Britain, for it lies at the very foundation of our civilization. Diana, the goddess who guides the first human beings to these shores, is a threefold divinity: she is the bright moon as Queen of Heaven and Earth, celestial traveller and mighty huntress, but she is also the dark moon as Queen of the Underworld. Hence Milton's Brutus, following Geoffrey of Monmouth, invoked her as Goddess of three reigns.

The realm of Britain, which Diana is instrumental in founding, reaches the apogee of its ancient glory in the figure of Arthur, who, whether or not he was originally a deity or a historical warlord, is certainly our greatest legendary king. His myth reveals him also to have a threefold reign.

He is not just king of the earthly realm of Logris; after his death he becomes, like Diana, a supernatural hunter. He becomes the King of the Woods, who is sometimes heard in the forests, hunting with his hounds. But if he is the Wild Huntsman, a Lord of the Earth, he is also a celestial traveller, riding his chariot, which is the Bear that gives him his name, or he is Arcturus, the Guardian of the Pole.

Thus Arthur, after his death, is found both above and below, but he is also in-between, in that intermediate realm that can only be perceived by the Imaginative Eye. To the modern psychological mind, it is the unconscious, the symbolic world of psychic images, but to the medieval imagination, it was the elf realm, Annwfn in Welsh or Faerie in English, Avalon in its uniquely Arthurian incarnation. Where Diana is the beautiful goddess of shades, Argante is the fairest of elves, Queen of Avalon, and in that Fortunate Isle blest by the Fates, Arthur dwells with his Faerie Queen. Arthur's myth takes us from Albion to Avalon, across the sea to the Otherworld; it leads us down into that underworld of the soul where we too can be touched by the glamour of Faerie and cease to hear the mind-forged manacles. Here we encounter the Sleeping Lord. Folktales tell of the danger of awakening the sleeper before his time, but not what that time is, or what the inner meaning of his awakening may be.

For Blake, the awakening of the Sleeping Lord on his death-couch is a resurrection, which he sees as a vision of the Last Judgment. This will occur when our spiritual traditions are finally ground up by the dark satanic mills of a mechanistic universe, the shrunken universe that can be seen with the "single vision" of literalism and materialism: when, as Blake puts it, "Imagination, Art & Science & all Intellectual Gifts" are despised. We must remember that Blake is not against science, any more than he rejects reason. Just as he warns against the monster that reason turns into when it is divorced from imagination, so he warns against the "fixing" of science into a materialist ideology, into scientism. By contrast, "sweet science" is one of "the Gifts of the

Holy Ghost" (*BCW*, 604). When we reject these gifts, the Last Judgment begins.

But though, from this, it would appear that the Last Judgment occurs at an end point in linear time, bringing about the end of time ("the Savior ... appear'd to Me as Coming to Judgment among his Saints & throwing off the Temporal that the Eternal might be Establish'd" [606]), it is also an event that we can experience in vision, seen by the Imaginative Eye. Although this event occurs when society ("Which is Humanity itself") reaches a spiritual nadir ("A Last Judgment is Necessary because Fools flourish"), it can be experienced by each of us, conversely, when we, amidst the chaos that is the sleep of Albion, embrace the gifts of the Holy Ghost: "What are all the Gifts of the Spirit but Mental Gifts? Whenever any Individual Rejects Error & Embraces Truth, a Last Judgment passes upon that Individual." But "a Man Can only Reject Error by the Advice of a Friend or by the Immediate Inspiration of God" (612–4). Blake's equation of friendship with divine inspiration as the source of Truth is perhaps surprising, until we remember that Blake always sees, at the spiritual core of every individual human being, the Eternal Great Humanity Divine whose archetype is Jesus the Imagination.

From whatever source inspiration comes, it brings with it a vision that is different for everyone "according to the situation he holds" (604), since "Every body does not see alike .... As a man is, So he Sees" (793). For Blake, the artist waging mental war against the materialist delusion, the Last Judgment is "an Overwhelming of Bad Art & Science." In his painting of this, as with his other "stupendous visions," Blake attempts to put his art at the service of Eternity, burning up the "outward Creation" that is seen *with* the corporeal eye. By seeing *through* the physical sense of sight, Blake sees instead with the Imaginative Eye, so that "Truth or Eternity will appear" (617).

He sees Jesus, who *is* the Human Imagination, throwing off time in order to establish the Eternal. Among "the Images of Existences" that he can comprehend "in their Eternal Forms in the divine body of the Savior" (605f), he sees the aged patriarch Albion ("our Ancestor, patriarch of the Atlantic Continent, whose History Preceded that of the Hebrews & in whose Sleep, or Chaos, Creation began") being awoken by his aged wife, Britannia (609).

Since Arthur is the manifestation of the sleeping Albion, the awakening of the aged patriarch is also the long awaited return of the once and future king, the wounded Messiah, not as a spectre but in tenfold splendor. Arthur's return is the restoration of the Golden Age, which is the goal of Blake's visionary work: not as a future event, but as an imaginative experience that throws off the temporal so that the eternal can appear.

The appearance of Eternity, in that hour when Arthur returns, transforms the world we know. For, though some believe that he is buried in Glastonbury, there is no grave for the mythic Arthur, whose wondrous presence touches hills and caves, rivers and lakes, forests and meadows throughout Britain. Wherever he and his knights were fabled to fight and love, wherever Merlin prophesied or cast his enchantments, wherever Logris borders Faerie—wherever the messianic king is believed to sleep, his awakening brings the landscape to life. And everything that lives is holy.

But if Arthur's return restores to its eternal reality every place touched by the myth of the Sleeping Lord, what of the people who dwell there, within the embrace of the outstretched limbs of the giant Albion? As Scotland and Wales rediscover their nationhood, the second Elizabethan Age is also beginning to see the emergence of a new sense of Englishness. Who better to provide us with a myth of England than "English Blake," as he called himself (187), whose words to "Jerusalem" arguably deserve to be the English national anthem.

But Blake's imagined Englishness is not something narrow or parochial; rather, it is through his inspiration that the English can see renewed their own sense of themselves as Britons, as Europeans, as humans. For the myths of Arthur, like the myths of all nations, speak to the Imagination, which is "the Human Existence itself" (*BCW*, 522).

Blake's vision of England stretches back beyond the Norman, Saxon, and Roman conquests, to the ancient Britons and their Druids, who received the Everlasting Gospel of Jesus and knew it to be the Gospel of the Imagination before the fall into literalism, when the stars fled from Albion's Druid rocky shore. The story of Albion's incarnation as Arthur, who promises to return in tenfold splendor, is the story of the reversal of the Fall, and the promise of return is kept alive by bards or poets. In the intervening centuries, the foundational work of English poets such as Layamon and Spenser in establishing an English mythology is brought to its fruition by Blake, who illuminates the Matter of Britain through his visionary art.

"The Ancient Britons," had it survived, could be seen as the final part of a group of pictures illustrating the legendary history of a Britain that would become "England." The first picture in this group would be Blake's 1773 engraving of Joseph of Arimathea among the rocks of Albion; the second, his watercolor of 1779 depicting Brutus landing on the shore of Albion; the third would be his colored etching of 1794, showing Joseph of Arimathea preaching the Everlasting Gospel to the ancient Britons; and the final part would be the lost picture of the Last Battle.

But in order to complete our gallery of Blake's pictures of the Matter of

Britain, this group needs to be viewed next to his famous painting of Albion rising up at dawn ("Glad Day," 1794), which is a both a self-portrait of the poet himself, transfigured, and, at the same time, a visionary landscape, the embodied land transformed. For the land promised to Brutus is not just over-run with giants; the land *is* a sleeping giant. We await not just the return of Arthur, but the awakening of Albion. Only then can he be reunited with his "other half," Jerusalem, which was built here in the time before time, once upon a time, among the "dark Satanic mills" of a mechanistic universe, and will be built again, when time is no more—not because time has reached the end of the line, but because it has been transcended, through vision.

When Blake asks whether Jesus walked upon England's mountains, he is not concerned with history as Gibbon understood it, but with a visionary event that occurs on the threshold of the soul world, the *mundus imaginalis:* the Otherworld that English poets from Layamon to Spenser and on into the present day have called Avalon or Faerie. To believe in Faerie is to believe vision.

There was no "England" in the literal sense when Jesus lived on earth, in the early days of the Roman Empire, any more than there was when Brutus landed twelve hundred years earlier or when his son Locrinus founded Loegria, Arthur's Kingdom of Logris. Arthur's Logris becomes England after the Last Battle, when the Spectre of Albion changes his life. Thus Los, the Eternal Prophet, sees "The Briton, Saxon, Roman, Norman amalgamating ... into One Nation, the English; & taking refuge/In the Loins of Albion" (*BCW*, 739). The four peoples who fought each other to make the English nation are like the four Zoas who fought each other to make the sacred history that is the death and judgment of the Eternal Man. In the awakening of vision that is Blake's Last Judgment, the four are made one and Albion becomes whole once more. Thus, where Brutus's Britain is a place of glorious conquest and Joseph of Arimathea's Logris one of religious conversion, Blake's England is a place of epiphany.

Jerusalem will be built again, Albion made whole, when we believe vision, for in Blake's Promised Land, there is no gospel but the imagination.

# *Appendix: Masterful Images*

Those masterful images because complete
Grew in pure mind, but out of what began?
—W. B. Yeats, 1939

Throughout this work I have argued that, while there is no conclusive evidence for the historical existence of King Arthur, his story continues to maintain a powerful hold on the western imagination. In fact, this hold may be all the more powerful precisely because the story is not limited to the historical record. Early British kings such as Cunobelinus or the Emperor Carausius, who we know "really" existed, have no such legacy.

The story of Arthur, I maintain, is best described as a legend, because it inhabits the mysterious intersection of history and mythology. A legendary character is one whose historicity (however solid or tenuous in the first place) has been overtaken by its mythical attributes, but to understand what this means, we must also ask what we mean by "myth."

## "What, then, is myth?"

This question was asked at the outbreak of the Second World War, in front of an international audience of European scholars by a German professor of classical philology, Walter F. Otto (1874–1958). The occasion was an annual gathering, which continues to this day, at which experts in various disciplines meet to share their researches into the wisdom of the past, many of them in the hope that we can learn how to renew our western tradition. This gathering is called "Eranos," a Greek word meaning a banquet at which everyone would bring food to share, and it has been held every year but one since its inception in 1933. The year that Professor Otto attended was 1939, and the theme that linked all the contributions was "The Symbolism of Rebirth."

Otto's lecture focused on the Eleusinian mysteries, the most famous and longest-lived of the Mediterranean mystery cults that offered eternal life through rebirth to its initiates, a thousand years before Jesus Christ extended the offer to all who would believe in Him. In his lecture, Otto (29) gave a powerful answer to his own question. Myth, he said, is:

> An old story, lived by the ancestors and handed down to the descendants. But the past is only one aspect of it. The true myth is inseparably bound up with the cult. The once-upon-a-time is also a now; what was is also a living event. Only in its twofold unity of then and now does a myth fulfill its true essence. The cult is its present form, the re-enactment of an archetypal event, situated in the past but in essence eternal.

The accuracy of Otto's definition would to some degree be borne out by events that were taking place all around the neutral enclave of Switzerland, where the Eranos conferences are held.

In 1933, in Germany, a myth that developed in the Near East and the Mediterranean but that, thanks to Christian evangelism, has now spread throughout the world—the Myth of the Redeemer—began to be reenacted in the Third Reich, which its supporters hoped would last as long as the Eleusinian Mysteries, through the cult of Nazism. In 1939 this cult attempted to bring about, through the Second World War, the death and rebirth of the West.

The sacred center of this cult was a castle in the northern Rhineland that was rebuilt by the SS in order to serve as the *axis mundi* or "world center" of the victorious, spiritually renewed Germany that would emerge after the war was won. At the Wewelsburg Castle in Westphalia were invoked the names of King Arthur and the Grail (Goodrick-Clarke, 125f), an archetypal figure and a symbolic image that constitute the most numinous elements in a western European version of the Myth of the Redeemer, in which the vessel containing Christ's Holy Blood, the Sangreal, becomes the object of a mystical quest; while, for lovers of "Nazi Mysteries," it becomes the object of an unholy quest undertaken by the Ancestral Heritage Division of the SS (122f).

If Arthur is the British Messiah, Hitler was, for many of his supporters, the Germanic Redeemer who had brought about "national salvation and rebirth" (Kershaw, 840) and who would go on to save the West from International Jewry and Bolshevism. There could be no capitulation to these forces, but only a heroic resistance to the end, even if it meant the destruction of Germany as well as its Führer (740)—for the land and its leader are one. If Hitler was prepared to take the world with him (747), his heroic sacrifice would lead to a renaissance of National Socialism (822), while his acolytes saw his struggle against Underworld powers as a Wagnerian "twilight," to be followed by a rebuilding of the citadel of the gods (789).

The Wewelsburg was de-sanctified in 1945, when the Third Reich fell, but the legend of Himmler's "Black Camelot" lives on in the popular imagination, and key events from the history of the Nazis are celebrated and reenacted by the spiritual descendants of the cult. There are even now "esoteric Hitlerists" who believe that the "ultimate avatar" is still waging esoteric war against the forces of the Demiurge (Goodrick-Clarke, 188–90): "What was," as Otto puts it, "is also a living event."

We may dismiss the political and spiritual continuity of the Nazi cult as the activity of a "lunatic fringe," but it is nevertheless a testimony to the "twofold unity of then and now" of which Otto spoke. If the Nazi cult reveals the dark side of the Myth of the Redeemer, it is no less an indication that the "once-upon-a-time is also a now" than is the powerful presence within twenty-first-century culture, if not within our belief system, of the image of the Sleeping Lord. King Arthur is the once and future king who will awake at his country's greatest time of need; he is the archetypal image of the hero who is "situated in the past but in essence eternal."

## The Lost Continent

Otto's definition of myth is by no means the one most commonly used, so it is necessary quickly to dispense with another answer to his question, because unfortunately it is one that is ingrained (perhaps for explicable reasons) in modern usage. Nowadays, when we say that something is "just a myth" we mean, invariably, something that is widely believed to be true but that is, in fact, false.

But for the Eranos scholars, this is "just" wrong. A myth is precisely a story that is widely believed to be false but that is, in reality, true.

The reason for this paradoxical state of affairs is not hard to find. We moderns in the West accept only one level of factual reality: the material, which must have its location in secular time and space, in history and geography. A story that cannot be located in either must, therefore, be false.

We have lost our sense of the reality of other worlds. Our conscious lives have become "a sleep and a forgetting," in Wordsworth's phrase (*WPW*, 460). By contrast, as we saw in Chapter Four, ancient western peoples experienced three universes. What we today would call the "real" world, the physical world of sensory phenomena, is only the lowest of these; there is also an intermediate world of psychic images and a "higher" world of archetypes.

One of the scholars who gravitated to Eranos after the Second World War, the Romanian historian of religions Mircea Eliade, saw archetypes as institutional models and behavioral norms for the people of "traditional and archaic societies," who believed them "to have been 'revealed' at the beginning of time" and who, consequently, regarded them "as having a superhuman and 'transcendental' origin" (Eliade, xiv). These transcendental exemplary models and superhuman paradigms are thus the archetypal basis of religion and culture, while the idea that the archetypal images of mythology return to haunt the dreams and fantasies of modern, agnostic humanity was a theme explored particularly by Eliade's colleague at Eranos (and the inspiration for its founding), Carl Jung.

Jung (1946, 410–26) thought of archetypes as "psychic instincts," by which he meant the primordial matrices from which human thought and behavior evolve. While Jung always insisted that the archetype is unknowable in itself, he explored in numerous writings the way in which archetypes reveal themselves in the soul by clothing themselves in images drawn from sensory perception. These archetypal images, what Yeats called "masterful images," are thus a bridge between the higher and lower worlds, reflecting one to the other, as the soul acts as a bridge between body and spirit in the traditional threefold model of the human being.

But during the Middle Ages, this threefold model of being was gradually replaced by a binary one: body and soul, mind and matter—opposites pulling apart and in conflict. An ancient harmony, the balance of the cosmos, was lost; the human being became a divided self.

All that did not fit into the one reality was dismissed as merely imaginary, while the true power of the creative imagination to transform consciousness was dismissed alike by religious fundamentalists and by the apostles of scientism, for both of whom there is only one reality: for the religious, the literal truth of sacred texts; for the scientific materialists, what can be observed either through their bodily senses or through the technology produced by their minds.

Myths, on the other hand, are the products of the creative imagination. They come from the intermediate world, so they speak to the soul. And they speak of truths that cannot be limited to the straightjacket of literalism, whether religious or scientific. For those whose "mind-forged manacles" can be heard in their voices, myths speak only of falsehood, but for those who acknowledge a separate reality, the lost world of the soul is heard through the imaginative voice of myth.

If myths speak from and to the soul, we can understand that a world without soul is one where myths are seen as "really" false. But for the scholars at Eranos, there are other worlds, and throughout much of the twentieth century, they explored those worlds on behalf of "modern man in search of his soul," meeting every year at Ascona in Switzerland, on the banks of Lake Maggiore. There, at symposia to which each speaker brought a gift of insight, they presented the fruits of their researches and revealed their discoveries.

A presiding spirit of Eranos in its first decades was Jung, who believed that, in order to truly *be* in the soul (*esse in anima*) it was necessary to hold the tension of the opposites: to surmount their destructive dualism by making of them, in Blake's phrase, *contraries* without which there is no progression. He believed that the opposites could come together in a sacred marriage, a *coniunctio oppositorum* that is itself a form of death and the necessary prelude to rebirth. Such a death and rebirth, he argued, was essential not just for the modern individual, but for western culture.

It was Jung who did perhaps more than anyone else in the twentieth century to rescue mythology from the "rag-and-bone shop of the heart"[1] to which so many of the treasures of pre-scientific culture had been consigned. Myths are, he argued, as "true" on their own plane of reality as the theories of natural science (the stories we tell ourselves about the nature of the physical world) are on theirs (1967, 159). They only appear to contradict each other because they are the products of different planes of reality, of different universes.

To put it another way: science deals with literal facts, myths with symbolic truths. And it is above all the symbol, the "masterful" image, which bridges the gulf between the material and the archetypal worlds. And here it is necessary to clarify that, by *symbol* we do not mean a mere sign or representation in a different form of something we already know. The true symbol, on the contrary, is the only possible expression of a reality that cannot be apprehended in any other way. In effect, it gives perceptible form to that reality.

Thus Jung, in a lecture he delivered at Eranos during the Second World War, explained that a symbol is "the best expression possible," given the human tendency for anthropomorphizing, "for something suprahuman and only partly conceivable." Nevertheless, "it ranks below the level of the mystery it seeks to describe" (1940, 278). Jung was clear that a symbol is not merely an allegorical image or a simple sign: "The symbol ... is so far beyond the grasp of language that it cannot be expressed at all in any unambiguous manner" (319).

The importance of symbolic images to the soul was also stressed by Henry Corbin, who, like Eliade, was a regular lecturer at Eranos after the Second World War and who, like Jung before him, was keen to stress the difference between symbol and allegory. Thus "the allegory is a sheathing," he wrote, "or, rather, a disguising, of something that is already known or knowable otherwise, while the appearance of an Image having the quality of a symbol is a primary phenomenon" (Corbin 1995, 18). That is to say, it cannot be reduced to anything else, although it can be understood on many different levels.[2]

As I showed in Chapter Four, Corbin is the scholar who revealed to modern man a world that had become lost in the West during the Middle Ages, the "imaginal" world, or *mundus imaginalis,* an inner universe with its own faculty of perception. This world, Corbin explained in a lecture he delivered at Eranos in 1965, is "an intermediary world" between the material world we perceive with our physical senses and the abstract world we apprehend with our intelligence. As the soul is the intermediary between spirit and body, so the *mundus imaginalis* is "the kingdom of subtle bodies," the place "where spirit takes on body and where the body is spiritualized." It is perceived by the cognitive power of the active imagination (1986, 186).

In his exploration of the active imagination, Corbin was walking in the footsteps of Jung, who already, in his Eranos lecture of 1935, had contrasted the *imaginatio vera,* or "true imagination," of the medieval alchemists, which enabled them to achieve their goal of creating the Philosopher's Stone, with the "fantastic imagination" that leads the soul astray—into a fantasy world with which the modern world is only too familiar, deluged as it is with images that do nothing but attach us further to the material world and its allurements and whose evocation is the inversion of the true imagination. By contrast, the "active evocation" of images that express an inner reality is the true alchemical *opus* (Jung 1935, 395f).

This alchemical work, as Corbin has explained, sustains a universe, that world whose organ of perception is the *Imaginatio vera,* the world he calls the *mundus imaginalis*—a term he coined, as he pointed out in a lecture given in 1974, "in order to avoid any confusion with what is commonly designated *imaginary.*" But this imaginal world, for us in the West, "has for some centuries been a lost continent" (1986, 265).

The reason for this, according to Corbin, is twofold. In the first place, there was the loss of the threefold model, whereby the human being was understood to consist of body, soul and spirit. This "anthropological triad" was replaced in the thought of the Christian West with "the dualism of soul and body ... of thought and extension." Secondly, there was the triumph of a rationalistic philosophy, which entailed the overthrow of the sovereignty of the active or "true" imagination and, with it, the in-between world of the soul.

"What remains," Corbin laments, "is an imagination whose products are now declared to be merely *imaginary,*" that is to say, fantastic or unreal. And, lacking the Imaginative Eye of the soul, our vision of the cosmos becomes reduced or *shrunk,* as Blake would say, to that mechanistic universe operated by dark Satanic mills. We perceive only "the desacralization of the world"; we become disenchanted (276).

## Return from Exile

But if man has lost his own soul, where now is it to be found?

The answer, according to Jung and to James Hillman (the founder of the Post-Jungian school of archetypal psychology and Eliade's and Corbin's colleague at Eranos during the sixties and seventies), is that it has been exiled to the unconscious psyche and has been replaced as the center, the heart of our being, by the ego, that discriminating "I" that is, in the modern world, the center of consciousness.

As Hillman explained in his Eranos lecture of 1967, the ego has an "affinity for light," but wherever it focuses its harsh glare, it creates a greater darkness at the edges (13). Whereas archetypal reality "is ambivalent and paradoxical, embracing both spirit and nature, psyche and matter, consciousness and unconsciousness," the ego has a tendency to see things in black and white, to turn the archetype's "continual dawning" into the sharp contrast between day and night, to harden the archetype's potential for polarity into conflicting opposites (12). This conflict, says Hillman, "is tearing the soul apart."

Traditionally, as we have seen, the soul had always been the "third factor" that held the tension of the opposites, existing "half-way between Heaven and Hell, spirit and flesh, inner and outer." It is the soul, not the ego, which "holds polarities in harmony," or which, for example, as I have discussed elsewhere,[3] connects or "conjoins" the knower with the object of his knowledge, whether it be the natural world, other people, or his own inner spaces. This "conjunctive knowledge," which is the basis for that innate sympathy between man and nature that enables us to live in harmony with our environment, is in contrast with what Hillman calls the "disjunctive rationalism" of the ego, which "makes divisions where the soul gives feeling connections and mythic unities."

As a result, the potential for polarity of the archetype turns into a deep split, which only the soul can heal, if it is allowed "to return from its exile in the unconscious" (14). Now, Hillman is speaking theoretically, as well as from his experience as a psychotherapist. But it is very striking that this splitting of the primordial, archetypal wholeness was vividly described in mythical images by Blake, writing over a hundred and fifty years earlier, as the murder and dismemberment of the divine body by "the Sons of Albion":

> They take the Two Contraries which are call'd Qualities, with which
> Every Substance is clothed; they name them Good & Evil;

From them they make an Abstract, which is a Negation
Not only of the Substance from which it is derived,
A murderer of its own Body, but also a murderer
Of every Divine Member: it is the Reasoning Power,
An Abstract objecting power that Negatives everything.
This is the Spectre of Man ... [*BCW*, 629].

The Holy Reasoning Power, when separated from the whole, becomes an abomination: an imbalanced and murderous Spectre that negates the Imagination—which *is,* for Blake, the Divine Body. Thus, when Albion falls from eternal wholeness into divided creation, his "sons" turn "contraries," what Hillman calls harmonious polarities, into "negations" that are tearing the soul apart. But "Negations are not Contraries: Contraries mutually Exist; /But Negations Exist Not" (639).

Albion finds that his archetypal reality is being negated and that he is in danger of falling into non-existence, but through divine mercy, he is given a material form: he becomes a physical giant who, at first, stretches out over the whole world but who gradually shrinks into the island that once bore his name but that is now called Britain.

His sons become the giants who once ruled this island, while the fallen Albion himself, though he lies in a deathlike sleep, projects his "spectrous" self into a series of kings who, at different pre-historical and historical periods, rule Britain after the defeat of the giants. One of these kings is that Dark Age prince called Arthur, who is a renowned giant-killer.

Thus, for Blake, myth does not negate history, and vice versa ("Eternity is in love with the productions of time" [151]). King Arthur is both a historical fifth-century prince *and* the spectre of the mythical giant Albion; he is one of the manifestations of the Eternal Man in time and space.

# Chapter Notes

## Prologue

1. Gawain is descended from the Welsh hero Gwalchmai, "a figure of folklore of some antiquity" (Green, 190), if not, as earlier scholars speculated, a Celtic solar hero or sun god (Weston, 13–7).

2. The case for an influence has been made by Judith H. Anderson, 192–4.

## Chapter One

1. Lawrence, 175.

2. The text of Milton's *History of Britain* is available from the Online Library of Liberty: http://oll.libertyfund.org.

3. *WPW*, 80f.

4. To avoid confusion I will use the traditional English spelling of the name of Arthur's queen throughout. Layamon in fact calls her Wenhauer and Blake, Gwiniverra. Both spellings are ultimately dependent on a Welsh original, as I show in Chapter Six.

## Chapter Two

1. *WPW*, 80.

2. Entry under "Termagant": Skeat, 499.

3. For a discussion of Gnosticism and its relationship to the Grail legend, see Weston (1993) and my *Gawain and the Grail Quest*.

## Chapter Three

1. *DC*, 71f.

2. Rachel Bromwich, the editor and translator of the Triads of the Island of Britain, says that Welsh poets do not distinguish between Helen of Troy, the Empress Helena, and Elen of the Hosts (*TYP*, 343).

3. According to Bromwich, Elen "appears to have been a character of early Welsh mythology who was particularly associated with the Roman roads in Wales (hence her epithet *Lluydog* "of the Hosts"). The Roman roads are known to this day as *Sarn(au) Helen*" (*TYP*, 342). She may have become identified with the British bride of Maximus, from whom the ruling families of Dyfed and Powys claimed descent, because she was, in origin, an ancestral deity of ancient British mythology (442f).

4. This is the position of Jeffrey Gantz (*TM*, 118), as stated in his introduction to "The Dream of Maxen," which he has translated into English for the Penguin Classics edition of *The Mabinogion*.

5. For Helen as a goddess, see Kerényi 1959, 326f. The stories of the twice-abducted Helen (238) and the curious legend of her being whisked off to Egypt while a phantom took her place in Troy (360) must remind us of the oft-abducted Guinevere, whose name means "white phantom" (as we will see in Chapter Six).

6. "Gnosis was not ... a simple Christian heresy of the first centuries of our era; rather, it is something that existed long before Christianity. There was a gnosis in Christianity; there has been one, and perhaps there still is, in Islam—and perhaps it may yet provide for an unforeseeable spiritual encounter between Orient and Occident. For gnosis itself, in all

its manifold forms and variants, also deserves to be called a *Weltreligion*" (Corbin 1983, 192f).

7. For the twentieth century's re-evaluation of the early heresies, see the Appendix ("Gnosis and Gnosticism") to my *Gawain and the Grail Quest,* 183–190.

8. Gibbon's lament for this "endarkenment" is characteristically eloquent: "By the revolution of Britain, the limits of science, as well as of empire, were contracted. The dark cloud, which had been ... dispelled by the arms of Cæsar, again settled on the shores of the Atlantic, and a Roman province was again lost among the fabulous islands of the Ocean. One hundred and fifty years after the reign of Honorius, the gravest historian of the times describes the wonders of a remote isle, whose eastern and western parts are divided by an antique wall, the boundary of life and death, or, more properly, of truth and fiction" (*DF* 2, 505f).

## Chapter Four

1. See Dixon, 120–139.

## Chapter Five

1. In an essay entitled "Arthur and the Academics," the British historian Ronald Hutton gives an entertaining and salutary overview of the changing fortunes of the proponents and opponents of a historical Arthur throughout the twentieth century. He expresses unease at "the current tendency among specialists to write off Arthur altogether" since it "begs the enormous question of how a character who may never have existed came, within three hundred years of his presumed lifetime, to be the greatest hero of his people" (Hutton 2003, 58).

2. The association of Arthur with Hercules may be traced back to Breton sources that predate Geoffrey of Monmouth (Green, 104). For Spenser's presentation of Arthur as the "rival of Hercules," see Hughes, 216–25.

## Chapter Six

1. The *Morte Arthure* is an anonymous poem dating from c. 1400 CE. It used the alliterative verse form that was typical of Anglo-Saxon poetry but was also used by Layamon, who, along with Wace, was one of the author's sources. The poem in turn was used by Malory for "The Tale of King Arthur and the Emperor Lucius," which constitutes Book V of Caxton's edition of *Le Morte Darthur.* In this and the following chapter, I have used the *Morte Arthure* to supplement Layamon's account of the Roman War and the end of Arthur.

## Chapter Seven

1. According to Geoffrey of Monmouth, Merlin prophesied of the Boar of Cornwall that "the House of Rome will tremble before his rage" (*HKB*, 144).

2. Merlin prophesies that Wales and Cornwall will say to Winchester, "the earth will swallow you up ... the day is at hand when your citizens will perish because of their sins of betrayal ... woe to the treacherous people, on whose account a famous city will fall" (*HKB*, 152).

3. "Then the foreigners will be slaughtered, the rivers flow with blood, and the hills of Brittany burst forth and be crowned with Brutus' diadem. Wales will be filled with rejoicing and the Cornish oaks will flourish. The island will be called by Brutus' name and the foreign term ["England"] will disappear" (*HKB*, 148).

4. A translation with a very useful commentary is provided in Loomis 1956, 131–78. He understands it as "a mosaic of Welsh bardic lore about the Other World" (177). The Welsh text, along with a modern English translation by Sarah Higley, is available from the Camelot Project online at: http://www.lib.rochester.edu/camelot/annwn.htm.

5. I am indebted for my interpretation of the symbolism of the number eight to an essay ("The Christian Mystery and the Pagan Mysteries") by the Jesuit scholar Hugo Rahner, which was originally delivered as a lecture at the 1944 Eranos meeting (for which, see the Appendix).

6. This tradition derives less from the sparse canonical sources than from the apocryphal *Acts of John* (Watts, 166–9).

## Chapter Eight

1. The abduction of Guinevere by Meleagant, Prince of Gorre, is reprised by the French prose Romance of Lancelot and forms the bulk of the Nineteenth Book of Caxton's edition of Malory.

## Chapter Nine

1. Quoted in Watts, 19.

2. "It is no longer possible for an assumption to be made that Arthur 'must have' existed. Instead the opposite appears to be true—there is no remotely reliable evidence for his existence and rather the balance of probabilities lies very heavily with him being a figure of folklore, myth or legend historicized by, or in, the ninth century" (Green, 177).

## Epilogue

1. *BCW*, 780.

## Appendix

1. Yeats, 392: This phrase, along with the motto to this Appendix, are taken from "The Circus Animals' Desertion," one of the last poems of W.B. Yeats, who was one of the first to recognize the importance of Blake's "masterful images."

2. Similarly Gershom Scholem, the Israeli historian of Jewish mysticism who lectured at Eranos in the fifties and sixties, argued that allegory is "the representation of an expressible something by another expressible something," whereas the symbol expresses a "hidden and inexpressible reality" which is "the true transcendence.... Where deeper insight into the structure of the allegory uncovers fresh layers of meaning, the symbol is intuitively understood all at once—or not at all.... It is a 'momentary totality' which is perceived intuitively in the mystical *now*—the dimension of time proper to the symbol" (Scholem, 27).

3. See Dixon, 28–30, in which I discuss the theory of "conjunctive" versus "disjunctive" knowledge and suggest that the interweaving of pagan Celtic oral lore with verse romance in medieval France provided us with a "beautiful conjunction" in the form of Arthurian stories.

# Bibliography

## Primary Sources: Texts and Translations

*AGW*—Butler, H. E., ed. and trans. *The Autobiography of Gerald of Wales*. Woodbridge, England: Boydell, 2005.

*AR*—Owen, D.D.R., trans. Chrétien de Troyes, *Arthurian Romances*. London: J.M. Dent, 1987.

*BCW*—Keynes, Geoffrey, ed. *Blake: Complete Writings*. 2nd ed. Oxford, England: Oxford University Press, 1979.

*BH*—Morris, John, ed. and trans. Nennius: *British History* and *The Welsh Annals*. *Arthurian Period Sources* Vol. 8. London: Phillimore, 1980.

*DC*—Myrone, Martin, ed. *William Blake: Seen in My Visions: A Descriptive Catalogue of Pictures*. London: Tate, 2009.

*DF*—Womersley, David, ed. Edward Gibbon, *The History of the Decline and Fall of the Roman Empire*. 2 vols. Harmondsworth, England: Penguin, 1994.

*FQ*—Hamilton, A. C., Hiroshi Yamashita and Toshiyuki Suzuki, eds. Edmund Spenser, *The Faerie Qveene*. 2nd ed. Harlow, England: Longman, 2007.

*HBG*—Bryant, Nigel, trans. *The High Book of the Grail: A Translation of the Thirteenth-Century Romance of Perlesvaus*, Cambridge, England: D.S. Brewer, 1978.

*HKB*—Reeve, Michael, ed., and Neil Wright, trans. Geoffrey of Monmouth, *The History of the Kings of Britain: An Edition and Translation of De Gestis Britonum* [Historia Regum Britanniae]. Woodbridge, England: Boydell, 2009.

*LA*—Barron, W.R.J., and S.C. Weinberg, eds. and trans. *Layamon's Arthur: The Arthurian Section of Layamon's Brut*. 2nd ed. Exeter, England: University of Exeter Press, 2001.

*LAL*—Day, Mildred Leake, ed. and trans. *Latin Arthurian Literature*. Cambridge, England: D.S. Brewer, 2005.

*LB*—Allen, Rosamund, trans. *Lawman's Brut*. London: J.M. Dent, 1993.

*LG*—Lacy, Norris J., ed. *Lancelot-Grail: The Old French Arthurian Vulgate and Post-Vulgate in Translation*. 5 vols. New York: Garland, 1993–6.

*MA*—Stone, Brian, trans. *King Arthur's Death: Alliterative* Morte Arthure *and Stanzaic* Le Morte Arthur. London: Penguin, 1988.

*MCW*—Vinaver, Eugène, ed. *Malory: Complete Works*. 2nd ed. Oxford, England: Oxford University Press, 1971.

*MG*—Bryant, Nigel, trans. *Merlin and the Grail*. Joseph of Arimathea, Merlin, Perceval: *The Trilogy of Arthurian Romances Attributed to Robert de Boron*. Cambridge, England: D.S. Brewer, 2003.

*MMWT*—Ford, Patrick K., trans. *The*

*Mabinogi and other Medieval Welsh Tales.* Berkeley: University of California Press, 1977.

*NHL*—Robinson, James M., ed. *The Nag Hammadi Library in English.* 3rd ed. Leiden, The Netherlands: Brill, 1988.

*PL*—Fowler, Alastair, ed. Milton: *Paradise Lost*, Rev. 2nd ed. London: Longman, 2007.

*PT*—Ricks, Christopher, ed. *The Poems of Tennyson.* London: Longman, 1969.

*RB*—Weiss, Judith, ed. and trans. *Wace's Roman de Brut: A History of the British*, 2nd ed. Exeter, England: University of Exeter Press, 2002.

*SPW*—Robertson, J. Logie, ed. *Scott: Poetical Works.* London: Oxford University Press, 1904.

*TLC*—Thorpe, Lewis, trans. *Two Lives of Charlemagne.* Harmondsworth, England: Penguin, 1969.

*TM*—Gantz, Jeffrey, trans. *The Mabinogion.* Harmondsworth, England: Penguin, 1976.

*TYP*—Bromwich, Rachel, ed. and trans. *Trioedd Ynys Prydein: The Triads of the Island of Britain.* 3rd ed. Cardiff: University of Wales Press, 2006.

*VM*—Clarke, Basil, ed. and trans. Geoffrey of Monmouth: Vita Merlini: *Life of Merlin.* Cardiff: University of Wales Press, 1973.

*WPW*—Hutchinson, Thomas and de Selincourt, Ernest, eds. *Wordsworth: Poetical Works*, Rev. ed. London: Oxford University Press, 1936.

*WSG*—Shepherd, Stephen H.A., ed. "The Wedding of Sir Gawain and Dame Ragnell for the Helping of King Arthur." *Middle English Romances.* New York: Norton, 1995.

*YCP*—Yeats, W.B. *Collected Poems.* 2nd ed. London: Macmillan, 1950.

## Secondary Sources

Ackroyd, Peter. *Blake.* London: Sinclair-Stevenson, 1995.

Anderson, Judith H. "Arthur, Argante, and the Ideal Vision: An Exercise in Speculation and Parody." Rpt. in *Arthurian Women*, ed. Thelma S. Fenster. New York: Routledge, 2000, 191–201.

Ashe, Geoffrey. "Glastonbury." *The Arthurian Encyclopedia*, ed. Norris J. Lacy. Woodbridge, England: Boydell, 1986, 237–43.

Barber, Malcolm. *The Cathars: Dualist Heretics in the Languedoc in the High Middle Ages.* Harlow, England: Longman, 2000.

Barron, W.R.J., ed. *The Arthur of the English: The Arthurian Legend in Medieval English Life and Literature*, Rev. ed. Cardiff: University of Wales Press, 2001.

Bentley, G.E., Jr. *The Stranger from Paradise: A Biography of William Blake.* New Haven: Yale University Press, 2001.

Broek, Roelof van den, and Wouter J. Hanegraaff, eds. *Gnosis and Hermeticism: From Antiquity to Modern Times.* Albany: State University of New York Press, 1998.

Brooks, Chris, and Inga Bryden. "The Arthurian Legacy." In *The Arthur of the English*, ed. W.R.J. Barron, 247–64.

Bromwich, Rachel, A.O.H. Jarman, and Brynley F. Roberts, eds. *The Arthur of the Welsh: The Arthurian Legend in Medieval Welsh Literature.* Cardiff: University of Wales Press, 1991.

Campbell, Joseph, ed. *Papers from the Eranos Yearbooks*, Vol. 1: *Spirit and Nature*. Princeton, NJ: Princeton University Press, 1954.

_____. *Papers from the Eranos Yearbooks*, Vol. 2: *The Mysteries*. Princeton, NJ: Princeton University Press, 1955.

_____. *Papers from the Eranos Yearbooks*, Vol. 4: *Spiritual Disciplines*. Princeton, NJ: Princeton University Press, 1960.

Carley, James P. "Arthur in English History." *The Arthur of the English*, ed. W.R.J. Barron, 47–57.

Corbin, Henry. "From the Gnosis of Antiquity to Ismaili Gnosis," Trans. James W. Morris. *Cyclical Time and Ismaili Gnosis.* London: KPI, 1983, 151–93.

_____. "*Mundus Imaginalis*, or, The Imaginary and the Imaginal." *Swedenborg and Esoteric Islam*, Trans. Leonard Fox. Pennsylvania: Swedenborg Foundation, 1955, 1–33.

_____. *Temple and Contemplation.* Trans. Philip Sherrard. London: KPI, 1986.

Damon, S. Foster. *A Blake Dictionary: The Ideas and Symbols of William Blake*, Rev.

ed. Hanover, NH: University of New England Press, 1988.

Darrah, John. *The Real Camelot: Paganism and the Arthurian Romances.* London: Thames & Hudson, 1981.

Dixon, Jeffrey John. *Gawain and the Grail Quest: Healing the Waste Land in our Time.* Edinburgh: Floris, 2012.

Eliade, Mircea. *The Myth of the Eternal Return:* or, *Cosmos and History.* Trans. Willard R. Trask. Princeton, NJ: Princeton University Press, 1971.

Faivre, Antoine. "Renaissance Hermeticism and Western Esotericism." *Gnosis and Hermeticism,* eds. Broek and Hanegraaff, 109–23.

Godwin, Joscelyn. *Arktos: The Polar Myth in Science, Symbolism, and Nazi Survival.* London: Thames & Hudson, 1993.

Goodrick-Clarke, Nicholas. *Black Sun: Aryan Cults, Esoteric Nazism and the Politics of Identity.* New York: New York University Press, 2003.

Gorski, William T. *Yeats and Alchemy.* Albany, NY: State University of New York Press, 1996.

Green, Thomas. *Concepts of Arthur.* Stroud, England: Tempus, 2007.

Harbus, Antonina. *Helena of Britain in Medieval Legend.* Cambridge, England: D.S. Brewer, 2002.

Hillman, James. "Senex and Puer: An Aspect of the Historical and Psychological Present." Rpt. in *Puer Papers,* ed. Cynthia Giles. Dallas: Spring, 1979, 3–53.

Hughes, Merritt Y. "The Arthurs of the *Faerie Queene.*" Rpt. in *King Arthur: A Casebook,* ed. Edward Donald Kennedy. New York: Routledge, 2002, 205–28.

Hutton, Ronald. *The Pagan Religions of the Ancient British Isles.* Oxford, England: Blackwell, 1991.

_____. *Witches, Druids and King Arthur.* London: Hambledon, 2003.

Jarman, A.O.H. "The Merlin Legend and the Welsh Tradition of Prophecy." *The Arthur of the Welsh,* eds. Bromwich, Jarman, and Roberts, 117–45.

Jung, Carl. *Alchemical Studies.* Trans. R.F.C. Hull. London: Routledge & Kegan Paul, 1967.

_____. "Dream Symbols of the Individuation Process." (1935) Trans. R.F.C. Hull. *Papers from the Eranos Yearbooks,* Vol. 4, ed. Joseph Campbell, 1960, 341–423.

_____. "The Spirit of Psychology." (1946) Trans. R.F.C. Hull. *Papers from the Eranos Yearbooks,* Vol. 1, ed. Joseph Campbell, 1954, 371–444.

_____. "Transformation Symbolism in the Mass." (1940) Trans. R.F.C. Hull. *Papers from the Eranos Yearbooks,* Vol. 2, ed. Joseph Campbell, 1955, 274–336.

Kerényi, Carl. *The Gods of the Greeks.* Trans. Norman Cameron. London: Thames & Hudson, 1951.

_____. *The Heroes of the Greeks.* Trans. H.J. Rose. London: Thames & Hudson, 1959.

Kershaw, Ian. *Hitler 1936–45: Nemesis.* London: Allen Lane, 2000.

King, James. *William Blake: His Life.* London: Weidenfeld & Nicolson, 1991.

Lawrence, D.H. *Sketches of Etruscan Places and Other Italian Essays.* Harmondsworth, England: Penguin, 1999.

Loomis, Roger Sherman. *Wales and the Arthurian Legend.* Cardiff: University of Wales Press, 1956.

_____, ed. *Arthurian Literature in the Middle Ages: A Collaborative History.* Oxford, England: Oxford University Press, 1959.

Mac Cana, Proinsias. *Celtic Mythology.* Feltham, England: Newnes, 1983.

Meurs, Jos van. "William Blake and His Gnostic Myths." Rpt. in *Gnosis and Hermeticism,* eds. Broek and Hanegraaff, 269–309.

O'Loughlin, J.L.N. "The English Alliterative Romances." *Arthurian Literature in the Middle Ages,* ed. R.S. Loomis, 520–7.

Otto, Walter F. "The Meaning of the Eleusinian Mysteries" (1939). Trans. Ralph Manheim. *Papers from the Eranos Yearbooks,* Vol. 2, ed. Joseph Campbell, 1955, 14–31.

Rahner, Hugo. "The Christian Mystery and the Pagan Mysteries." Trans. Ralph Manheim. *Papers from the Eranos Yearbooks,* Vol. 2, ed. Joseph Campbell, 1955, 337–401.

Raine, Kathleen. *William Blake.* London: Thames & Hudson, 1970.

Scholem, Gershom. *Major Trends in Jewish Mysticism,* 3d, rev. ed. New York: Schocken, 1961.

Sims-Williams, Patrick. "The Early Welsh Arthurian Poems." *The Arthur of the Welsh*, eds. Bromwich, Jarman, and Roberts, 33–71.

Skeat, Walter W. *Concise Etymological Dictionary of the English Language*. Oxford, England: Oxford University Press, 1884.

Speck, W.A. *Robert Southey: Entire Man of Letters*. New Haven, CT: Yale University Press, 2006.

Starkey, David. "King Henry and King Arthur." *Arthurian Literature XVI*, eds. James P. Carley and Felicity Riddy. Cambridge, England: D.S. Brewer, 1998, 171–196.

Stein, Murray. "The Gnostic Critique, Past and Present." Rpt. in *The Allure of Gnosticism: The Gnostic Experience in Jungian Psychology and Contemporary Culture*, ed. Robert A. Segal. Chicago: Open Court, 1995, 39–53.

Stoyanov, Yuri. *The Hidden Tradition in Europe: The Secret History of Medieval Christian Heresy*. London: Penguin, 1994.

Viscomi, Joseph. "Illuminated Printing." *The Cambridge Companion to William Blake*, ed. Morris Eaves. Cambridge, England: Cambridge University Press, 2003.

Walter, Philippe. *Arthur: L'Ours et le Roi*. Paris: Imago, 2002.

Watts, Alan. *Myth and Ritual in Christianity*. London: Thames & Hudson, 1953.

Waugh, Evelyn. *Helena*. Harmondsworth, England: Penguin, 1963.

Weston, Jessie L. *From Ritual to Romance*. Princeton, NJ: Princeton University Press, 1993.

_____. *The Legend of Sir Gawain*. London: David Nutt, 1897.

Wind, Edgar. *Pagan Mysteries in the Renaissance*, Rev. ed. Oxford, England: Oxford University Press, 1980.

# Index